GOLD RUSH GIRL

Pioneer Life in the Black Hills

By
Sarah Elizabeth Taylor

Taylor, Sarah Elizabeth, *Gold Rush Girl: Pioneer Life in the Black Hills*

Copyright 2018 by Elisabeth Irene Quinn

Published by Willow Glen Publications

ISBN (paperback) 978-0-9998090-0-6

ISBN (eBook) 978-0-9998090-1-3

Library of Congress Catalog Number: 2018931158

To my Mother,
whose principles of honesty
and high standards
brought me
to a pure womanhood,
I dedicate this book
- Sarah Elizabeth Taylor

CONTENTS

PART V - Later Years

FOREWORD

In 2008, my parents moved from Virginia to Texas. Before their move, I offered to keep several boxes of genealogical records of my mother's family at my house. Out of curiosity I decided to leaf through the old records. One box contained hundreds of typed and handwritten papers. As I began reading through the pages I realized that I had found my great-grandmother's life story—a manuscript she had written chronicling her childhood in the Black Hills. In 2011, I began to dictate her manuscript onto my computer and organize it into chapters. I felt compelled to share her story as well as the story of others living in the Dakota Territories at that time. Where possible I have attempted to verify dates, names, facts and places. I apologize for any inadvertent errors or omissions.

I have a deeper appreciation for the woman I am named after and the faith that we share. I am struck by a thought that Sarah Elizabeth expressed, "God alone can look into the hearts of men and read the pages they have written." May you catch a glimpse of Sarah Elizabeth's heart as you read the story she has written.

It is my hope that no one is offended by some of the references or names that have been included in this book. Sadie, as she was known, lived and wrote in a different time. People were not as sensitive to the way in which different races and ethnic groups were addressed. To remain true to that time period, I've tried to avoid modifying words that would be considered socially, politically and culturally incorrect today. All photos included in the book came from my great-grandmother's private collection.

I am forever grateful for my husband, Michael, and sons, Taylor & William, as they encouraged me in this process; and for my father, Walter Kurth and my son, Patrick, co-editors and collaborators. I also appreciate the input my sister Sarah Edge provided. A big thank you is owed to Jennie Jang, my professional editor; Kimberley Eley of KWE Publishing LLC; and Butch Clarke of Alphagraphics for formatting the book. Thanks also to Debbie Vardiman, the Head Archive Volunteer at the Black Hills Mining Museum in Lead, South Dakota, as well as the Phoebe Apperson Hearst Free Library in Lead for allowing access to maps and research materials for this book.

Elisabeth "Betsy" Irene Quinn

PROLOGUE

When I decided to write the experiences of my life in the Black Hills, I wondered what to call the book. The tall pines covering the hills of the Dakota Territory form an unforgettable picture in my mind. Their brown cones, that drop and roll here and there to find resting places among the rocks of the hillsides, are similar to the experiences, places and people who have found resting places in my memory. I love the remembrances of my childhood and wish to bring to life, for my readers, the Black Hills and all their rugged beauty, cruel and terrible at times, but always sturdy and grand with a mystique that draws one into the very bosom of their life.

The Black Hills possessed many wonders for a child reared in its midst. Acres of grand old pines, beautiful pasque wildflowers that we called "goslings" and blood red anemone flowers that peaked forth with the last snow of winter (reminding us of the blood that Christ shed at his crucifixion). There were also countless shooting stars pointing their hearts toward heaven. These marvels instilled in my heart a love of that country that can never be replaced by any other land.

This land of my childhood was a laboratory of history and geology. Long before the formation of the Alps, the Himalayas, the Andes or even our own Rockies, geologists believe a huge batholith or dome began to emerge from the surface of the earth. That dome, later to be known as the Black Hills, began to rise through concentric circles of geological formations of shale, limestone, and sandstone. Finally arose, the great pinnacle of glory, the granite center known as the Needles with Harney's Peak the capstone (Mount Rushmore). Upon its face, the heads of the great founders and preservers of our country would be carved to become its crown.

Embedded deep within the granite heart of this land laid jewels, precious and semi-precious, including rubies, garnets, opals, beryls and topazes. Additional hidden treasures of coal, tin, gold, silver, lead, copper and other ores made this area known as the richest thousand square miles in the world. Thick forests of pine trees grew along the sides of those rugged hills, and from a distance it made them so dark that the Indians named the area the Black Hills.

No one knows who first claimed ownership of this treacherous, and yet great treasure chest of a land. Before the white man, many different tribes of Indians fought over and staked their claims. Indian legends handed down through generations describe how only someone with a brave and pure heart could pierce the black domain of the hills, return, and live to tell the tale of its conquest. One old Indian relayed this story: "An Indian chief, seeing the glittering pebbles brought by his noble brother returning from his warrior's tests, killed his brother and then rushed into the forest in search of more glittering treasure, but he never returned. Forever after, Manitou the Great Spirit roamed the hills and swallowed up all the evil ones and allowed only the good ones to return." The old Indian further elaborated on how the Great Spirit rolled down huge rocks from the top of the mountains as fortune hunters tried to climb the unknown heights. The ground would tremble and the earth would slide away under their feet and the evil-minded intruders would sink down to be devoured by wild beasts.

This is the land of my childhood! It is a rugged land feared by Indians, a land of shifting shale and formidable mountains; however, it is also a land of beauty and strength. This small circle of towns was my world: Lead City at its center, her satellites Deadwood, Central City, Golden Gate, Terraville and the smaller camps around. Not unlike the terrain, the inhabitants of this land could be rough and calloused; yet these pioneers survived and grew to appreciate the beauty of the land.

Prologue

It is my hope that in reading these pages you may see beyond the stereotype of the vices and degradation so typically relayed of "the Gold Rush days." I hope that you will catch a glimpse of the grandeur of the mountaintops and the beauty of the pines as portrayed in the lives of the men and women who lived in that territory during this period of history. May only the true, the noble, and the good in those lives, settle into your memory as they have in mine like the fallen pinecones of those great trees of the Black Hills.

Sarah (Sadie) Elizabeth Taylor

SADIE'S FAMILY TREE

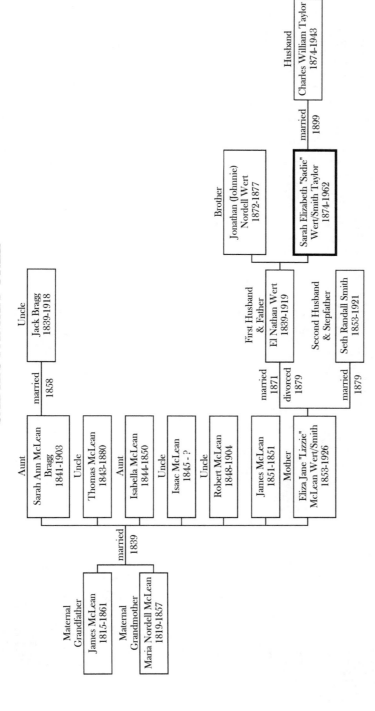

Husband Charles William Taylor 1874-1943	
married 1899	
Brother Jonathan (Johnnie) Nordell Wert 1872-1877	
Sarah Elizabeth "Sadie" Wert/Smith Taylor 1874-1962	

Uncle Jack Bragg 1839-1918

married 1858

Aunt Sarah Ann McLean Bragg 1841-1903

Uncle Thomas McLean 1843-1880

Aunt Isabella McLean 1844-1850

Uncle Isaac McLean 1845 - ?

Uncle Robert McLean 1848-1904

James McLean 1851-1851

Mother Eliza Jane "Lizzie" McLean Wert/Smith 1853-1926

First Husband & Father El Nathan Wert 1839-1919

married 1871

divorced 1879

Second Husband & Stepfather Seth Randall Smith 1853-1921

married 1879

married 1839

Maternal Grandfather James McLean 1815-1861

Maternal Grandmother Maria Nordell McLean 1819-1857

7

PART I

Family Beginnings

MOTHER'S ARRIVAL IN AMERICA

Sarah Ann Bragg and Eliza (Lizzie) Jane McLean

I n September of 1863, a little undernourished child named Eliza Jane McLean stood at the window of the reception room of the Charity Sisters Home for orphans in one of the big cities of England. In appearance, she looked about five years old, but in reality was nine. She was dressed in the school's somber brown garb and wore a small poke bonnet* over her mass of very black curls. Her peculiar black eyes, one very large and the other smaller as though stunted in its development, gave her face an elfin look. Her restless flitting made her seem like a small autumn nymph ruffled by the intermittent breeze coming in at the open window.

When Eliza was three, her mother, Maria (Nordell) McLean, died. There was a changing row of housekeepers after Eliza's father, James McLean, went to London. When he never returned to his children, Sarah (17), took in Isaac and Eliza. When Sarah left for America to join her husband, Isaac, Eliza's fifteen-year-old brother tried to hide her from the bobby* to prevent him from taking her to the Sisters of Charity orphanage. Their older brother Tom had already left for Scotland to seek help from their Grandfather.

Despite Isaac's efforts, eventually the bobby found her and took her to the orphanage. She was told that her father was dead.

Two years later, the child was watching for her brother, Tom. The Sister of Charity nun watched her with dreaming eyes, for she was trying to envision the future of this little waif that had been brought to their door by city authorities. The child had a brilliant mind and quick fingers. Her deep musical voice gave promise. She had a proud haughty bearing that distinguished her from all the other children in the school. What was her future? Would America give her the chance for development that the Almighty seemed to have fit for her? Would that sister to whom she was being sent be able to cope with that proud willful spirit that resided in the child's heart and give her the love and understanding she needed?

The child suddenly said, "There he is!" She dashed toward the door but was halted by the command, "STOP, come here." The door opened and with almost a sob the little girl hurled herself into the arms of the young man entering through the door. The brother and sister were lost to all but each other.

"You've come, you've come for me," the little girl said as her arms

---

*A poke bonnet is a hooded hat with a projecting rim on the front side that shaded the face of the wearer. All of the wearer's hair could be "poked" inside of it.

*The British term used for a policeman.

encircled her brother's neck. He lifted her off the floor and walked toward the waiting Sister. Putting the child down he handed the Sister a paper and waited.

After reading the paper the Sister finally said, "Everything is right and you may take her now for she is ready. She has said her goodbyes and here are her belongings." With hurrying feet, they hastened down the walk to the massive gate that led them out of the stone walls that had been like a prison. What a sigh of relief escaped her as she got the answer to her question, "I'll never have to go back there again?" Her brother answered her, "No."

She asked, "Where are we going?"

"Southampton."

"Right now?"

"Yes."

"Will I see Bob and Isaac?"

"No."

"Why?"

"Not time."

"Won't I ever see them again?"

"You will be with Sarah and maybe we will come to America too."

"And there will never be a workhouse anymore," the child whispered as she gave a joyous skip.

For to her, the Charity Sisters Home had been the workhouse, for it was charity and all the children had to work. She had learned to sew and knit and mend. She had to clean her part of the dormitory before she could play.

Now...finally, Tom had come back for her with a letter that included passage money from her 22-year old sister, Sarah. Eliza was to come to America on a big ship to live with Sarah and Sarah's husband, Jack Bragg.

Jack Bragg, her brother-in-law, a quiet little Englishman with "itching feet," was the first member of her family to enter the "Promised Land of America." As a boy of seven, he spurned his father's right to apprentice him to a baker, who made him knead his bread dough by tramping it with his bare feet. A few years later, he hid himself aboard a wind-jammer that was provisioning in his home harbor of Poole, England, and after two days at sea, he appeared before the captain with the statement that he wanted to see the world. For four long, sorry years he worked his way as a cabin boy.

On his return he landed in Manchester, England, where he apprenticed himself to Eliza's father, a custom shoemaker. Her father, James McLean, kept close to twenty men busy in his shoe shop, while her mother assisted by fine finishing the ladies' shoes with her long, slim hands. In 1858, Jack Bragg married Eliza's 16-year-old sister, Sarah Ann McLean. The following year he received his journeyman's papers. One year later, his "itching feet" called for new lands to conquer, so to America he went. He arrived in Charleston, South Carolina, a day before the Civil War blockade began.

On landing, he was asked his name, to which he responded John Bragg. A Confederate military guard immediately took him into custody. The military court sentenced him to be hung as a Union spy masquerading as General Bragg's son. The next morning, standing on a gallows with a rope around his neck, he saw the Union Jack flying from a mast and demanded British protection. He had recognized his old ship in the harbor and one of the sailors down on the street. The sailor was called forward, and recognizing Jack, declared him to be Johnnie Bragg of Poole, England. The noose was unfastened and Jack was given twenty-four hours to leave southern territory.

He went north and eventually arrived in Philadelphia, and a few months later, his wife Sarah joined him. After spending two years in the orphanage, it was to their care that Eliza was being sent.

"What is America like, Tom?"

"It's a great country but there is a war there now and it has been hard even to get a letter from there until now."

"Would you like to go there?"

"Would a duck like to swim? I'll be going someday and so will our brothers if we have to work our passage. But Jack says there is lots of money there and after a while he'll send us the money."

The two trudged on to the wharf in Southampton. They were children of a custom shoemaker, the son of a feudal Lord of Scotland. Their father had refused an education and gone his own wild way against his father's wishes. He married a French girl of noble birth whose father disowned her for marrying a Protestant, and he, in turn, was disowned for marrying a Catholic. Thus, both were cut off from noble heritages. Their children were left to fight the world alone and find their haven in America. Proud of their blueblood and bound to make a good life and be independent, they moved forward as so many others have done to make a better America.

Therefore, in the early Fall of 1863 the little black haired black-eyed girl of nine, holding tightly to the hand of her brother, stepped onto the deck of a White Star liner that was headed for the far-off shores of the United States. To the boy, really, only a lad, and the girl, the ship meant AMERICA in capital letters.

"May I see the captain?" The boy asked the sailor who accosted him.

"The Captain is busy. What is your business?"

"The Captain will see us," the boy answered. "Tell him that Captain Nordell's nephew waits on him."

The sailor looked at him in protest but the boy's clear eyes brooked no delay and the sailor left them standing there. A few moments later he returned.

"The Captain will see you in his cabin, sir. This way please." Upon entering the cabin, the Captain arose and looking at the two, said, "You must be Maria Nordell's children, though you both take after the Scot. Tell me, what can I do for the Nordell kin?"

"My sister Sarah is in America. Our parents are both dead and I wish to send my little sister to her in Scranton, Pennsylvania. Sarah will meet her in Philadelphia. I am to place her in your charge as you were a friend of our uncle."

"Yes, boy, a friend of both your uncles, God rest their souls, for they were both grand men and 'tis a great loss that they went down in that bitter hurricane but that is a lot we seamen may all meet. Have you notified your sister?"

"Yes, sir. I was in Scotland when the letter and the money came to send the little one and I wrote at once saying I was sending her with you, sir. I hope I was not overacting sir."

The Captain replied, "For her uncles' sake I will take the wee one and do the best I can in these troublesome times. You understand there is a war over there and it is always a question how we make port with blockades and fighting but we should land at Philly and with God guiding us I will hand her over to your sister as I would one of my own."

A few more words were exchanged and Tom McLean bid his little sister goodbye until the time when the good brother-in-law, Jack Bragg, could send money for passage for himself and his younger brothers left in Manchester.

We will say nothing of the heartache at parting or the strange life on board the ship. Upon Eliza's arrival in America, an accident she had suffered while living in the orphanage had somewhat disfigured her, so much so that her sister Sarah did not recognize her and almost refused to claim her. Two years had changed the idealized looks of the little sister. The high-strung, self-willed child became the dictator of her own life for the easy, happy-go-lucky John and Sarah Bragg. They could not cope with the will of the child who had run her own life for two years, and they did not try to do so. Eliza could always rely upon John and Sarah, however, and they stepped in when needed.

Jack's "itching feet" carried him many places through the years that followed. In 1869, Jack, Sarah and Eliza, with several of the men from Scranton, Pennsylvania, where they were living at the time, moved west. Jack started a boot shop at 16th and Harney Streets in Omaha for a short time. Next they moved to Wichita, Kansas, where he built a home and shop. While he never disposed of his property there, Wichita could not hold him for long. Leaving his wife and Eliza behind in Kansas, he headed to the gold fields of California.

(EDITOR'S NOTE: Although the book says Eliza left from Southampton on the White Star Line, it is more likely that she departed from Liverpool on a different ship line.)

A MARRIAGE, MOVE, DEATH & DIVORCE

When Uncle Jack left for California, Aunt Sarah and my mother remained in Wichita. In 1871, my mother, at age seventeen, met and married El Nathan Wert, age 30. They settled in Humboldt, Kansas, where my brother, Johnathan "Johnnie" Nordell Wert, was born on June 12, 1872, and I, Sarah Elizabeth "Sadie" Wert, on March 18, 1874. Soon after I was born, my father found himself unable to cope with my Mother's indomitable will. He deserted us for another more congenial woman and demanded a divorce. My mother refused to grant him one.

Due to my mother's failing health, the doctor ordered her to move to the mountains of Colorado. Since Uncle Jack was gone, Aunty joined us in Pueblo where she opened a millinery shop. While we were in Colorado, my brother became gravely ill and died.

After my brother died, my father was determined to get a divorce, and tried to kidnap me to force my mother to agree. I hid under a bed in a dark room without an opening except the door. I stayed there all day without food or water. Not even my mother knew where I was. Eventually I heard Mother say, "Sarah, why can't we find her? I know he did not take her on the train when he left." She was like a crazy woman pacing the floor when I crawled out to her. Sobbing I said, "He can't take me now." I was only three but that agony stayed with me all my life.

Later, when my mother remarried, I realized why she could not give her consent to my stepfather's adopting me. I also knew she would never give anyone a right to take me from her without a battle, not even my husband. On September 18, 1878, unbeknownst to my mother, my father filed for divorce claiming my mother had deserted him, and conveniently married his third wife, Frances Scanlon, the following day. It took months for the news of the divorce to reach my mother in Colorado. Upon receiving the news, she traveled to Kansas and on March 15, 1879, she filed for divorce due to adultery. The judge overruled my father's divorce and my mother was granted custody of me. I never saw my father again.

From here on it is best that you know the child who relates the story. Born a girl, when my father desperately wanted a boy, within the next five years I had lost my older brother by death and my father by divorce. My sad-eyed mother reared me alone, she who had only seen the darker side of life. Despite her poor health, up to this time I had never been out of my mother's sight.

Picture me, a child quite undersized but exceptionally straight and active, pale from too much indoor living, and that whiteness accentuated by very black hair cut short like a boy. I was given the nickname of "Tommy." My peculiar eyes seemed to form half my face. My hands, with which I did most of my talking, and my feet, encased in fine, handmade kid* shoes, preferred to move with a run, a skip, or a jump. My ringing laugh that was always ready to burst from my throat told of that pent-up love and a joy of life that could not be suppressed by the hush-hush of elders.

My clothing, the envy of all the children, was a little print wrapper in the morning, a finely embroidered Swiss or dainty wool dress - as the season demanded - in the afternoon, and if taken out in the evening, a daintier dress and accessories to match. My mother was the town dressmaker and I was her advertisement.

In Pueblo, I was never allowed to play with other children. My sole playmate was a shepherd dog that stood guard over me day and night. People spoke to and treated me as a grown woman, with the exception that I must be seen but never heard. Privy to all fitting room gossip, I was never allowed to repeat any of it.

---

* Leather made from a young goat.

One day some girls, older than myself, came with their mother, and while our mothers were busy, we played in the next room. I impersonated a certain patron and repeated racy gossip that was then relayed back to my mother who impressed upon me the need to keep my mouth shut with the lash of a riding quirt on the back of my legs. Needless to say, I knew better next time and became a very good judge of what to tell and what not to by watching what my mother told others.

Mother was a good listener, but not much of a talker. When she spoke, it was always to the point. Her tongue was like a whiplash when she wanted to use it, and, as I grew older, I preferred the riding whip every time to a scolding, for the whip sting was soon over but the tongue-lashing was seldom forgotten. Every word was made to cut deep into the heart and lived for a lifetime. I also grew up to never worry my mother unnecessarily but to take care of and amuse myself. I was always hearing from strangers how bright and remarkable I was for my years, but was continually criticized by Mother.

El Nathan Wert

Eliza McLean Wert

Jonathan Nordell "Johnnie" Wert

Sarah Elizabeth "Sadie" Wert

BLACK HILLS GOLD RUSH

While we were living in Pueblo, the Black Hills became open for mining. Trappers and fur traders, returning with their furs, were the first to tell of Indians having gold nuggets in the Black Hills area that was part of their reservation, sacred land for the Sioux and Cheyenne Indians. In 1874, as the rumor spread, the government fitted out an expedition under General Custer with a troop of cavalry to explore the Black Hills. These men made their first camp in the Black Hills proper at what was then established as Custer City. From there expeditions were sent out to different parts of the hills and up the gulches.

The men found small deposits of gold around Custer and as they progressed, larger findings were reported. Government officials tried for a time to keep the report secret. As this information became known, prospectors began moving in, even crossing into Indian Reservation land. After the Battle of the Little Bighorn in 1876, the boundary lines were changed to place the Black Hills outside the reservation and the Hills were officially opened for settlement that same year.

While the first gold prospectors came in from the Montana gold fields around Helena and the Big Horn Mountains, the larger influx of men and money naturally came from the east and southern rail points. During the human stampede of 1876-1880, many trails led off from the Union Pacific and came through Nebraska and Wyoming. Each trail offered some advantage over others in the way of terrain or outfitting supplies. Many came from Nebraska...Grand Island, Ft. Kearney, Sydney and Plum Creek (although this was only a river crossing for beef herds). The Grand Island, Ft. Kearney and Plum Creek trails came together a few short miles after crossing the Loupe River and all headed via the Spotted Tail Agency. However, Cheyenne, Wyoming Territory, and Sydney (via the Red Cloud Agency) proved to outfit most prospectors as travel was much shorter via their trails. Reduced travel time was a tremendous incentive to those who expected to "pick up their gold and return pronto."

When word spread that gold had been discovered in the Black Hills and the area had been opened to prospectors, Uncle Jack and his boon companion, another Englishman by the name of Billy Hayes, were living in Sacramento, California. They packed their shoemaker's kits, leather, and findings and took the Union Pacific Railroad to Laramie, Territory of Wyoming, where they purchased a buckboard, horses, blankets, and provisions and set out for the Black Hills.

To use Uncle's own expression, "The trail was naught but two ruts most of the way with herds of buffalo crossing and re-crossing it." Many times, they were compelled to steer their course by the sun and the buttes* or at night by the stars. They cooked their food over a campfire and slept rolled up in their blankets under the buckboard. Their horses were hobbled or staked out nearby as precaution demanded.

One night they slept so soundly that they awoke in the morning to find their horses gone, probably driven off by thieves. They immediately realized that they were stranded on the open prairie. Two days later, a freight outfit with extra horses came along that sold them another team and piloted them into Deadwood, Dakota Territory, in the spring or early summer of 1876.

Until the fallen logs and trees were chopped down and sawed into lumber at Judge Dudley's sawmill, initially, the Main Street of Deadwood was not passable by wagons. When Uncle arrived, Deadwood was a one-street town with a towering wall of rocky hillside behind rude shacks. Down this one street came freight wagon trains pulled by oxen or mules, men on horseback, and at times pack mules.

---

* Buttes are hills that rise sharply from the surrounding area with sloping sides and flat tops.

Dressed in mackinaws with trousers stuffed into high boots, most men carried packs on their backs. The gamblers wore Prince Albert's and fancy high-heeled boots. The men and the few women and children all made their way through mud or snow, around piles of rough lumber, logs, hitching racks, and debris as they attended to their business. Deadwood in 1876 was a conglomerate mass of people, from college graduates to Chinese coolies, all bent on making a stake or adventure for themselves. Saloons, dance halls, and brothels were quickly built. Deadwood even developed a small section akin to San Francisco's Chinatown.

Deadwood was the fitting-out place for miners and prospectors, the rendezvous for hard characters who preyed upon honest workers, the hell-raising spot for the fellow who wanted to celebrate when he made a stake, and the place to lose it all to human sharks who infested the gambling dens. Never a mining town after its short life of placer digging, Deadwood always lived upon the output of the surrounding camps. From the beginning, it was notorious. In later years, it also became the home of many prosperous mining, business, and professional men of the Black Hills region.

To reiterate, the Hills were not formally opened for settlement until 1876, but many prospectors had filtered in with General Custer's Expedition and shortly after. Among those early prospectors were Joe Ingoldsby and Bill Gay who, on December 9, 1875, found fifty-cent prospects in their placer wash at No. 5 claim above Gayville. Camps sprang up overnight along every creek. Claims were staked and claims were jumped. The best placer claim was on Deadwood Creek and netted its owners $180,000 in four months' time. These developments contributed to the Black Hills opening for settlement in 1876. Human life was often the price paid for a few ounces of gold washed out in the miner's pan. A man would be shot on sight if found stealing horses or provisions from another man. The law of the revolver was the law of the land and questions were seldom asked.

Many great tales recount the findings of those early days, but placer finds soon gave out and the miners went out into the Hills themselves, looking for the mother lode from which the gold had drifted.

To these adventurers, Indians were troublesome until sometime after the legal opening of the Black Hills region in 1876. The last real difficulty in the heart of the Hills was at Camp Crook and was known as the Crook Massacre. Reverend Henry Weston Smith was the first man killed by Indians, on August 3, 1876, while on his way from Camp Crook to preach in Deadwood. Reverend Smith was the first preacher in the Hills and was much loved and respected by everyone. He was buried in the little cemetery laid out in the gulch, but after a flood his body was moved to a more protected spot, high on Mount Moriah, where he rests not far from Wild Bill Hickok.

That same day, Ike Brown and two others were also killed. A wagon train from Bismarck pulled into Crook just after the massacre and a posse of men from the train tried to track a group of Indians, but located only one. They returned to the wagon train and went on to Deadwood before night.

Located down the creek from Deadwood, Elizabethtown was established before Deadwood in April of 1876. The town was named in honor of Elizabeth Carl, a young girl with the Elizabethtown pioneer group, and its pioneers had many rules and restrictions incorporated in the town planning. Those who preferred more freedom moved to Deadwood and eventually Elizabethtown morphed into a ghost town.

Uncle Jack and Billy Hayes began a thriving business in Fred Zipp's shop in Deadwood. One of Uncle Jack's first jobs was making a pair of boots for Wild Bill Hickok. Standing in the doorway of the shoe shop, Uncle Jack witnessed the killing of Hickok in the saloon across the street.

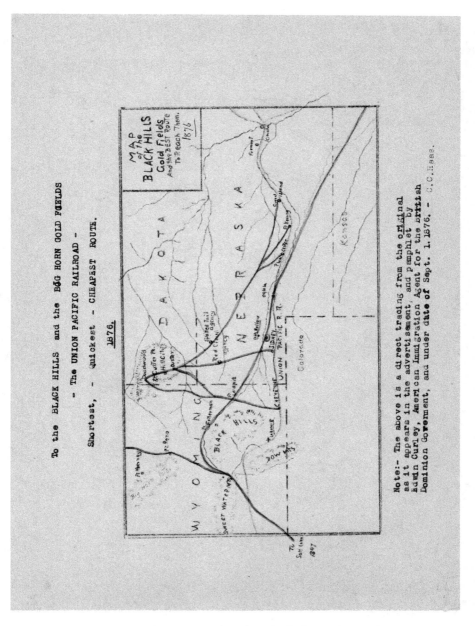

The above map is a direct tracing by Edwin Curly (American Immigration
Agent) from the original Union Pacific pamphlet dated September 1, 1876
C. C. Haas.

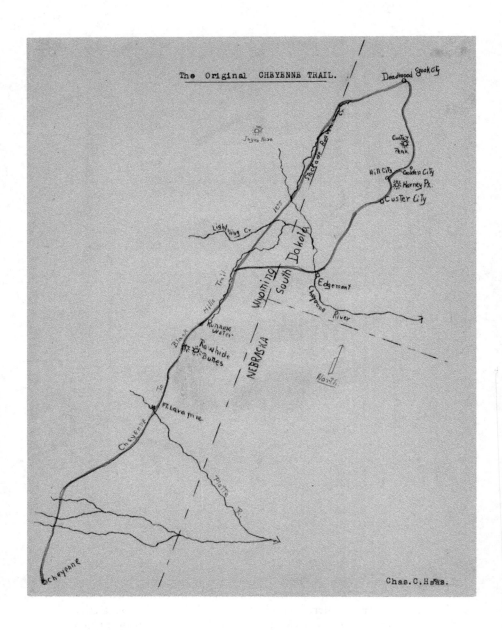

The CHEYENNE-DEADWOOD Route - 1877

STATIONS and DISTANCES

Eating Stations to Deadwood, marked - #
Eating Stations to Cheyenne, marked - o

Stations	Miles	TL Miles	Water
Cheyenne	0		
Nine Mile	9		
Pole Creek - o	9	18	Good Water.
Horse Creek	10	28	Good Water.
Bear Springs	10	38	Good Water.
Chugwater - # o	14	52	Good Water.
Huntons Ranche - #	14	66	Good Water.
Eagles Nest - o	12	78	No Water.
Ft. Laramie - #	17	92	
Brackenridges - # o	4	99	Good Water.
Government Farm - o	12	111	Good Water.
Rawhide Buttes - #	12	123	Alkali Water.
Running Water (Niobrara River)	14	137	Good Water.
Hat Creek - #	14	151	Good Water.
Indian Creek - #	16	177	Good Water.
Alum Creek	14	191	Good Water.
Red Canyon - # o	15	206	Good Water.
Spring on Hills	12	118	Good Water.
Pleasant Valley	14	232	Good Water.
Custer City - # o	9	241	Good Water.
Twelve Mile Station	12	253	Good Water.
Mountain City - #	12	265	Good Water.
Rapid Creek	12	277	Good Water.
Head of Whitewood Creek	12	289	Good Water.
Deadwood	3	292	"THE EL DORADO"

Coaches each way daily. More when required.
Gilmore & Salisbury, Owners.

By 1877 stage coach service was available between Cheyenne and Deadwood. This was the probable route of Jack Bragg and Billy Hayes after they left the railroad.

AUNT SARAH BRAGG

Aunt Sarah Bragg

Uncle Jack left Zipp's shop in Deadwood to open his own shoe shop in Lead. Once settled in Lead, Uncle Jack sent for his wife Sarah in the summer of 1878. Aunt Sarah left the millinery shop in Pueblo for my mother to run. She then left for Kansas City, Missouri, where she purchased a stock of hats and trimmings and started for Lead.

Sarah Bragg was a little Englishwoman whose veins carried the blueblood of Scottish chieftains and French nobility. Measuring scarcely five feet tall and weighing less than one hundred pounds, she was a born lady. Her bonnets and tiny well-shod feet spelled FRANCE in capital letters, while her business instincts and thrift were truly Scottish. Every ounce of her petite being was vivacious energy. When she took the stage, she was the only female passenger with eleven men packed in seats intended for nine.

One night, unable to rest in the crowded coach, though her male companions slept soundly, she determined to get out and stretch her legs at the first stop. At last her chance came. The stage slowed up and stopped. She pulled the flap aside and hopped out. She had hardly touched the ground when the driver swung his whip and, with clanking harness, the horses dashed off into the darkness.

My aunt, for a moment dazed, stood alone on the open prairie. The stage had only stopped to give the horses a breathing spell. At midnight, and alone, she sat down in the trail to think and look around. Way off in the distance a small flame leapt up, died down, and then leapt up again as if someone was putting fuel on a campfire. Were they white men or Indians? Were they desperadoes or honest men? She reasoned, if Indians, they would find her at daylight. If white men, they would likely not harm her, so she walked as silently as possible toward the fire. One man heard her step and instantly rolled into the shadow, but she had seen he was white so she spoke, telling her plight. Stepping into the light to be visible, she begged him to take her into Deadwood where her husband would pay him well.

The man stood up, as did also his partner, whom she had not noticed before. They explained that horse thieves had driven off their horses and all they had was a pack mule. She talked and pled. Finally, the men, after a lengthy conference, caught the mule that was hobbled nearby. One climbed on and his partner then lifted her up astride behind him. Holding the man around the waist so she would not slide off, they started toward the nearest stage station several miles ahead.

When the stage reached Ash Hollow, the men, roused from their sleep, noticed that their lady passenger was missing and gave the alarm.

Remembering the short pause several miles back, the driver turned the coach back to look for her. They met up with Sarah and her escorts shortly after they took the trail. A grand rejoicing swelled in everyone's hearts. When she tried to pay her escorts, the men refused, and they never claimed recognition in Lead. Whether the two turned back or reached the Hills she never knew. Their names were shrouded in mystery. During the rest of the journey, the driver and passengers kept a close eye on her. They delivered her unharmed at her destination to her smiling young husband.

On her arrival to Lead, she opened her trunks, and thus, the first millinery establishment in the town. Aunty and Uncle's house and shops were in a long building, built like most of the others, of rough pine boards running up and down and batted with smaller boards. The sides lacked windows, but the front had large windows and two doors with glass. The windows did not open and were used instead as show cases.

A partition divided the front of the building into two rooms: Uncle used the smaller room for his shop and Aunty, the larger one for her store. Behind the two shops were three bedrooms with six-foot partitions dividing them and the parlor. The bedrooms lacked openings except doors. A stovepipe provided heat that carried over the partitions from the front room stove to the chimney in the kitchen. The kitchen was a lean-to affair extending two-thirds across the back of the main part of the building. This lean-to was made of the roughest kind of boards nailed to the studding and covered with tarpaper to keep out the cold, and had two half windows and a door.

A window in the front of the long parlor gave a view into the store and a window at the back looked out upon the backyard. The main part of the house had muslin tacked on the studding and was covered with paper, making it one of the best buildings at that time. Here, Aunty furnished the Easter bonnets for the ladies of the town for many years.

S.R. SMITH

Among the early settlers of Lead were Seth Randall Smith and Howard Mealy. On May 1, 1877, the two opened the first exclusive grocery store in Lead under the name of Mealy & Smith on the south side of Main Street. They brought in their stock of goods in covered wagons, drawn by mules and oxen.

Both young men hailed from Minnesota. Mealy was the son of Senator Mealy of that same state, and Smith, born in Maine, had spent his boyhood clearing his father's farm in Minnesota near the source of the Mississippi River. At age 17, he left home to follow lumber camps as a lumberjack, and eventually became a boss in the Washburn Lumber Mill of Minneapolis. He left the lumber field to become interpreter and trading-post manager among the Chippewa Indians. This on-the-job training equipped him to face further adventures of a developing frontier.

One interesting event brought about Mr. Smith's departure from the Indian Reservation. Howard Mealy visited the reservation to see Mr. Smith. Mealy enjoyed teasing Indians, especially an old fellow known as Black Bear. Mr. Smith was absent from the trading post one day when Black Bear came in to buy a plug of tobacco. Black Bear went to the counter and said, "tobac." Mealy pretended he did not understand and offered him a bag of salt. Black Bear shook his head, "No, tobac." Mealy responded with several other articles and laughed. No laugh came from Black Bear. His eyes smoldered while his face remained unchanged. As Mr. Smith came into the room he realized the situation had escalated. He advised Mealy to return to

Minneapolis the next day with him, since he had plans to pick up a load of flour for the Reservation.

They started early the next morning and as they came to an open space in the thick timber, Mr. Smith caught a gleam of sun on metal. He turned quickly to find the source and yelled in Chippewa "Put it down" just as Black Bear had his tomahawk raised over Mealy's head. Black Bear dropped back, quoting Mealy's usual remark when rebuked by Smith for teasing Black Bear, "I just fun!" Of course, it would not have been fun if Smith had not been so quick to recognize the danger.

While on their trip, the two young men decided to open a store in Lead. With the New Year, they began preparations to accumulate a stock of groceries hoping to reach the "promised land" by early summer. In Fargo, North Dakota, other wagons joined them, and again in Bismarck. After many delays, the long train finally started its final trek.

The details of that eventful journey were often relayed to me, but only the high points are fixed in my memory. Approximately four hundred people in the train left Bismarck. The Mealy and Smith outfit brought up the rear. Men on horseback, leading pack horses, were going in to prospect; men with wives and children were going to make a start in the new field; men with stocks of goods planned to start trading; and some men and women were solely bent on adventure. The train pulled out of Bismarck early in March. Snow covered the ground and the crunch of the wheels and crack of the whips made a merry song for those expectant souls starting on the long journey to a land where all hoped to become millionaires.

After several weeks travel, a rumor of Indians emerged. The dreaded Sioux were on the warpath. A sharp lookout was kept and proof that a group of Indians was on their trail began to show. How big a band? They did not know. The members of the train became panicky and Smith was chosen to take charge. Ox and mule teams moved slowly, under good conditions, ten to twenty miles being a day's journey. While the ground was frozen most of the time, on some days, warm winds blew and the snow melted, leaving the trail soft and heavy. Streams had to be crossed on the ice, or forded, often causing long detours and delays for the wagons.

Rumors that Indians were drawing closer caused the train to accelerate more rapidly. The objective was to reach a high stretch of ground on the other side of a river. They came to the river early in the afternoon just as the lookout reported a small band of Sioux advancing in the rear.

A stampede followed, and the ice that ordinarily would have allowed one wagon to cross at a time gave way with the weight of several. A wagon went through. The stream was too deep to ford with high banks on either side. This catastrophe left the train divided with the smaller contingent at the mercy of a group of Indians as night approached. Here is the story as told by S. R. Smith:

"In one of our wagons were great coils of heavy rope to be used in sinking shafts. We got them out. I pulled off most of my clothes and, with the ends of two of the ropes, waded and swam to the wagon, passed the ropes under the box, one on each side, and made for the opposite shore. I had unhooked the animals first and they swam ashore. We fastened the two ends of the rope to trees on the banks close to the ground. I swam back and, taking another rope, fastened it to the tongue of the wagon. Horses were hitched to the other end and thus were able to pull the wagon out.

By driving the other wagons astride the ropes, and having men steady the wagons on the downstream side, we got every wagon across before dark. Most of the women and children went over in the wagons, but one woman refused to go that way, so I carried her across astride my neck. I made fourteen trips across that stream and was up to my armpits in the water most of the time, with no chance to get warm except by moving.

My own wagon was last to cross, and no food ever tasted as good as the stew and black coffee the women had prepared that we ate in the darkness that night, and no clothing ever felt so warm as the old mackinaw I crawled into after the ropes had been cut so the Indians could not follow us.

That night our camp was in darkness, but on the opposite side of the river in the distance, we could see the Indian campfires. With daylight, the Indians had disappeared and were not seen again.

When we came in sight of the Black Hills they looked like a black cloud on the horizon many, many miles away. Distances are deceptive there. The men became anxious to push on more rapidly. Realizing that a blizzard was brewing, I advised an early camp and the group gave heed except for four men, prospectors with pack animals who determined to push on to the mountains that looked so near.

About three o'clock in the afternoon I ordered the train to draw their wagons up in a circle, and prepared for the storm. Seeing a herd of antelope taking shelter in a nearby grove some of the men shot several and brought them into camp. Others gathered all the available wood they could obtain.

While we were eating supper, the storm swooped down upon us, a blizzard of intense fury that lasted for three days. Only the precautions taken in making camp saved our stock and our own lives. Every available box and object had been used to form a closed circle and the snow drifted high up on the outside of the circle. On the inside the stock huddled in the shelter of the wagons out of the wind. We people, rolled up in blankets in the wagons and tried to gain warmth from each other. When the storm was over, the wood and venison came in mighty handy, for it was several days before we could break camp.

After the storm, a search party was sent out to look for the four who had gone ahead. We hoped to find them alive and bring them into camp. Two had killed their horses to make a windbreak for themselves and had holed up by their horses' bodies where they had been covered by the drifting snow thus saving their lives. Their hands and feet were so badly frozen that the one man lived but a few days and was buried near our camp. The other lost both legs and for years went up and down the streets of Deadwood seated on a board set on wheels and guided by a stick.

The bodies of the other two men were found by wagon trains that came over the trail later. The men had wandered in circles, for their equipment was found scattered in that way. At one time, they were within three miles of camp as one body was found near our camping place.

The blizzard seemed to open the doors for spring. While the roads were heavy and even terrible through the Badlands region, the weather turned warm and spring really came with green valleys studded with blood blossom along the hillsides."

At Camp Crook, the company began to break up. Some staked out farms in the valleys, while others went on to Deadwood and Lead, with Mealy and Smith in the last group. In January of 1878, Mealy grew weary of roughing it and returned to Minnesota. About that same time an epidemic of mountain typhoid began to develop, and Seth Smith was one of the early victims. He had built a large cabin upon the South Mill Street hill and stocked it with groceries from his store. When he became ill, a prospector came and took care of him in return for food and lodging. The man stayed only a short time, stocking himself up with provisions. He went off prospecting never to be seen again.

In his delirium, Smith kept calling for water. One day he crawled out of his bunk and made his way to the water bucket, albeit too weak to get up on his hands and knees. When he reached for the dipper, he accidentally pulled the bucket over on himself. Exhausted by the effort, yet cooled off by the splash of water, he lay on the floor for some time and dozed off to sleep.

When he became conscious, the first thing he remembered was a gallon-sized can of peaches on the floor. He used his hunting knife to cut a gash in the can, out of which he sucked all the juice and then laid on the floor cradling the can in his arms as he fell to sleep. Upon waking, he cut an opening in the can and managed to get his fingers in for some of the peaches, eating them until the can was empty. He always said that the peaches cured him.

Passing the cabin one day, Mrs. Alexander heard Mr. Smith and gave him aid. He never forgot her kindness. Mrs. Alexander cooked some rice and brought it to him. He asked her how to cook it and she told him just to put the rice in boiling water with a little salt and let it boil until it was tender. He thought that her rice was the finest food he had ever eaten. When he got up he went to the sack of rice, took a scoop full and poured it into a kettle of boiling water. In a short time, the kettle was full, but the rice was not yet tender. As a result, he put the rice in his dishpan with more water. That became full and began to boil over, so he took a wash boiler he had and dumped the rice into that with more water. When all was said and done, he said he ate rice for over a week. After that incident, he never wanted rice unless it was mixed in and masked by other ingredients.

OUR MOVE TO THE BLACK HILLS

My mother was supposedly dying of consumption.* Realizing her condition, in May 1879, Mother determined to join her sister Sarah in Lead in the Dakota Territory. Her rationale was that my aunt would be available to look after me when the end came.

As you can imagine, when we moved to the Dakota Territory my mother took a somewhat precocious brat with her. I was all that she had and I must be perfect, the best in every way. Stern reality ruled all things. I often heard her say: "What she gets while I am alive, I know she will have, but after I am gone, she may have nothing." All my life I was pushed and pushed to learn with little gentleness or tenderness; yet, I was her very life and nothing else mattered. Health, happiness, almost life itself, had to sidestep her insatiable ambition for me and for herself. Her motto, "The child must never be allowed to be ashamed of the mother," was as much of her creed as "The mother must always be able to be proud of her child."

Although five years old at the time of these travels, I have no recollection of how we managed to get from Pueblo to the stagecoach in Sydney, Nebraska. While trains were an old story in my young life, this move was the first time we had ever tried the stagecoach. The stage seemed such a small place in which to stowaway thirteen adults and two children with all their luggage, while still leaving space for the driver and express messenger with his gun, bags of mail, and express.

---

* Consumption was a lung problem similar to tuberculosis.

Up to June 3, 1879, when we arrived in Lead, my knowledge of the Black Hills was comprised of stories handed down by relatives and friends. From that time, however, my memory has framed many pictures that seem to stand out more with each passing year.

A year after Aunt Sarah's wild trip to Lead, the old stagecoaches improved with a few more comforts. Roads were better and the distances to travel between railroads and terminals diminished. The first picture of my trip to the Black Hills is from the cubby* of the stagecoach.

The trip from Sydney to Deadwood was devoid of thrills for the adults except for the tale of the hold-up and stealing of the bullion from another coach while it was waiting for departure. Later, when the Express Office burned down, the stolen bullion was found in a hole under the floor. The express agent was implicated for the robbery. Since the thieves had not yet sold the bullion, they never gained anything from their crime.

While eating dinner at a way station we heard about a hold-up that had occurred there. One of the station help was killed and the passengers were robbed of their jewelry and money, and then sent on their way. These depredations were always attributed to a gang of outlaws operating in Nebraska and Kansas, guilty mostly of cattle rustling.

In view of the reports told in Pueblo and written from Lead, my mother sewed her money inside the lining of my dress and put some bills under the insoles of our shoes. She considered that robbers would hardly search a child, and also felt confident that I would keep my mouth shut. I did not know about the money sewn in my dress, however, for mother finished that task on the advice of her old friend Judge Richards of Pueblo after I fell asleep.

The stage was of reddish-yellow color, like a great swinging boat perched on four wheels, with heavy canvas curtains to shut out wind and rain. Small baggage could be piled on top and at the back was a platform suspended by huge leather straps where trunks and boxes were secured. Perched high on the back was a seat where two could sit and brace their feet on the trunks. In front, high up over the cubby, the front of which made a

---

* A cubby was known as the front boot, made of leather and used as a baggage compartment. It extended off the main coach body and was located under the driver's bench.

brace for feet, was the driver's seat. There, three could sit without being crowded. The express and mailbags were placed in the cubby over which rested a thick cushion of straw and blankets. There, Willie Price, the only other child on the trip, and I spent our sleeping and most of our waking hours on that eventful journey. My mother only weighed seventy-six pounds when we left Pueblo so she won the sympathy and assistance of everyone on the trip. She was almost entirely relieved of my care throughout the trip.

Inside the coach were three seats. The back seat and front were fairly comfortable, except that one had to ride backward when sitting on the front seat. The middle seat lacked a back, except for a wide leather band attached at each end to the center posts of the coach and suspended straps fastened to the ceiling. These three seats held nine grown people daily, but in stormy weather, twelve crowded in, drawing the canvas curtains closed, placing the travelers in darkness regardless of time of day.

The driver's seat extended out over the cubby, and when the leather apron was buckled down, the driver and messenger fastened it over their laps to keep their legs dry when it stormed. In the cubby, Willie and I were as cozy and warm as the proverbial "bugs in a rug," far more comfortable than inside the coach.

In pleasant weather, we stood up between the legs of the driver and the messenger (also known as the express man responsible for delivering express packages) and held onto the dashboard. From this vantage point, we could look out over the horses' backs and to the sides for miles and miles, with views of deer and buffalo grazing in the distance. My talk and actions, very much like a little old woman's, kept the stage driver and messenger chuckling, and made me somewhat proud. I discussed the trip in detail with them, much to their amusement. One day, when a hill loomed in the distance on the prairie, they turned to me with sober faces, saying: "How far do you think that is from here?" I screwed up my eyes and with a wise look guessed "Five miles," a great distance to my young self. The messenger slapped his leg and explained, "Gol darn! If she didn't hit it exact!"

I soon lost the prestige I had won, for when a wolf howled in the distance, I vanished in terror into the cubby. I shall never forget that howl, just after sundown, while it was still light. The crunching of the stage frightened away the wolf from his supper, but the snarl in that howl sent Willie and me under the blankets in the dark cubby. Though much bigger, Willie was younger than me. We both crouched down together until the old wolf was gone. We never knew what happened after that because we fell asleep. Our first recollection was being awakened and dragged to an early morning breakfast at a roadhouse.

The stage was generally pulled by six horses driven at top speed for sixteen or eighteen miles depending on the difficulty of the roads. We would drive up to a station with a "hip-hip-hurrah!" Fresh horses would be changed for the next drive. Three times a day, we stopped for meals, and once at night, when the station keeper served coffee, and usually something stronger. The station boss looked after the horses and had the new ones ready to hook on as soon as we drove in so that the stage would lose minimal time.

Drunkenness was frowned upon for drivers or guards, as a clear head, sharp eyes, and steady hands were necessary if we should meet Indians or road agents.

I was looking over the dashboard when we reached the top of Deadwood Hill, almost a mile straight down with a high bank on one side of the road and the creek bed below on the other, with hardly enough room for one vehicle to make the grade. Down we plunged with a whoop, a shot from a gun, a cracking of the whip, the rolling of stones, with sparks flying from the shoes on the horses' feet, and wild shouts of men. A throng of people filled the street to watch the stage come into town and to hear the latest news from the outside world.

On the right side of the street as we entered Deadwood were low, squatty buildings, or rather, in reality, one long building almost a block in length, comprised of Chinese laundries, opium dens, and Chinese stores of different sorts with a ceiling that could not have been over seven feet high. A solid boardwalk lay in front of the building, and above the walk extended a three-foot balcony that gave egress from the rooms above the business rooms. On this balcony, the Chinese flower girls sunned themselves and bade for patronage. This was Deadwood's Chinatown, and on that day as we rolled down the Deadwood Hill, the Chinese flower girls poured out onto the balcony dressed in brilliant flowered costumes. Their fans and black hair adorned with brilliant little fans and ornaments made for a bright picture.

I had scarcely recovered from the wild ride down the hill and the glittering array of Chinatown, when the coach stopped at the Express Office and I was handed down to my mother since she was one of the first to alight. Aunt Sarah and Willie's dad, David Price, the largest man I had seen up to that time, met the stage at Deadwood. A large black hack* stood nearby with two beautiful, sleek, brown horses. Our baggage was loaded and we were soon transferred for the last four miles of our journey to Lead.

---

*A hack is another name for a buggy.

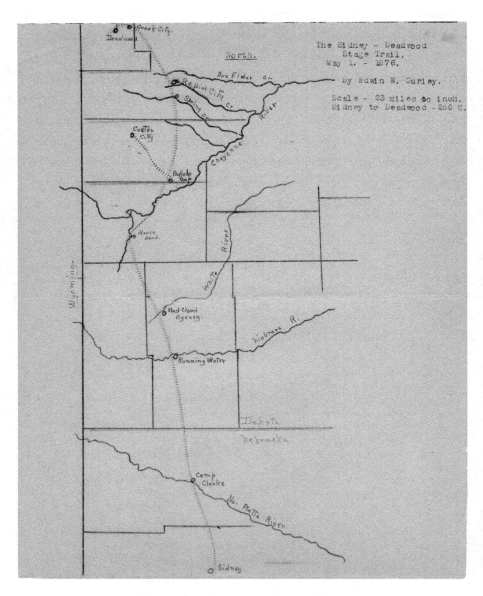

Sidney to Deadwood Map--1876 E. W. Curley

The SIDNEY-BLACK HILLS Route - 1876

E.W. Curley

Stage leaves Sidney every morning at 8 a.m.

Stations	Miles	TL Miles	Time
Sidney	0		
Water hole	12	12	
Camp Clarke	28	40	
Niobrara River	51	91	
Red Cloud Agency	18	109	
Horsehead	45	154	20 Hours
Buffalo Gap	17	171	
Rapid River-City	43	214	
Crook City	32	246	
Deadwood	10	256	48 Hours - 8 a.m.

It took 48 hours of travel time to go 256 miles from Sydney, Nebraska to Deadwood. More than half of that time was spent on the last 1/3 of the journey.

Early pictures of Lead

ARRIVAL IN LEAD

During the trip to Lead, we children were seen but not heard. Strangely, I have no recollection of Willie's mother, Sarah Price, except that she became very ill a year later. The start of the ride from Deadwood to Lead had a slight downhill trend and the road was wide and decent until we reached the tollgate, now Pluma. A long pole lay across the entrance of the bridge. A man came out of the cabin by the side of the bridge and the driver gave him some money, after which the pole was swung up into the air and we crossed.

Then the road changed, becoming increasingly steep, rocky, and narrow with a bank on one side and a raging creek some ten feet below on the other side. The road had been dug out of the side of the hill, barely wide enough for one wagon. Every four hundred feet or so, a turnout was available for another wagon to pass. In one place, we met a wood-rack and another hack. Another team and wagon were following us. The heavily loaded woodrack drew into the turnout allowing both of us to pass. The wagon that had followed us then backed into the turnout after the wood-rack pulled out. We then pulled around the other hack. The space was so narrow that before passing, all the passengers climbed out and walked while the men steadied the hack on the edge of the bank to keep it from going over. We then climbed in again and continued to our destination without mishap.

When I saw Lead for the first time, before me to the north of the road and east of the new mill was a small settlement of small houses, cabins, and stores. This area made up the original town that had been called "Washington" and later "Poverty Flats" or "The Flats." As the road swung west we passed the brick home of Sam McMaster, the Superintendent of the Homestake Mining Company, with the company assay office and barns. A small creek flowed between them and the main part of town. A good boardwalk followed the road from the brick house to its junction with Mill Street that ran north for about a block to the main opening of the Homestake Mine. As we turned south on Mill Street we passed a fine new brick store that had just been completed. This building was known as the "James Block" and housed the Hearst Mercantile Company store. The store at that time employed eleven men, and conducted $300,000 of business yearly, selling everything - food, liquor by the demijohn or barrel, clothing, hardware (even prospecting supplies), and for a short time, furniture.

From the "James Block," the business part of town continued on a level street for about two blocks to the next brick building, the bank, which had just opened in the spring. Across the street was a sudden drop to the town's main creek. For the first two years, this creek, along with a few shallow surface wells, served as the town's water supply. Soon thereafter, the creek water became contaminated, resulting in a typhoid epidemic.

I first set foot onto Lead soil at the corner of Mill and Main. At that time, the buildings still had space between them, to be filled in eventually. They were mostly one-story, sided in front and batted over tarpaper on the sides. Uncle Jack and Aunt Sarah's house stood about ten feet above street level, with her millinery shop and his shoe shop in the same building.

Here, I found myself at home, with my Aunt's familiar black walnut parlor suite upholstered in black horsehair and covered with crocheted tidies, the marble-top table, and three-cornered whatnot. Also familiar were the little china shepherdess and king's-herald, and the little vases Aunty had brought from England, along with the bouquet of hair and wool flowers under the glass dome. Over the floor lay a bright red velvet carpet over six inches of straw, providing a soft cushion to my feet and a nice warm stove. I danced and laughed, for after a long, hard journey, being home again felt so good.

The walls of the house bothered my senses as the tarpaper gave off a distracting odor. Aunty said the smell kept down the bedbugs that infested all the new pine lumber. While the muslin and paper made the walls look more attractive, they also provided the grandest nesting places for bugs and created plenty of work for the housewife. My mother would say: "It is no sin to get bedbugs, but it is a crime to keep them." Thus, a continual war of extermination broke out. I well remember seeing Uncle follow the seams of the ceiling with the lamp a short distance below. The bugs would drop into the flames as they emerged from hiding, drawn by warmth. Often the throat of the chimney would be filled with dead bugs before he finished his trip across the ceiling, as the bugs were in plentiful supply.

The distance between houses on our side of the street was usually about two feet, and we were often awakened at night by some poor drunk trying to find a way out of the wind between the two buildings. He would usually give up and sleep there until morning. At first, this frightened my mother, but we soon became accustomed to it.

PART II

Life in the Black Hills

LEAD LOCATION

Lead was first laid out in 1876 when Smoky Jones and others conducted a preliminary survey of the town. J.D. McIntyre resurveyed it in May 1877. Lead received its name from the gold quartz leads centering within her borders and is pronounced "leed," not "led" as so many try to say.

Heavy fallen pine trees, boulders, and underbrush made driving a team into the town impossible. Even on horseback, the early pioneers could hardly make their way over nature's obstacles. In spite of this, the community became the home of a great mining company.

Early pioneers stopped at nothing when gold was in sight. Little camp settlements eventually merged to create Lead City. Placer mining along the creeks soon became a thing of the past and prospectors headed for the mountains, digging into drifts and sinking shafts in the hope of finding the real source of the golden fruit.

As the population outgrew its boundaries, a larger field of operation was sought. Lead began to spread west of the mills and up the main gulch. Buildings north and south of Main Street covered the hillsides, in some cases to the very top of the hills. Nice buildings began to replace the shacks and by 1879 the town presented a very credible appearance and became the metropolis of the Black Hills.

The first frame building was erected in June 1877 by James H. Long and was the first hotel in town under the name, Miner's Hotel. Mrs. Mary Long, a motherly Irish woman, filled the office with flowers and tended them like children. Great red geraniums and big leafed begonias created a homey air in contrast to the rough pine interior. From the office, the stairs led to the bedrooms upstairs while at the back was the dining room with its long plank tables. There, girls of the best families in Lead served the substantial food of those times. These girls married and later became leaders in the town's social life. "Slinging hash" or working for Mrs. "So and So" yielded an honest day's work and was a badge of honor.

As mentioned earlier, Mealy & Smith opened the first exclusive grocery store in 1877. Peter A. Gushurst and others also opened grocery stores. A year later, Mr. Smith sold the grocery store and in 1878 opened the first furniture establishment.

Oscar Silver brought a stock of goods from Denver as far as Custer, where he was forced to open up shop and was bought out by the U.S. soldiers. He then returned to Denver, bought another stock of goods and opened the first dry-goods store under the name of Silver Bros. He sold the first block and tackle and rope used by the Homestake Company.

Thomas Jones opened the first meat market in 1877, located next door east of my aunty's millinery store on Main Street. Thomas Uren, who later bought Jones out, was a clerk there. I bought many a pound of meat from both men.

As mentioned earlier, in the spring of 1879, the first bank was established with John "High John" Ainly in charge. This building was the first to stamp its image on my memory there in Lead.

As I recall, the first woman and child in Lead were Mrs. Carter and her little daughter Josie who died in the diphtheria epidemic of 1880. She was a little black-eyed black curly haired youngster, always laughing and loved by everyone. Pearly McCoy was the first baby born in Lead. My Aunt Sarah Bragg ran the first millinery store, and Pencus Cohen opened the first clothing store. This store expanded as years went on and Cohen took on different partners. While originally on Mill Street, the store ended up on Main Street with Joe Chamison in charge as a partner.

Reverend Smith was the first preacher, a Methodist, and Indians killed him. The first church was Roman Catholic and was built in May 1879 on the hillside back from North Bleeker Street just under the old water tank. It was a frame structure with siding that ran lengthwise and was painted white. It had a tower tipped with a cross. The paint, the siding and the tower proclaimed it "the peer of all" in those days, along with many steps to reach its doors - a flight, then a platform, another flight and a platform to rest, then another and another. Later, a new street ran from Bleeker around the hill and it left but two flights when one went by the road. Some very pretty homes were built, leading to the start of Sunnyside.

The post office started in 1877. George Noyes was appointed the first postmaster and George H. Holden was made deputy immediately after the first delivery on July 29, 1877. Wesley Alexander was the mail and express carrier. In the first year, the office sold stamps to the amount of $574.50. A money order office was established August 3, 1879, under W.H. "Billy" Fawcett. By 1881 the volume of business done was as follows:

Stamps sold	$	2,087.52
Paper wrappers, stamped envelopes, postcards	$	442.20
Registered fees and packages	$	95.20
Money orders issued	$	35,238.41
Money orders paid	$	5,603.11
Money orders repaid	$	216.00

Add to that the income from box rent $548.00, and you get a picture of the rapid growth of Lead in three and a half years. My mother collected and wrote down the above facts at different times during her life in the Hills.

A reliable source of water was essential both for human consumption as well as for mining operations. Up until 1878, the creek running behind the main street of the town plus a few surface water wells served as the main water supply of Lead. The principal well was located just under the brow of the hill upon which the Catholic and Protestant cemeteries were laid out side-by-side. The creek and the wells soon became contaminated with disease and the mine tailings that drained into the creek. To supplement the water supply in the immediate area, additional water was brought in from water rights owned by miners outside of Lead. Water rights, like placer and lode rights, were precious commodities.

By 1878, the Pioneer became the principal source of water for Lead. Owned by McLennan and Webb, these water rights were bought by the Homestake Company for $40,000. Another source was the Whitewood. The water was brought from springs and small creeks in the mountains through flume or sluice boxes. One sluice box emptied into a large wooden tank on South Mill hill and the other into a wooden tank on Sunnyside. From these tanks water ran downhill to the mills and homes of the town.

In town, the sluice boxes were covered affairs, but outside of town they were open troughs three feet wide made of 2 x 12 boards. Walking along the side of the trough, I occasionally saw dead animals lying in them with water washing over their rotting bodies. Thoughtful persons would generally remove the bodies.

I well remember when one of the old tanks was cleaned out and replaced by a new one. Papa described the tank as a third full of muck with the bodies of dead cats and dogs. He buried the bodies of three newborn babies taken from that muck. Such was the first water supply of Lead.

After our arrival, Uncle Jack moved his shoe shop around on Mill Street next to the then outstanding hotel known as the Homestake House. It was located across from the mill and what was later known as the "open cut." Many of the unmarried mill and mine officials roomed and boarded at the Homestake House while other rooming and boarding houses cared for the miners and workmen. On the west side of the street the buildings were rather scattered. Green's lumberyard took up most of the space, with the bank, Long's, Silver's and a few others on the same side.

By expanding from the bank corner west on Main, North Mill Street had gradually become the business street. South Mill hill became the residential section and later West Main. The leading hotel for transients was the Springer House, the pride of the town, built several blocks to the west on Main. A meal in its spacious dining room was quite the social event in the lives of the locals.

The homes of the town dotted the hillsides south and west of the business section. Residents aimed to get as far away as possible from the eternal pounding of the mill stamps, thump, thump, day and night every day with never a break in the rhythm.

MEETING MARIE BUCHMANN
& SAM McMASTER

My first formal call in Lead was made one Sunday afternoon. My aunt was dressed in a much be-ruffled black silk gown, its huge bustle effect protruding under her wide skirt, made still wider in appearance by the use of a wire hoop skirt frame suspended from an eighteen-inch waistband. Over the tight-fitting bodice, Aunty wore a heavily jet-beaded shoulder cape, held in place by a fancy black silk elastic belt while the huge puffed sleeves of her bodice made the cape's lace ruffles give a broadening affect to her shoulders. As a result, she looked somewhat like a large hourglass.

On her head, Aunty wore a miniature creation of a famous New York milliner, and carried in her finely gloved hands a tiny sunshade that had spread out about eighteen inches. This was used more to hide her face from the too curious rather than to ward off the sun. Unaccustomed to the climate, I wore a brown velvet coat that covered my dress entirely, a velvet hat to match, brown kid gloves, and high bronze kid shoes. Aunty's gown swept the ground, but she raised it daintily when the need arose to protect it from the dirt on the sidewalk or at the street crossing.

We made our call on Miss Marie Buchmann, a young woman, the daughter of a well-to-do family of Schleswig-Holstein, Germany. She was irked by her stepfather's treatment. Having an independent disposition, she resolved to come to America, and landed first in Chicago. There, she learned of the Black Hills and took the train for a point west where she joined a wagon train into the Hills as the only woman. She had been well trained in all the housewifely arts and was an exceptional cook. She soon found work and was soon made the housekeeper for Samuel McMaster, the first Superintendent of the Homestake Mining Company in the Black Hills.

We knocked on the kitchen door, for the front door was seldom used, and on the call to "Come in," opened the door and walked into a large combination kitchen, dining room, and living room. A man, wrapped in a huge grey blanket, sat in an old-fashioned, wooden rocking chair, his trousers rolled above his knees and his feet in a tub of hot mustard water. Mary, as she was always called, from time to time added more hot water from what seemed to be a huge iron teakettle, while the man drank a glass of steaming hot "toddy." Mary put the kettle on the red-hot kitchen stove and came forward to shake hands. Aunty introduced me very formally to Miss Buchmann who, in turn, introduced me to Sam McMaster, who apologized for being caught in such a shape by saying, "Mary insists on treating me like a baby to break up this damn cold."

Another time when I was visiting Miss Buchmann, Mr. McMaster came into the room from his office, and on seeing me, patted me on the head saying, "Don't you let Mary get your feet in hot water or she'll take all the hide off them," and chuckled and then added: "But she sure can knock a cold."

In those early days, I believe one could say that Sam McMaster was the most important man in Lead. He was a tall, raw-boned Irishman, blunt and outspoken. He had few words, but when he spoke, he meant what he said. He was just and kind-hearted to the extreme but at the same time, harsh and severe when the need arose. Miss Buchmann was one of the grand characters of those early days, a friend in times of trouble and a faithful adherent to the laws of her church and the country she had adopted. She had no use for those who deliberately did wrong, and never minced words in telling them so, but she had the finest, most sympathetic heart when it came to innocent unfortunates.

Miss Buchmann became a tried and true friend. She was not socially inclined, but distinguished looking, honest and true, and ran Sam McMaster's house in a thorough manner. She looked after his interests as though they were her own; guarding his health, his house, and his purse with conscientious integrity. Her tongue was sharp for the evildoer, but her heart was a haven of rest for those in misfortune. The evildoer learned to shun her, but others loved her, for a truer, nobler soul never trod the streets of Lead.

Another member of the McMaster household was Harry Teer. When we first knew him, he was the master of the Homestake stables, and he would bring peals of laughter to our childish lips by his many absurd antics. With a grand flourish, he would call upon my aunt to witness how he proposed to Mary each day, but she would have none of him. She picked up the broom and chased him out of the house amid peals of laughter from us all. He was very kind to children and loved by everyone.

MR. SMITH BECOMES
A PART OF OUR FAMILY

Seth Randall Smith

Eliza McLean Smith

W e had not lived in Lead very long when S. R. Smith came into our life. One day Aunty went to Deadwood on business, and Mother was looking after the store. A customer wanted to see a hat on a shelf beyond Mother's reach. Mother stepped up on a three-legged stool to get it down but the stool tipped. She grabbed at the shelving that gave way, and had it not been for the counter in front of her, Mother would have been crushed under it. The customer's screams brought Mr. Smith to Mother's rescue. Lifting the boxes, he met my Mother for the first time.

At that time, Mr. Smith was a co-owner of the Smith & Gould Furniture establishment. He began calling regularly on my mother as did other young men of the town. Some I liked very much, but I paid little attention to Mr. Smith. One day I admired a little red chair sitting on the walk in front of his store and he told me that if I would be his girl he would give it to me. I looked him in the eye and very decidedly said, "NO!" and went home. Clearly, our relationship had a rough start.

Five months later, my mother and Mr. Smith were married in Uncle Jack and Aunt Sarah Bragg's parlor. When mother told me that she was going to marry Mr. Smith, I cried and begged her not to, saying, "He's bad, Mama. No! No!" Perhaps that is why I was not present at the wedding for I might have made a scene.

I didn't know they were married until the next morning when Maggie, Aunty's hired girl, told me that I was going to live with my new Papa. I simply turned and walked into my aunt's dark bedroom and crawled under her bed. I was later found fast asleep with a tear-stained face and my aunt's kitten clasped in my arms. From my perspective, my mother had deserted me for another and I never forgot it. Her marriage severed the close tie between us, and from that day on I lived my own life. Although I was only five years old, I kept my troubles and my joys to myself.

I never accepted Mr. Smith as a father but I did call him Papa. He was usually very kind to me but I never let him "step over the mark." He did not allow the world to know my feelings toward him, and he always resented Mother's and my actions. He seldom failed to make us feel his resentment. The outside world could not know the hurt that cut the deepest, especially into my mother's heart.

I accepted life as it came and learned very early to keep my chin up and my lips smiling no matter how deeply hurt I might be and did not allow my temper to rule me. My aunt once said to me, "Always remember it takes two to make a quarrel and a word once spoken can never be recalled so shut your teeth tight and go away until you forget to be mad - but don't forget to laugh, darling, no matter what happens." Later, I laughed when she fell on the ice and Aunty snapped, "She'd laugh if I killed myself." I answered, "Shall I cry?" and then she laughed.

Thus I learned to practice the precepts laid down by my elders, especially these two: 1) Keep smiling no matter what the weather, and 2) Don't speak when you are angry. The result has been peace and harmony through many trying events.

Seth R. Smith now began to figure in a large way in the life and development of Lead. His origin and early life caused him to develop into the man whom few understood, kind and generous to the needy and those who could do his bidding, but a man who could hate while yet appearing to love. He had but few friends, loyal to no one because he could trust no one, a man who had many admirable qualities and few vices, yet one who wrecked his own life by the secret hates and passions which poisoned him.

A study of his childhood elicits pity. He was born in Bangor, Maine, before the Civil War. His mother, Eunice Blake, was of good colonial stock, a woman beloved by all her children and friends. His father, Benjamin Smith, was also of good colonial stock, but a dictator in every sense of the word. He ruled his wife and children with an iron hand and allowed no one, friend or foe, to oppose his slightest act. During the Civil War, Benjamin served his necessary time in the Army, then moved west taking up a homestead on the banks of the Mississippi near Monticello, Minnesota.

At this time, Seth was eleven, with a family comprised of four boys and five girls. The work of the farm consisted primarily of chopping down trees and grubbing out the stumps. Playtime or schooling for the children or rest for their mother were all scarce. The oldest boy, Edmond, split his foot open when felling a tree and bled to death on his twenty-third birthday in 1881. Phylinda, the eldest girl, died of diphtheria that same winter.

His mother was heavy-set and tied at home looking after the necessary work of caring for her family and the work of the farm-- washing, ironing, milking, churning, raising chickens and turkeys, slopping the pigs, and sewing and mending without any modern convenience.

The older girls married young and Seth's father found frequent trips to town necessary as he was the only one permitted to do the trading or business for the family. Upon leaving, he would call the two older boys and tell them to dig twelve to sixteen stumps out of the field or take a licking when he got back. They knew they could not dig all those stumps and that a licking would follow. Seth's brother Charles would say, "What's the use, you're a fool to try Seth... you might as well go hunting. Pa 'ill lick us anyway."

One day, while driving the cows to feed in the timber, Seth came across a deer run. That night when he went for the cows, he took wire and his gun. Barefoot, he crossed the deer run with dreams of a pair of boots and a chance to go to school that winter. He set a trap with the wire so that when the deer would touch it, the trigger of the gun would be pulled.

Early the next morning, he heard the gun go off and running out of the house he raced to the gun to find the deer, a fine young buck. "I got him, I got him," he yelled and dragged the dead buck to the house. He skinned it, tacked the hide to the side of the barn, sold half of the meat to a neighbor and took the other half to his mother for the family. Expecting to collect his money, he learned that the neighbor had gone home with the meat without payment.

He worked hard to clean the hide properly and with hopes of going to town with his father on Saturday and sell it to buy boots. When Saturday came, his father gave him the job of digging out fourteen stumps or receive a thrashing. His father then took the hide to town with the promise of buying the boots only to bring back two boots that were not mates. One was a good boot but the other was cheap; when it got wet, it shrank up so that it pinched Seth's foot.

Since the farmer to whom he had sold the deer meat lived near the schoolhouse, Seth asked if he could work for his board and sleep in the loft. He also landed the janitor job at the school to pay his tuition. That worked very well but he needed books, so he asked the neighbor for his deer money to discover that his father had taken it. As a result, Seth set another trap for a deer and killed it. This time he carried the hide to town himself and acquired the money for his books.

Mr. Smith Becomes a Part of Our Family

When summer came, the farmer hired him, but when he went to draw his pay his father showed up and demanded it. The farmer said that if he could not pay the boy he would not pay the father. That night Seth went home to bid his mother whom he almost worshipped farewell and left for good. His father tried to follow him but everyone covered for the boy and he got away. He was seventeen and very large for his age, and soon found work as a carpenter. After several years, he had a little nest egg laid away in the bank.

Seth figured out what he thought his time was worth to his father until he turned twenty-one. Homesick to see his mother, he visited home with the money in his pocket. He was well-dressed in a fine coat, to which his mother received him with open arms. However, she told him to hide the coat or risk his father taking it when he got home. After supper, Seth shoved the dishes to one side saying, "Pa, what will you take for my time until I am twenty-one?" His father answered, "What you earn is mine." "Oh, now," said Seth, "Get it." Realizing he had been too hasty, his father answered, "But I'm willing to take one thousand dollars." Seth drew out a paper on which was an agreement that Benjamin Smith and wife, for the sum of one thousand dollars, surrendered, etc. etc., to the earnings of Seth Randall Smith. He pushed it over for his father to sign. His father drew back. "Where's your money?" Pa asked. Seth piled up two stacks of five one hundred dollars each in front of him. His father reached for it. "Oh, no. Sign first." His father drew back while his mother watched both of them. Avarice got the best of him and Benjamin signed the paper and Eunice after him. Seth took the paper and his father reached to scoop up the money. "Oh, no. You only own half my time and mother the other half," as he pushed one pile to his mother while his father grasped the other pile. Then, kissing his mother goodbye, he put on his coat and walked out of the house for good.

Next, Seth found work in a logging camp. Starting as a chopper, he rose to be a boss logger. When he saved enough, he bought a spring seat for the family wagon and sent it to his mother so that she could ride to town in comfort. His father appropriated the seat and put a board across the top of the wagon sides for his wife to sit on. That was the last gift Seth ever sent home. When his mother died at the age of 57 in 1881, no one told him until three months later when his sister requested money for a tombstone to which he complied.

(EDITOR'S NOTE: Eunice Smith is buried in Riverside Cemetery in Monticello, Minnesota.)

DISASTER FOLLOWS
THE DEADWOOD FIRE

Life was not easy for Papa. On September 26, 1879, two months before he married Mother, a disastrous fire occurred in Deadwood. That night the mill whistles began to pour out a continuous blast and to the east the sky was blood red. Deadwood was aflame! Deadwood was burning! Deadwood was swept away!

To rebuild, lumber, clothing, food, and furniture were all necessary, Lead had to furnish them all. Within a week's time, the Gould and Smith furniture stock practically sold out. Mother bought ticking from Silver Brothers and the James Store to sew mattress ticks that Papa then filled with straw and excelsior. Rush orders were sent to Omaha, Chicago, and Minneapolis for more furniture.

With all the firm's money, Silas Gould took the stage to Bismarck, where the goods would be shipped by rail and then hauled by team with ox or mule to Lead. On arriving in Bismarck, Gould bought up mule teams and wagons at high prices and waited on the arrival of the furniture. He also rented a vacant warehouse and as the goods came in, he stored them there until enough teams were available to ship them to Lead.

When Gould procured an outfit, he loaded it with the items that would fit most compactly such as table and chair legs, sides of beds, and dresser mirrors. He stored bulky pieces including dresser bodies, tabletops, and chair seats and backs until he could acquire more and larger wagons. He sent on the initial wagons with the smaller items. Then, a fire swept through the Bismarck warehouse and destroyed its contents. Unfortunately, Smith

& Gould did not have insurance to cover their losses.

Papa hired an old cabinetmaker by the name of Marcus Gurney and went to work. Together, they made seats and backs for chair legs, and head and footboards for the bedsides that had already arrived. They made tabletops and chests of drawers and used up what had come through but this was still not enough.

Papa offered Gould a "buy or sell" proposition for $400. Gould refused. He evidently still had some of the firm's money left for he went gambling and lost dearly, caring more about cards than business. He eventually took the $400 and left town.

Papa mortgaged the house to raise the $400. Later, when bills and scorching letters began to arrive in the mail, he learned that Gould had not paid for the furniture that was burned, and that the firm was financially broken. When the bank refused to give Papa credit, and with no furniture to sell while still owing his creditors, I saw him pick up his revolver and start for the basement. Mother caught him as he went down the stairs. She took the gun away and told me to go to bed.

The next day, Mother, with Mr. Gurney's help, took over the management of the store, while Papa earned money as a carpenter. The business weathered the storm. Mother wrote to all the creditors promising payment in full with interest. Beebe and Runyon's of Omaha, Nebraska, shipped a duplicate order to restock the store.

During this time, Mother clerked in Papa's store and sewed bindings on strips of Brussels carpet for the tailing* room of the Homestake Company. She earned good money for her job at the Homestake Mill, and also made dresses and gave music lessons on her organ, all while keeping our rooms over the store in apoplectic order. How her frail little body endured the strain no one knows. Papa worked from seven in the morning until the six o'clock whistle blew, and then came home. Then, he either delivered the furniture on his back that mother had sold during the day, or made or trimmed a coffin, or made mattresses from the excelsior that had come in

---

* Tailings were the gold flecks not taken up by the quicksilver plates in the mill.

the packing. One day I remember mother prepared a casket for a child, and watching her I remarked, "That's just big enough for me isn't it, Mother?" My Mother dropped the hammer and sat down on the floor with her apron over her head. She cried as though her heart would break. That was the only time I saw my mother break down and cry during that long hard winter. In two years, she paid all the bills from the money that Papa earned as a carpenter, along with the proceeds from the store.

Twice after that, Mother was compelled to take over the management and save the business. Papa could manage business successfully alone but when he joined with another person he failed. In later years he would say, "I tried many partners in my life but the only one that paid out was the partnership with my wife." Somehow Mother was always able to get the money needed when Papa was turned down, and they would come through.

Most of the goods sold to boarding houses and hotels were paid for in trade. As a result, we always had one good dinner meal a day. The rest of the time we alternated cornmeal mush and graham mush with sorghum or milk for our supper at ten or eleven o'clock at night when the store closed. In the morning, hot pancakes and coffee gave us a good breakfast. We lived on mush and mush and more mush except for Thanksgiving.

Near Thanksgiving, the men had a turkey shoot and each man paid a quarter to shoot at a turkey's head when it popped up between the slats of a crate that stood a hundred feet away. Papa won a turkey and Mother made a nice dinner and invited several friends. One friend was Mr. Roberts, a gentleman she had gone out with before she married Papa. Papa served at the table and gave Mr. Roberts only the neck of the turkey, offering no other part to him. Mother protested but Papa claimed that the neck was the sweetest meat on the fowl, and continued with his dinner. I never remember Mother ever inviting another guest to our table though Papa often brought men and even women home for a meal without any previous arrangement.

I can still see my mother take blue and white twine and sit and knit in the minutes between customers. She knit my stockings or Papa's socks. She often unraveled old socks to reuse the best wool to make another pair. She could knit without watching her needles and read a book aloud, while Papa,

Mr. Gurney and I would listen. She was always busy and raised our ideals of life for better living. Other people paid her to sew and she used all of her earnings to pay the creditors and mortgage. That was a hard winter.

I well remember the dresses I wore, made from several different pieces of material, outer flannel waists with the back and front made from different colored pieces of cloth while the skirt that showed under my aprons was made of good wool. My everyday aprons were gingham while Sunday's apron was made of white muslin. The first nice dress I had was made from a piece of pink cashmere and some blue silk that my Aunt gave Mother. The dress had some pearl bead trimming taken off one of her own dresses. I was to "speak a piece" at church and I felt dressed for the occasion.

Shoes were a problem. I was hard on shoes and Uncle had always made my shoes before they left Lead. My feet were accustomed to soft kid, and new shoes cost $5 a pair. I remember overhearing an argument between Papa and Mother that ended with his words, "Well I'll buy her next shoes" and he did, a pair of copper-toed cowhide two sizes too big for me that I certainly resented. I kicked every stone that came in my path. By the end of the week the $3.75 shoes took a one-dollar mending. The next week the same happened and the third another mending, and when Papa saw, he yelled, "Well, buy her shoes yourself." By that time, I had corns on every toe and a broken big toe but Mother never knew until long after the heavy shoes were discarded.

That was the only time I ever knew of Papa's objecting to pay for any of my clothing. I was always one of the best-dressed girls of the town, though I doubt very much if my clothes cost as much as those of the other girls. Many of my dresses were made from mother's cast-offs or remnants picked up at odd times and always made by her.

Papa never used liquor or tobacco, as Mother was bitterly opposed to liquor. I shall never forget one night when Papa came home from a hard day's work building the Savage Tunnel house and stopped halfway up the stairs. I was hanging over the railing. He looked at my mother and said, "I want a glass of beer." She shook her head. "I want a glass of beer and I'm going to have to it," he repeated and started down the steps. Mother never said a word. Halfway down, he stopped and said, "If I want beer so bad that I have to have it, it's time to let it alone." From that moment he never touched liquor in any form and he fought the liquor interests, even defending his buildings and our lives with the point of his gun.

Those were days of poverty or gold. Mother and Papa stood side-by-side in the struggle whether we were living on cornmeal mush and milk or on the fat of the land in later years. Through hard work they rose to be among the foremost people of Lead financially and socially and helped to build the city.

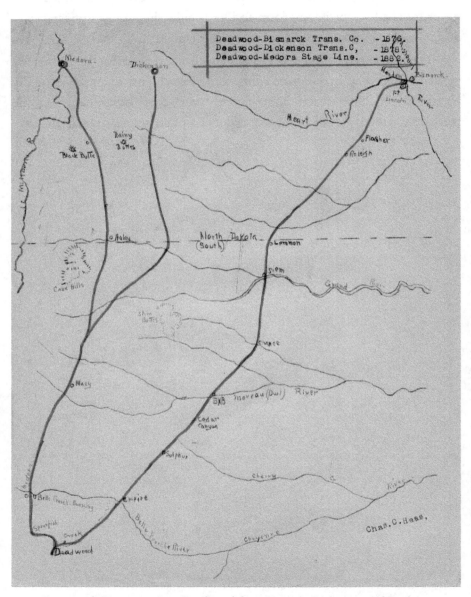

Stagecoach Lines came into Deadwood from Bismark, Dickenson and Medora.
This would be the route Silas Gould took from Deadwood to Bismark.

The <u>BISMARCK-DEADWOOD</u> Stage Line - 1876

N.P.R.R. Operators & Owners

Bismarck	
Mandan	
Ft. Lincoln	
Flasher	
Raleigh	
Cannonball River	
Seim (Grand River)	
Chance (No. Fork Moreau River)	
BXB Ranch (So. Moreau River)	
Cedar Canyon	
Sulphur	
Empire (Belle Fourche River)	
Oak Grove Ranch	
Crook City	
Deadwood	265 miles

UNDERSTANDING MY MOTHER

After Uncle moved his shoe shop, Mother assisted Aunty in the millinery store and became a very busy dressmaker filling a void in the little city. As a result, she had little time to devote to her wayward daughter; yet, that daughter was never long out of her sight.

At that time, my little mother was scarcely four feet eleven inches tall and weighed but seventy-eight pounds. Her blue-black hair, which she wore in natural curls, and her black eyes and fair skin accentuated by bright red cheeks made her a striking figure. Proud and haughty in manner, she was somewhat unapproachable to the free and easy inhabitants of a mining camp. Her dresses were generally severely tailored but very stylish.

I was showered with the best of every plaything on the market. Men predominated, and many of them were clean, lonely souls who took notice of a little child and were grateful for her smile and a cheery "how-do" that warmed their homesick hearts.

One such man, on going back to England, sent a package to his landlady marked, "For the little girl next door who is always laughing." The package housed a beautiful little genuine Delft sixteen-piece tea set that I cherished for several years without breaking a piece. A few years later, my stepfather took it out of the box where I had packed it and gave it to a girl unfamiliar to me when I was on a visit to Kansas with my mother. Thus, even my toys were never my own. If my stepfather had a notion, they could be taken away, even birthday gifts.

In the eyes of the townspeople, I had everything. In reality, I owned nothing, a fact I realized over time and consequently learned to hide things securely that I prized. I truly learned the lesson Mother wanted me to learn - "Never love anything or trust anyone to the point that it would hurt to give them up."

Mother never allowed me to play haphazardly with other children, and in Lead, she was even stricter about my associates. Grown-ups showered me with gifts of all description, and when children were allowed to come and play with me, I often tempted them to stay longer than they really desired by giving one of my toys to them unbeknownst to my mother. Instinctively social, I longed for companionship.

I was never popular among other children. In spite of a happy democratic nature, I insisted on being the leader. So, owing to my own disposition and my mother's strict supervision, I had few friends among the children. As a result, I was a lonely child, but too proud to let that loneliness be known. Year after year, I drew more and more into my shell. I played by myself, inventing my own games and living a life even my mother knew little of. I knew little of my mother's love or thoughts. I once heard her say to my aunt, "Sarah, I hope and pray I can teach her never to love or trust anyone but to be independent of all the world. Then she will never be hurt."

At that time, I did not realize what she meant. I learned years later what my mother's life had been like, the heartaches that had transformed her into a stone image. My aunt was the only one I could go to for unstinted affection, and even then, never in the presence of my mother. Mother was the dictator, the arbitrator of my life, and none dared to interfere. Her intense jealousy for me caused me to fear rather than to love her and caused her to be overly harsh and demanding of me.

As mentioned earlier, she was the youngest child of a Scottish chieftain's disinherited son and a French nobleman's granddaughter. Having lost her mother when she was three and her father shortly later, she was placed as a ward of the state in a religious school until age nine. Sent alone to America to her sister Sarah and her husband Jack Bragg, she never forgot her family heritage, though she never mentioned it. Proud and haughty, she allowed herself to make but few friends, and even then, only of her rank.

Unfortunately, despite her high standards for friends, she was not a good judge of men, and her marital life was unhappy. She had to be the dictator of her husband's life along with mine. Due to her fine analytical and business mind, time after time she demonstrated her superiority over her husband. Few men were able to tolerate that situation and thus her married life was continually plagued with friction.

As drink was a main cause for her father's estrangement from the family, Mother compelled all family members to be total abstainers. This influenced her whole life's actions in the Black Hills. She fought liquor interests with every mental and physical force she could muster up. No one could associate intimately with her and also drink or tolerate the saloon. She had great pity for a drunkard and referred to drunkenness as a disease acquired because of a weak will and bad associates.

I look back at my mother and see one of the strongest wills and characters I have ever had the privilege of coming in contact with. No dictator ever ruled with more of an iron hand. She never vaunted her power or lauded herself but quietly forced those around her to do her will or "get out." Her servants worked with her for years and respected her. They were loyal to her as she was always loyal to them, but she "hewed to the line" in all things and "let the chips fall" where they would.

The only fear I ever seemed to experience was of my mother. Darkness or high places, thunder, lightning or wind held no terror for me. I loved to watch a storm even as a tiny child but the terror of my mother's anger left me speechless and unable to defend myself, even when innocent of the act under question. I took many a punishment for things I never committed. I knew she would not believe me if I declared myself innocent, for she only believed her own opinions as true. All else was false and a lie.

Mother was a dictator for the first twenty years of my life, but my inmost thoughts and ambitions I kept to myself until I could be financially independent. My aunt was my haven for emotional overflow. I could go to her with my troubles and joys and find sympathy and softness. And my old uncle, quiet and good, gave me a faith in the goodness of humanity that I never learned in my mother's home. My mother's will ruled everyone, especially her child. OBEY was spelled in capital letters in our house.

Mother was well aware of the sins that thrived in the mining camp and was certain that they must never touch her or her child.

I carried a fear of my mother's displeasure were I to fail her in any way. I was but a sickly little pine tree nourished by a determined mother who could never give up on herself or see me falter. To her, my head must never bend and I must be able to hold my place among the best. Mother was hard, cruel at times, denying herself a softening of affection toward, or accepting affection, from me. Yet, today, I honor and respect her for who she was and what she did for me.

Mother and Aunty had very different personalities. Aunty was smiling, blue-eyed and fair while mother was the daring, silent, black-eyed, black-haired dictator of the Scotch Highlands, born to rule. Mother was the haughty Scotch father and Aunty the lively, dancing, happy French mother who made friends everywhere and filled her home with feasting and jolly company. Uncle, too, liked friends and a crowd around him and when the day's work ended, music filled the house.

In my aunt and uncle's home, I found happiness and an unfamiliar freedom. While Mother never relaxed her vigilance over me, I found my aunt and uncle's home a constant source of relief from the strict discipline of my mother. Aunty would take me on business trips to Deadwood while leaving Mother in charge of the store. Often, a friendly call would loom up when too strict a confinement made me restless, and at these times Aunty would take me with her on an outing.

One day, I surprised my mother by describing a certain house and its surrounding houses and several of the people. I asked her, "Where was that house and who were the people?" "Who has been talking to you?" she asked in a strained voice. "Who told you about such a place?" I said, "No one. I just remembered it." My mother could not believe my answer, but finally told me that it was the house where I was born and that I was only two and a half years old when we left.

This talk led to my recounting other recollections, and I told my Mother that a certain man in town looked like my father. Mother had never mentioned my father to me or allowed anyone else to do so. When Mother met the man later, she recognized that I should be told the true conditions of my life. From that day on I realized that she would never allow anyone but herself to come into my life if it was within her power. I was hers and no one would ever take me from her. My past was buried with that talk until many years later.

When thinking of her I recall a woman with a fear of the unknown, never trusting anyone; a woman eternally watching for something unexpected to face her. She prepared for the worst, never trusted anyone, and always had her chin up to face the inevitable without revealing the awful fear that plagued her. Mother seldom smiled and I do not remember hearing her laugh. To most people she was a stone image with a sympathetic face that a lonely heart might go to in trouble, but with a manner that forbade trouble to touch her own heart.

Naturally, having an active brain continually prodded by my mother, I became a somewhat precocious brat. At the age of five I talked the language of adults, for I was never babied. I would often stand off and be shocked at the antics of children older than me. I wanted to join them but my mother's hand seemed always on my shoulder and her voice was always saying "No." These facts may explain why my childhood scenes are so vivid in my memory.

OUR HOME OVER THE STORE

The marriage of my mother to Papa changed the tenor of my life, for it brought me into contact with people from all classes. In most ways, I was still sheltered from the general public, but I learned the ways of life in a most unique manner.

At that time, Papa owned the furniture store building, in addition to a four-room house on South Mill Street. Since the house was occupied, Papa rented rooms in Thomas Jones' new house until his house could be vacated. The Jones had a boy, George, and a girl, Pauline, my age. Pauline and I became very good friends.

Papa decided he could remodel the rooms over the store so we could live there and still have the rent from the house coming in to pay off the mortgage. When Mr. Jones sold his meat market and the family moved away, their move hastened our own relocation to the second floor of the store.

Our three rooms were always very comfortable. I spent most of my time alone for I was not allowed to have many playmates. I had more toys than most children so Mother never favored other children around unless she could be present and know exactly what we were doing. My very democratic tendency was a constant worry to my mother who was rather exclusive where friends were concerned.

The common sights that I, a six-year-old, could see from our apartment windows were many, especially at night. Looking out of the kitchen windows at the back of the apartment revealed the sordid life of the brothel and down-and-out prostitutes. Vice, drunkenness, and disease were everywhere. Saloons flanked our building, with three more directly in front and houses of prostitution on every side.

A long, narrow building known as a second-rate lodging house was near us, with a front entrance and one opening on the alley in back of Papa's place of business. In the late afternoon or evening, one could see men too proud to be seen entering the front door furtively sneak into the lodging house through the back entrance. Some windows did not even have blinds to hide the sordid lives of the prostitutes.

Ramshackled cabins stood behind this lodging house where the dregs of society wore Mother Hubbards and carpet slippers.* These women sold their diseased bodies to the riff-raff who would give them food and a place to lie as they eked out their last days in squalor and filth, along with the lowliest of the mining camp.

The bright lights of Main Street lit up our front room so that when mother went downstairs to help with customers, I did not need a light. I loved to sit in our big chair and watch the sights of the street and the building across the way. Mrs. Fran Baldwin's and Mrs. Eliza Hayes' small building gave way to a two-story frame building that housed the Family Liquor House. The upstairs was divided into a sort of reception room with small rooms and booths leading from it.

From our front windows, I could look across the main street into the nightlife of the town. Every other door opened into a saloon with doors swinging continually. Women with rich gowns, jewels, and painted faces paraded the street. In her bright green silk dress, Russian Alice, her diamonds flashing from hands and throat, would walk up the street, enter a saloon and take her seat at a poker table. The men would crowd around. I learned later that she was a notorious poker player and gambler who spent her time between Deadwood and Lead.

Alice was a little below medium height in size, with golden blond hair and brilliantly painted cheeks. I never saw her in the daylight or was close

---

* A Mother Hubbard was a full loose gown, usually fitted at the shoulders, while carpet slippers were house slippers made from carpet material.

enough to see her eyes but heard men remark that she saw everything... even through her opponents' cards — and thus knew what they held. Her spectacular dress and jewels would dazzle anyone and take his mind off his game. Alice became known as Poker Alice, the poker shark of the west. Her reign soon ended, however, and she left the scene before we moved to the house on the hill.

I watched the flow of men and girls drinking at the tables on the second floor of the Family Liquor House. Many then drifted into the exclusive booths along the side of the long room. Bright lights, money jingling, liquor flowing, combined with songs and laughter made up the nightlife of the dives of Lead in those early days.

Our home over the store was quite thrilling not only in what I saw and heard but in the way it was built. The big front room had large windows, in the hall stretched a heavy wire from the living room door casing back to the kitchen-dining room door casing. From this wire hung a long curtain that made for a bedroom behind the curtain. This room received light from a skylight that opened onto the roof. From the skylight, a ladder-like stairway dropped down. Papa could drop the stairs down, open the skylight, and walk out on a two-foot walk that ran the length of the roof. In the winter, one could raise this walk above the slope of the roof to let the snow slide under and off the roof. Here, Papa could rush to see where a fire was located when the mill whistles made their announcement. Papa was Chief of Hose Company Number Two for a while.

I was not allowed to play up there, but one day while Mother was working in the basement I found the skylight was open to air out our rooms and the ladder was down. Hearing voices, I climbed up and the boys playing on the roof of the next building dared me to come out. I never took a dare but out I went. The boys walked the ridgepole of their store and dared me to do the same on ours. I was six and complied, finding a thrill, and I did it again but in turning at the end of the roof to return, my weak ankle gave way. Down I slid, under the walk. I grasped the edge of the planks and hung suspended three stories above the ground.

My mother heard the boys scream, rushed out in the alley and looked up. The larger boy kept his head and hurried along the walk to my assistance. He and one of the others grasped my wrists and pulled me back up before Papa could reach us through the skylight. Then the boys disappeared over the roof of the next building. While I escaped the whipping I really deserved, I received a good tongue-lashing and was never allowed to go up on the roof again.

The front room of our living quarters had a big closet that extended the full length of the room. The roof sloped down to within three or four feet of the floor in the back of the closet, and in this space, Papa stored his factory-made coffins and caskets. These coffins were nested one inside another, with the smallest, infant-sized and the largest for an adult.

About this time depredations were taking place upon very young girls of the poorer class. Finally, a high-up mill man was accused and arrested. His friends claimed that he had been framed because the miners disliked him. One night a mob formed, intent on hanging the man, but when they got to the lock-up as the little jail was called, the mill man was missing. The mob began to search the town continuing through the next day.

When Papa brought the accused man in, I was sitting in a big armchair in front of the window with the back of the chair toward the room. Papa hid him in one of the coffins way back in the dark end of the closet and then stacked several nests of coffins behind the door, and none too soon. About an hour later the room filled with angry men who yanked open the closet door, only to confront the coffins. They fell back with oaths and did not search further. They acted as if they had stared at death and had had enough. That night, the accused man was spirited out of the Hills, and rumor has it he went out to the Pacific coast where his wife joined him later.

A year later Papa again used a coffin for a hiding place. An old drunkard had made a habit of slipping into our basement and climbing up on the stack of mattresses stored there to sleep off his jag. Papa tired of it so he decided to fix the old fellow. Papa was six-foot-two and "strong as an ox," while the drunkard was a little square-built German. One night when Papa went to lock up, the old drunk was there again on the mattresses. Nearby was a stack of cheap coffins. Papa lifted the fellow gently and laid him in a casket putting the lid on it in such a way as to still give him air. The next morning, Mr. Gurney, the cabinetmaker, was working at his bench when the old German awakened. When he found himself in the coffin, with a wild oath, he climbed out and rushed out of the basement never to return. He always claimed Papa wanted to bury him alive.

CHILD'S PLAY IN LEAD

Sarah Elizabeth "Sadie" - age 6 with
her dog, "Nip" (around 1880)

One day shortly after reaching Lead, a lady took me into a store that had a lot of dolls and I was told I could have any one I wanted. These included beautiful French dolls with real wigs of golden hair and wonderful dresses that the lady held up for me to see. I shook my head, for there was one doll that looked like my mother. It was only a small china doll with no clothes but she was so white with red cheeks and such black hair that she was my mother.

The lady reached into the showcase and took the doll out. "You don't want this one, why she is just a cheap little dolly. Now look at this beauty" and she held up a very expensive bisque doll for me to admire. I shook my head and held out my arms for the little doll. When I looked at it more closely, I sighed and in a disappointed voice said, "But she has blue eyes." Pointing to my mother I said, "She has black eyes." I looked into my mother's eyes, but I held the doll and would take no other. To me the doll was my mother in miniature and I wanted no other.

Our friend gave me the doll with the expression, "She is a queer child and will soon tire of it. Don't you want to take this one for her when she does?" My mother shook her head and, clasping the naked doll in my arms, we walked out of the store. I thought that my doll's blue-black hair and her colorless face with the bright red spots on her cheekbones made her skin look all the whiter by their brilliance.

The second winter after Mother and Papa were married was exciting to a small child like myself. Papa built me a sled. While I could not handle it by myself, he would take Mother and me down the hill on it in the evenings and on Sundays.

The jokes and laughs and clean sport in the frosty air gave us a fine refreshing sleep, when we got between our warm blankets on our good old featherbeds with, perhaps, a warm down or goose feather comforter on top. I had that sled for years. It was the fastest on the hill, and desired by all the boys. I seldom rode a bobsled because of the sled Papa had made for me. Nip, my little fox terrier dog, sat on the front of my sled and rode down the hills with me, then helped pull the heavy sled back up the hills. He knew that sled very well. One day, my wonderful sled disappeared. We searched in vain for it.

After my sled disappeared, I trusted generous playmates for rides until one day, two boys came up the hill with a bright new brown sled. Mine had been grey. Suddenly, my dog Nip dashed out into the road and snatched the sled rope, then started toward me. In the tussle that followed, the sled was turned over with the runners up. On the side of the brace was clearly burned "Sadie Smith." The sled was mine and my dog had recognized it!

The boys had stolen it and their father had painted it brown but he had never examined the underbracing. Nip had recognized the sled and insisted on bringing it back to me. Knowing the dog was right, the boys ran off and we never saw them on that hill after that. Their father never tried to claim the sled.

About this same time, I had my first lesson as to whom I was to associate with and whom not. It had been a dirty, slushy morning, but finally the sun came out, and I was permitted to go out on the walk. For a while I stood and watched a little girl playing in the street. I longed to join her but knew I must not, for I had been dressed to go visiting with my aunt.

Suddenly, the little girl slipped and rolled into a mud hole. I rushed to her, helped her up, and using the skirt of my clean white dress, wiped the mud off her face and hands and led her to my mother to clean her up properly. My mother washed the child and sent her home, then turned to me. I shall never forget her face. My aunt could not contain herself any longer and said, "I'd whip her, Lizzie, bringing a little guttersnipe in here like that. Just look at her!" My mother shook her head sadly, "No, not for being kind to others. There's enough heartache in life without that," and she turned to wash me and change my clothes again for the promised visit.

That little girl was the child of a prostitute, but she became one of the finest women in her community in later life. At her funeral in Los Angeles, her friends filled one of the leading churches of that city in tribute to her noble womanhood and loaded her casket with flowers.

In those days, very little class distinction was apparent, especially among the children. With sandwiches, cake, and a few apples, it was off to the hillside on Saturday or over to Flag Rocks to climb their rugged faces and to peek into the cave under them. Winter set in with its first snowfall on Labor Day and the ground remained covered until the last of June. We went sledding on the hills all in happy companionship. For some reason, we had more snow those early years than they have now.

Among the little folk, birthday parties provided a constant source of good times, always held in the afternoons with all sorts of games. As a general rule, no social lines were drawn. At those parties, children usually arrived at two o'clock with a suitable gift for the honored child. Games were played, children showed off in their respective ways, cake and ice cream or some other dessert was served, and then the children went home. These were simple, innocent parties that brought happiness to the hearts of young and old. As the children grew older, the young people had parties and played old-fashioned games.

One colored family lived in Lead in the first days. They had a little niece, Julia, who made her home with them. The townsmen considered the men of this family the best barbers in the town. They were somewhat accepted on par with many whites, so Julia was invited to most of the parties given by children.

One birthday party especially comes to my mind. A little girl from a rough, uncouth Irish family had invited me for her two o'clock party. Mother did not want me to associate with her, owing to her rough language, but she purchased a pretty gift for the child and told me that I could go when I finished my work.

After my dinner dishes were done, Mother gave me a dust cloth and told me to do my dusting since it was Saturday. For a child, I worked very carefully and when Mother inspected the job she found dust on the chair rungs. She made me do it again. Again, she found dust and again I had to repeat my chore, "For I must learn to do my cleaning well." At about four-thirty, my dusting was accepted. I then took my bath and dressed in my clean clothes. With my gift in my hand and sad tears in my throat I was sent to the party only to meet the other children coming home. I had to tell the little girl's mother why I was late, that I had not done my work correctly and had to do it over. I added, "Because Mother could not abide a dirty house." I gave the message and turned around and ran home in shame to my own room. I put my cat in my arms and Nip also snuggled up against me. Mother "saved face" as our Chinese laundry man would have said, but I had read her heart. Years later I met that same girl. She had become a novitiate at a Catholic convent.

Child's Play in Lead

In that raw western atmosphere, a group of girls thrived and grew, starting with Ann, the little German girl, blonde, plump, merry and loved by all. Martha followed, the little household drudge and mother to her little brothers and sisters. She was thankful for any kindness and worshipped at the feet of Aunt Sarah. Mary, Sue, Maud, Maggie, Ellen, Lizzie, Susan, and Pauline were also part of a host of girls who needed to be watched over and trained. Some bettered themselves and some were led astray by waywardness.

DOCTORS & LAWYERS IN LEAD

One day, the Deadwood hack deposited three rather distinguished looking men on the bank corner: the first doctor and one of the first lawyers in Lead or Deadwood. These men included Doctor Hile Howe, Attorney Judge George Monroe, and Casper. Word spread around town that they were three Harvard men who had come to live in our midst.

Dr. Howe was a good doctor; George Munroe had a fine legal mind and education. Casper appeared to be a fine Southern gentleman in his broadcloth suits, finely polished boots, and large Southern colonel's hat. His voice, rich and low-spoken, told of the orator he might have been. Drunk or sober, he always had a clean, white handkerchief at his command to wipe off the brim of his hat when an impish boy would send it rolling into the ditch. We never knew Casper's real name. At the bank, the first of every month, a New York draft arrived, to be delivered to "Casper." That was all; and at his death, a pine board at the head of his grave bore only one word, "Casper." His two friends never told his story or true name.

One day in 1879, my mother was dressing me for a trip to Deadwood, when I fainted. Black diphtheria had reached home. Mother laid me on the bed and rushed for Dr. Howe. Locating him in one of the saloons, she found him dead drunk, under a pool table. With the help of the bartender, they dragged him out and got him on his feet. She then led him, staggering, to Aunty's kitchen, where she plied him with black coffee and poured cold water on his head. At last, she brought him to the bedroom. He sniffed the air, slapped his hands on his pockets, then turned and dashed out of the house. My mother threw herself on her knees beside me sobbing and prayed. She had done all she could. A few minutes later the door opened, and Dr. Howe returned with quick orders, "Hot water, lots of it, and towels." Lifting me onto the dining room table, he worked to clear my airway by performing a tracheotomy and saved my life.

From that time until the epidemic was over, he worked night and day and left the drink alone. Ninety-six deaths marked our little community that spring. Funerals were held at the church and friends traveled from camps around to attend. Mountain typhoid, scarlet fever, diphtheria, and smallpox epidemics followed each other with regularity. With the first smallpox cases there was no virus, so the early doctors vaccinated those not infected with the scabs of those infected.

George Monroe knew law and was a brilliant persuader, drunk or sober. Drink was his one vice. He respected women, loved children, and cards fascinated him little. He ventured into the silent hills prospecting for weeks at a time, but was never successful. He finally died alone in his mountainside cabin, and was laid to rest not far from his friend, Casper.

After these men left, Dr. Henry Bruhns, the little old German doctor and druggist who seemed able to raise a man from the dead, arrived in town. Another time I was ill, I recall him pacing my bedroom floor, muttering to himself and watching the hands of his great old silver watch, counting the seconds and listening for the click of the gate for Papa's return with life-saving medicine. Twenty years later, I saw him as a broken down old man, yet still with the nerve to declare four doctors as traitors to their calling and then saving my own child's life. Did the people of Lead love Dr. Bruhns? Yes, although he became a to-be-pitied drug victim, for morphine became his curse.

Later, doctors who could actually keep their minds and desires under control came to Lead. The Homestake Company built its own hospital and Doctors J.W. Freeman and D.K. Dickinson were in charge. There the men and their families were cared for by the small sum of one dollar and a quarter per month, deducted from their wages for medical care and drugs.

(EDITOR'S NOTE: Dr. Hile Howe, Attorney George Monroe and Dr. Henry Bruhns are all buried in the South Lead Cemetery. There is also a Casper Barth buried in the South Lead Cemetery - but it is unknown whether he is the Casper referred to in this book.)

MY SCHOOL YEARS IN LEAD

Sadie - age 12 (1886)

I began school March 1880 after the Deadwood Fire. My first day was a disaster. School was held in two buildings with the playground in the backyard. The little folk went to school in a log cabin adjoining the two-story J.K. Searle home. In the "Big Room" on the second floor of the Searle building, Professor Darling taught the older boys and girls. They went to and from the playground using an outside stairway.

Miss Chapman was my primary teacher and our seats were made of planks nailed to sawn off pieces of trees placed on the hard-packed earth floor. We lacked desks and blackboards, but had a primer, a slate and a pencil, and were taught by the old ABC method of learning our letters backward and forward and printing the letters on our slates. When that was accomplished, we learned to spell "CAT" and other three-letter words by seeing the pictures beside the words.

During my first afternoon recess, I was standing at the foot of the "Big Room" steps watching the children play when two large boys came tearing down the steps. The first one, bumping against me, knocked me over and the other, coming so fast behind that he could not stop, tried to jump over me. Instead he landed with both feet on my back. Four of the older girls carried me home on an improvised stretcher made with my coat. My school days were over for that year, for I could not raise my head or move my legs for three months. The grownups never learned what really happened until I went away to college twelve years later. Those boys had broken my back, dooming me to a more or less quiet life. Mother attributed my condition to excessive weakness since no doctor was available to say otherwise.

One day Papa came home and, standing by my bed, told me to put my hand in his pocket. I did and then I jerked it out quickly. Then again, mustering up courage, I tried again and drew out a tiny fox terrier that became my constant companion for thirteen years. Papa had found him under the walk in front of the store. At the time, the weather was bitterly cold and the pup's little mother had brought it out and laid it at Papa's feet as if asking him to look after it. For weeks, she would come to the house and ask to come in. She nursed the pup and then slipped away until she finally weaned him. She belonged to an old drunken painter and knew the painter had no home for her pup.

Thus I had my first pet. Later I had many cats and birds, but none ever took the place of "Nip." Though I am now an old woman, no pet has ever taken his place in my heart. He died while I was away at college. He went to sleep on the rug in front of the piano where he used to lay countless hours when I was practicing. Papa buried him as he would have buried a child, for he was a faithful member of the family. Although Papa always seemed to like pets, after Nip's death he never had another pet.

While my back injury ended my school days that year, it did not stop my education thanks to Mother. She taught me those awful a, b, c, d's, and d, c, b, a's, a terrible task, the remaining months of that school year. I always wanted to say "...O, P, Q, S, R, T." You see Papa's initials were "S. R." and it never was right in my child mind to say "...R, S, T."

By helping me persist, when at last I recovered, I could already say my letters forward and backward and recognize them printed or written as small or capital letters. Papa gave me a silver dollar when I proved I really knew them and could enter Miss Chapman's primer class in September. Miss Chapman continued to have a special place in my heart. When her father struck a rich vein of gold when I was nineteen, she gave me a tiny neck chain and pendant made from gold taken from her father's mine. Mr. Barclay made the chain and I still have it as a precious keepsake.

Although I was six, I was as small or smaller than most four-year olds. The fact that I was able to read almost at once astonished my teachers. I had a good memory and when Mother read me the stories, I memorized most of the words.

Reading, however, was quite different from spelling and the latter proved to be my bugaboo throughout life. Words such as "cat" or "cot" were all the same to me. My Mother could not understand my confusion. I was just as liable to spell "cat" d-o-g as any other way no matter how much Mother drilled me. I was forced to stay after school daily to study my spelling.

Orally I could spell down the room but when writing I was just as liable to write "was" w-o-s as to use an "a." These days we would say "EYES" in capital letters but we had no oculists or glasses in those days. Several years passed before my mother realized my eyes were defective and I was given glasses for constant wear.

The following year the town bought the Catholic Hospital and made a school out of it. Three teachers taught an average of 156 pupils. Over time the school developed into a respectable eight-grade school divided into primary, intermediate and grammar rooms. My teachers over the years included Mr. Darling, Mr. Morgan, Miss Rogers, Mr. Driscoll and his wife (then Miss Barry), and Mr. Green and his wife (then Miss Frank).

When Professor Driscoll was my teacher, I made my first perfect attendance record for a month. I always suffered with terrible spinal headaches and would go home from school sick. In spite of that, Mother made me get my lessons for the next day before I could put my books up and go to bed. As a result, for the next day or two I would be too ill to go to school. I did, however, keep up my studies and would return to school ahead of my class.

When Professor Driscoll noticed that a headache was bothering me, he took my books and locked them up in his desk and sent me home to rest. When Mother went to him and demanded the books, he gave his opinion about my studying when ill. As a result, after a night's complete rest, I was able to go to school the next day. I actually attended school for three months in the spring of 1883 without any absence. I even won the school spelling bee and Papa gave me a small gold dollar. Paper money was unknown and gold was the coin of those days. I spent twenty-five cents of it for a china-headed doll that I still have. That doll was always my favorite, although I had many beautiful dolls.

In the fall of 1886, Professor Green took over the school. Miss Frank had been Mr. Driscoll's assistant the year before and she continued under Mr. Green. Shortly after school started, Mr. Green came into Miss Frank's room and asked if he could do anything for her. She answered, "No," but she did suggest that he take one of her pupils into his class. He looked over the class and noticing a couple of large girls and a large boy on the backseat asked which one. She called my name and I rose and the rest of the class settled back in their benches. "Not this one," said Mr. Green as he stared at me in astonishment, for I was so small that even a year later I was mistaken for a ten-year-old. Miss Frank smiled, saying, "You will find her well-prepared." As I was standing at the end of the seat next to him, he put his hand on my shoulders and led me out of the room without saying a word.

The clothing of a schoolchild in those days might be of interest. I wore a suit of long-legged, long-sleeved woolen underwear next to my skin; next to that, finely embroidered white muslin panties buttoned to an underwaist;* over that, a woolen petticoat sewed on a woolen waist, but also a heavy cotton drill waist to which was buttoned two or three fancy white muslin petticoats. Next came the dress of heavy wool and a long-sleeved apron or pinafore that covered all and kept one clean. A pair of heavy, home-knit stockings and high shoes completed one's winter costume.

Before going out, we put on leggings and high overshoes or boots, a very heavy coat, a hood, a muffler, and mittens, and mothers prayed that we would be sufficiently warm and not take cold. We lacked furnaces in those days, but had huge stoves that generally glowed red and roasted those who sat near, while those at the edge of the room froze.

In the winter, girls and boys wore rubber boots with felt socks inside. We took our shoes to school and put them on after we arrived, placing our boots by the side of our desks. My winter shoes were sixteen buttons high with a French cork sole above the outer leather sole. They kept my feet much warmer and dryer than the ordinary shoe and made me an inch taller.

The summers were short, really starting with the first of July and ending with the first of September, as snow flew all the rest of the time. I do not remember a year when we did not open school in a snow flurry and close the last Friday of June with the same kind of weather.

The Greens left Lead, but the Driscolls remained. Mr. Driscoll later became cashier and then President of the First National Bank and rose to be one of the most influential men of the community.

---

* An underwaist was a blouse to which undergarments such as stockings were buttoned.

DISEASES & FUNERALS

Shortly after the last note was paid off in the spring of 1881, the doctor advised that Mother take a vacation in a lower altitude for a few months. Unfortunately, she did not have the option because I could not leave school. Also at that time, Papa had begun the serious study of undertaking, or more explicitly, embalming. He needed Mother's education to help him, as he had never completed past the seventh grade. Although he always wanted an education, his father opted for the money he could earn instead.

The boy's desires had been thwarted at every turn. Now, the man's desires, with all the pent-up ambition of those suppressed years, had to be realized. Mother read the physiology lessons and I listened to and loved them. The names of the bones were music to my ears, and the circulatory system seemed like a wonderful stream of life. I was only seven but would study those big charts with a fascination that overpowered everything else. Finally, Mother forbade their being taken out and visible in my presence. I wanted to be a doctor, but Mother said, "No." And no was NO.

Several years later, when Papa went to Chicago and took a course in embalming, he spoke highly of an undertakers' organization through which the undertakers could influence legislation for the control of contagious diseases. The result of this experience was the eventual organization of the Nebraska-South Dakota Funeral Directors' Association. Mr. Heaton of Lincoln, Nebraska, served as president and Papa served as vice president. This organization existed for several years and Papa became the instructor of embalming at the annual meetings.

Papa worked with a woman who washed the bodies of women and children for him. She accidentally scratched her hand on a pin. Not having rubber gloves such as undertakers use today, her hand became infected by the poison secreted by the body of a woman who died of peritonitis. Mrs. Green's arm began to swell, and eight times was lanced and gangrene cut away. The arm was eventually saved but rendered almost useless, being left with little but the skin drawn over the bones. This experience taught him a necessary lesson of caution when handling bodies afflicted with contagious diseases. Sadly, in addition to disease, he learned that death exuded all kinds of poisons, so he studied to perfect a disinfectant to counteract its effect.

Papa fixed up a prescription that he felt would kill any poison and used it in all cases after Mrs. Green's experience. The prescription became a standard embalming fluid for those early days. This fluid contained a considerable amount of arsenic.

In the winter of a black diphtheria scourge, Papa foolishly handed the embalming fluid he had concocted to some women helping in a "house of death." He gave instructions to scatter it around and disinfect their hands with it after they washed the body of a dead child. The mothers of some of the children did more. They saturated cloths and bound them around the throats of the children and bathed them with the fluid. When a frantic little French mother accused Papa of letting her babies die while he saved her neighbors' children, he learned of the harmful practices. Almost in a panic, Papa gathered up all the fluids initially given out to the bereaved families and gave them different bottles of embalming fluid (with the arsenic removed). He did this in such a way that did not cause alarm.

Strangely, no deaths occurred where it had been used and the epidemic was soon stamped out. Papa used this same fluid for embalming with great success for his remaining years in the business. For a disinfectant, he removed the arsenic from the prescription and used it lavishly in all the homes he had cause to enter.

I soon learned to only be seen and not heard, but often I found it better to not even be seen. At times, I heard a great deal that was best not to be repeated. For many years Papa was the only undertaker in the town, and undertakers, like doctors, learn of many family skeletons. In this way I, too, learned things that never reached the outside world.

In times of sickness quarantine regulations were absent, so epidemics spread over the whole community like wildfire. Typhoid, diphtheria, scarlet fever, meningitis, and smallpox took their toll every year and filled the cemeteries on the hilltops.

One example of laxness at funerals, schoolchildren kissed the lips of a person that had died of diphtheria as they passed by the coffin. Papa hammered on the subject, along with doctors, and eventually worked up a sentiment to keep the caskets closed and enforce quarantine regulations. Almost five years passed to accomplish what today would be deemed the most lax regulations.

Funerals were public gatherings with the attendance of everyone in the community. When men died, especially among the foreign element, one or more bands played, preceding the casket to the grave. Usually, the "Dead March" was chosen, and the hearse and hacks and men moved to the slow dirge. The ceremony at the grave ended as the dirt fell upon the rough box, and then the band struck up a rollicking air, usually "When Johnny Comes Marching Home" or "Marching Through Georgia." Attendees stepped off at a lively pace to the center of town where they usually broke for the saloons for glasses of beer or whiskey to discuss the grand funeral.

On June 26, 1880, Fire Chief Rubin Miller and his wife, Hannah, buried their 5-year-old son, Raymond. Mr. Miller was the Chief of Lead No. 1 Hose Company, and an elaborate funeral ceremony was planned. At ten o'clock, No. 1 Hose Cart received the casket of the little boy and the men of the Company took their places at the rope, the tongue, and the bars. The cart was a two-wheeled affair on which hundreds of feet of three-inch hose were wound. At the front was an iron tongue that two men held up when moving, and to which was fastened a rope with handholds every so often. The men used the rope to pull the cart. Two men grasped a heavy bar at the back of the cart and acted as a brake to keep it from rolling upon the men in front as they went downhill.

The No. 1 Hose Cart served as the hearse that day and carried little Raymond Miller to the cemetery, with a band in full regalia leading the procession and playing "The Dead March of Saul." On their return from the grave, they played "When Johnny Comes Marching Home." This was the typical high-class funeral of those early days.

When a refined English family had a death and they issued invitations to the funeral, quite a sensation took place. These families did not have a band and everything went off in a very quiet, exclusive manner, with the general public thinking this terribly disrespectful. Yet, a few years later all the pomp and show for funerals passed out of the picture.

CATASTROPHES

Lead and Deadwood were no strangers to disaster. I recall a number of catastrophes. Floods, mine accidents, and blizzards all left their mark, but no crisis was more common and destructive as fire. Houses were built of pine boards. When the heat of the sun glared down on them, pitch oozed out in trickling streams. The pitch then settled in globules forming chunks of spruce gum that the children broke off and chewed as delicacies to be passed around among a chosen few. Early houses were fire hazards with a vengeance. A lit match could set a blaze to the pitch boards in an instant. Other hazards included old stumps left standing after trees had been removed, filled with rosin, chips and dried bark - wonderful for starting a fire in wood stoves that were used all year around. Scattered pine needles posed a danger but we thought little about it until the Deadwood fire. Only then did Lead become fire minded, for a bucket brigade provided insufficient protection.

The bucket brigade formed shortly after Lead was laid out. The need for some sort of fire protection became evident and a volunteer fire company was formed. No water system existed, although the creek and wells in different parts of town furnished the water supply until the Pioneer and Whitewood ditches were brought into town. Fire hydrants were installed in a few places principally to protect the mill and business houses. Hose Company No. 1 was then organized.

The town purchased a two-wheel hose cart and a few hundred feet of three-inch hose. Hose Company No. 1 became an independent fire company chartered by the territory of Dakota. In 1879, it had a membership of twenty-three experienced firemen with A. J. White as its foreman. The officers were elected semi-annually and the members were comprised of the town's businessmen. The fire company owned all the firefighting equipment. As the town grew it became evident that this fire protection was inadequate.

Another cart with hose and hose-house cost money, but a rival company was needed. "The boys are all right so far as they go but we need new blood." "How are you going to get it?" "The company will help. It's to their interest as well as ours." And that is how Company No. 2 came to be.

As the town loved getting together for programs of all sorts, to raise money for the new company, the men decided on a minstrel show. The new Miners' Union Hall was rented and preparations were made for the show. Brothers Romeo and Harry Marshall, Lead's two popular colored barbers, were the leading characters with their banjos and bones* and musical voices. The other men blacked up and dressed up. They practiced with bones, practical jokes, and quips, putting on a credible show.

The crowning feature was a Cakewalk with the big cake presented at the end of a caricature of Alexander's Ragtime Band. This show was put on entirely by the men of the community, netting the boys $400. Within the year, Hose Company No. 2 was launched with its house on North Mill Street. At the time of the big Homestake woodpile fire, Papa was chief and the two companies had their hands full to confine the flames and save the town.

Many other incidents of those first days stand out in my memory; however, I think few realize the terrible disaster that occurred in the dead of winter at the camp at Terry. It was a small camp and the miners lived in a long, flimsy shack built against the side of the mountain. They cooked and ate on the ground floor, and eighteen men slept in the loft above. As was the custom, the stovepipe from the stove below passed through the floor of the room above and out through the roof without a regular chimney to protect the building.

---

* Bones were used as musical folk instruments in minstrel shows. The most common bones were a pair of animal ribs or lower leg bones.

That winter we had extra heavy snows and, especially that week, the snow covered Lead so that the men tunneled between buildings. I remember Papa shoveled a path from our kitchen door to the street that left a wall six feet high on each side. The road was between three-foot walls of snow. The weight of the snow on roofs crushed many small shacks. At Terry, the roof of the mine shack collapsed and the pine-resin-filled boards caught fire from the stove. With the snow melting on the building, the snow from the hillside also began to slide down, and the men became trapped. Papa claimed he took out the remains of eighteen charred bodies after two days of digging in the ruins. Very few of the men could be identified.

I well remember two disastrous fires for the Homestake Company. The first was in the woodpile on June 24, 1893. The great boilers were fed cords of wood to keep the stamps and engines working. To supply this demand, the narrow-gauge trains brought in a steady stream of wood carloads from the hills miles away. From the cars, the wood was pitched into a chute at the top of the hill. As it struck the great bumper at the end of the chute, the logs leaped high into the air to fall onto a great pile. Chips from the logs fell through the crevices to the bottom of the heap to become tinder. Hundreds of cords of wood were thus piled into a huge stack of logs out of which smoke and then flames suddenly began to rise.

The men fought to save the mills for many days. They worked with masks of wet cloths over their faces, but to no avail. Finally, the firemen began moving the unburned wood. Wagons were loaded that carried the wood away to safety. Every man or boy who could lift a log worked. Business was at a standstill. Day after day they worked, and the pumps turned the water from the mines into the very heart of that great furnace, sending out a stream of lye water that burned the firemen's feet through their boots if they stepped into it.

For years that pile had never been moved, and the snows and rain that had fallen over time caused it to heat and rot until spontaneous combustion kindled the blaze. The company lost a million dollars, and weeks passed before the fire was put out, although it felt like a year.

The other great fire started in the "Old Abe" stope. The cause is still a mystery. All at once the mine was on fire. The town tried to flood the mine, but still it burned. Finally, firefighters bulk headed the stope by sealing up the burning part with earth and cement, and ultimately abandoning that part of the mine.

(EDITOR'S NOTE: Sarah Elizabeth was probably referring to the mine fire that began on Nov. 25, 1907, and burned for 44 days until workers extinguished the flames by flooding the mine.)

Speaking of fires, I will tell of a lesser fire and the rattlesnake story that occurred in our barn next to our house in South Lead one Sunday afternoon. To understand the situation, one must remember that the houses of Lead were built into the hillside. Most of them had a basement floor with one or two side openings onto the yard.

Our barn was a stone basement story that led into our backyard while the carriage room above opened onto the street. Papa kept his hearses and carriage in this carriage room while our carriage team and my saddle horse were in the basement. The rest of the space served as a hay room, with the hay brought in from the valley and sent down a chute from the platform above.

In the fall, the storage room was usually filled to the ceiling with hay, except for a small space, occupied by the oat box, next to the gate that led to the horse stalls. This arrangement made it easy for the stable man to pitch the hay into the mangers and the oats into the feed boxes.

On that unforgettable Sunday, my particular friend and her two younger brothers stopped by on their way to Sunday School. James did not intend to go as he had lost his Sunday hat, but I persuaded him to go home, change clothes, and go anyway as he would not wear his hat in church.

As he left, he shouted to his sister, "Watch Roy." My friend and I sat on the porch visiting and forgot all about the little boy. When James came running back he asked: "Where's Roy?" Just then Roy came running from the barn with his face as white as a sheet. He screamed in a shrill frightened voice. "The - there - there's a sna - snake in there." We ran through the house to see the snake that had climbed halfway up the stairs toward the floor above the backyard.

While my mother ran for Papa to come kill the snake, she left us to watch where it would go. It started down the stairs so I rushed around the house to close the stable door that was standing open. On reaching the door I saw that the hay room was a mass of smoke and flames. I forgot the snake. My thought was for the horses. James and I ran to them. By that time, others had noticed the smoke pouring out of the hay chute and came rushing over the hill to help. We coaxed two horses out but my saddle horse refused to budge. I finally threw the stable man's ulster* over his head and led him out.

Just then I heard a wild oath and scream. I learned after I escaped the barn with my horse that a burly Irishman headed a mob rushing down the stair only to meet the rattler coiled on the four-foot platform at the bottom. He could not turn back, so he jumped with both feet onto the center of that hissing coil and fortunately killed the snake before it could strike. It had eight rattles and a button.

Folks concluded that the snake had been brought in from the valley with the hay and had made its nest under the feed box all winter. Miraculously neither the stable man nor the horses were bitten. Since not much hay was in the barn at the time, due to the summer season, minimal damage took place from the fire owing to the stone walls.

For weeks, Roy saw snakes in his sleep but finally his confession came. He had found some matches in our kitchen and gone out to the hay room, built a small pile of hay in front of the feed box, lit his match and started the fire. As he was heaping more hay on the blaze, the snake stuck its head out and hissed at him. When he ran the snake followed him out of the barn. We always counted it as a very lucky fire.

Snakes were never found in or around Lead, but were sometimes, as in that case, brought in from the valleys in the loads of hay.

In addition to fires, flooding was a potential hazard. The Deadwood flood goes down in history as one of the great catastrophes of those early

---

* An ulster was a man's overcoat.

days, destroying most of the business section of Deadwood in 1883. The warm Chinook winds* in May brought the snowmelt from the mountains into the valleys and gulches much earlier than usual.

Mother and I had been in Deadwood and stopped at the tollgate to visit Mrs. Alice Chandler. She had been a teacher in Iowa for years and was engaged to Mr. George Chandler for a long time. Alice's father was Marcus Gurney, the cabinetmaker who worked for Papa after the Deadwood fire. Alice's mother, Emma, remained in Monticello, Iowa, with Alice and her siblings. Emma was a very nervous woman and claimed that if Alice ever left her she would die. She had her daughter believing it.

Mr. Chandler, for health reasons, left Iowa and moved to Deadwood. He became a part owner in the toll road and gate at what is now known as Pluma. After he had fully recovered from his lung trouble, Miss Gurney made up her mind and left Iowa to marry Mr. Chandler in November 1882. In the spring, they built a pleasant home upon the hill near the tollgate and expected to abandon the little house at the gate and move into the new home on May 15. We stopped to visit them and watched them pack. The next afternoon their plan was to visit Lead and she would stay with us while he got things settled in the new home.

The following day, however, the Chinooks came. Heavy rain loosened the snow, creating great rivers of water that crashed down the gorges. The elevation of Lead was high enough that the water soon subsided, but the tollgate was swept away where the Whitewater and Strawberry Creeks made their junction and swept onward towards Deadwood. There, joined by Deadwood Creek, the waters almost wiped out the town of Deadwood.

When the water began to undermine their home, Mr. & Mrs. Chandler tried to save their belongings. Mr. Chandler was on solid ground but, seeing the danger to his wife, he ran back into the house. Taking her in his arms, he reached the door when the dam waters threw the house backward and carried it downstream. Three days later, their bodies were recovered. They were buried together in a single grave in the Mount Moriah Cemetery in

---

* Chinook winds are warm dry winds that descend from the eastern slopes of the Rocky Mountains and cause a rapid rise in temperature.

Deadwood the next day. Eight lives were lost in that flood.

With the flood and the destruction of the dam, a new road from the tollgate to Lead had to be built. It became only a prolonged Main Street leaving the Superintendent's home, cutting off the mills and the little village of Washington from the main highway. The road was widened and the creek almost ceased to be, except when spring thaws brought snowmelt from the hillsides. The old springs at the head of Main Street seemed to have been washed out with only surface water trickling into the creek bed.

GRUBSTAKING & UNCLE'S INJURY

Among those early pioneers, it was common practice for a man who had a good paying job to grubstake* a prospector. Uncle Jack grubstaked Mike, an old prospector who had laid out a claim called the "Peach Lode." Mike brought in wonderful samples of ore to be assayed, but there never seemed to be much of it. A friend told Uncle that Mike was "salting" the claim to keep Uncle paying him. "Salting" was obtaining ore from another mine and claiming it was from their mine. One Sunday, Uncle walked out to the Peach Lode. Night came on and he did not return, Monday morning and still no Uncle. Night again and Uncle had not returned. On Tuesday morning Papa and his friends went to the mine but they did not find Uncle. They scattered out to search.

About four o'clock Papa found Uncle staggering up a gulch toward Lead. He looked as though he had been lying in a gutter, and was in a semi-dazed condition. He recognized Papa and asked if he was looking for him. Uncle never drank and Papa could not understand his condition. Uncle would not talk. Papa brought him home and Aunty thought he would be all right after a hot bath, a shave, clean clothes, and a night's sleep. It did not work out that way. On examination of the mine it was found that Mike had salted it from the Uncle Sam Mine a short distance away. After Uncle's return home, Mike disappeared. Later he was seen in Montana but we never saw him again.

---

* Grubstaking meant financing the prospect while the prospector did the labor and then split the profits with his backer.

Uncle's mind seemed to become blank for he never could tell what had happened. Aunty thought that a lower altitude and good doctors might help him so she took him to Wichita, Kansas. The doctors there advised a trip to England so to England they went. In London, he was taken to the King's doctor. On examination, the doctor diagnosed the case thus: He had been struck over the head with a heavy, blunt instrument, possibly a miner's drill, and then probably dragged off into the brush and left for dead. He had come to, and instinct had led him home. The broken skull had healed, leaving a deep depression along the top of his head, but the depressed part pressed upon his brain and caused a hardening of the brain tissue. At that time, nothing could be done for him, as brain surgery was unknown. The doctor said he might eventually gain his reasoning faculties, but those years would always be a blank. He continued to work at his trade but he seldom talked. He was a quiet, simple, kindly soul who would not harm a fly, but after his injury he would smoke his pipe and brood, day after day. What were his thoughts? We never knew.

Fifteen years before his death, in 1903, Aunty died. This seemed to rouse him out of his semi-stupor. He handled his business in Wichita himself, and left a small estate. At the age of eighty-one, he died. If he could have had the medical care of today on the day he was found wandering in the hills, he might have reverted to the same jolly Uncle Jack of my early childhood. With no care, he became a silent, simple hearted man whom everyone loved, but pitied. He died on August 19, 1918, and was buried beside his wife in Highland Cemetery in Wichita, Kansas.

MR. SAVAGE & THE SAVAGE MINE

Around the same time Uncle Jack was injured, a short, stocky man with crass mannerisms and a huge role of greenbacks swaggered along the main streets of Lead, offering hundred dollar bills to any woman who would kiss him. Needless to say, few took him up on his offers. Even prostitutes turned him down, and local authorities began to follow his record and dubbed him "The Kissing Savage" or "The Kissing Fool."

The man was named "Savage" (Peter W. Savage). He had located a very rich vein of gold in Strawberry Gulch. His family consisted of a dandy "simp" of a son, Eugene, who spent most of his time in the saloons and dives of Deadwood, and a very striking looking but reserved daughter, Gertrude "Gertie," who avoided the people associated with her father and brother. In fact, she seldom left her rented room at the hotel except for business purposes. She bought good books and evidently did very fine needlework, but unfortunately, she soon discovered opium. Originally used to induce sleep at night, opium became an addiction for her and drew her towards the dives of Deadwood's Chinatown.

The Savage Tunnel mine became quite a strike in mining circles and aroused the interest of the Homestake Company. Development of the Savage Tunnel progressed and Savage went on a wild spending spree by putting up a large boarding and lodging house at the mouth of the tunnel. Papa had the contract for constructing that building, and was paid in cash as the work progressed each week. About that time, one of Savage's workmen betrayed him and became a spy to investigate the tunnel for the Homestake Mine. He impersonated a common laborer, but in reality was somewhat of a mining expert. After learning the direction of the drift and collecting enough samples to assay, so as to estimate the value of the mine, he quit work and returned to his old job in the Homestake Mine. Repeated offers made by the Homestake were turned down by Savage and in a short time a prospect hole was sunk in South Lead. Before long, the workmen learned that the Savage vein had been tapped, and, according to mining law, it could no longer develop along that line.

Savage had trusted his luck too much and lost his stake. He was broke, with an absolutely useless boarding house as his only asset. Savage's beautiful daughter was already a patron of the Chinese opium dens, and Savage and his son, bums. Gertie died on March 28, 1885, in a Chinese joint and Papa buried her in a lonely grave in the South Lead Cemetery, with Mother and a female neighbor the only ones in attendance at the funeral. Peter Savage the father, Eugene the brother, the gravedigger, and Papa lowered the body while a Protestant minister offered a prayer.

Peter and Eugene were not seen much after Miss Savage's death. The old Savage Tunnel House remained their only monument. Peter died at the age of 64 on November 3, 1890, and was buried in the South Lead Cemetery by Papa.

THE HOMESTAKE MINE

Lead, like Rome, was built on seven hills and through those hills, the rich gold veins (or leads) converged at Lead City. The Homestake Mine in Lead was like the body of a giant octopus whose feelers became exposed in the outcroppings at Terraville, Terry, and other surrounding areas.

The Homestake Mine was the very heart, blood, and life of Lead and the surrounding country. Even the agricultural valleys of the Black Hills were dependent on the gold output for their support. Moses Manuel located and filed the mineral claim known as the Homestake and sold it to J.B. Haggin, George Hearst, and Lloyd Tevis in the fall of 1877 for $70,000. (Factoring inflation, this would be approximately $1.6 million in 2018.) This was the beginning of what was called the greatest gold mine in the world. Adopting the name of the mineral claim, the Homestake Company expanded by purchasing the Golden Star Mine from the Manuel Brothers for $45,000 followed by the Highland Mine from William Baldwin. The company later added the Old Abe, Deadwood, Terra, DeSmet, Caledonia, Pierce, Big Missouri and many other mines until what was known as the Homestake Group reached from the DeSmet Mine on the north to the Savage Tunnel on the south. This land became the richest hundred square miles in the world and represented, in improvements, an outlay of two million dollars (approximately $46.5 million in 2018 dollars).

Homestake Gold Mine stock became one of the longest listed stocks on the New York Stock Exchange. Quoting from one of the Black Hills papers dated November 14, 1902, the dividends to that date, 288 in all, amounted to $11,548,350 (approximately $80.00 a share). When Haggin and Tevis subsequently stepped out of the picture, Hearst became the primary owner with controlling interest.

(EDITOR'S NOTE: Although the Homestake mine finally closed in 2002, more than 40 million troy ounces of gold had been mined from its beginning in 1876 until its closure. Based on the 2018 value of $1,300 per troy ounce, this would amount to nearly $53 billion dollars.)

Even before and after the Homestake Company was formed, some placer miners from Custer, Deadwood, Gayville, Central, Golden Gate, and other camps gained rich rewards for their labor. Uncovered pockets and fissure veins paid huge dividends, such as the Hidden Fortune claim discovered by Otto Grantz. I well remember the day his discovery was made. He ran a dairy for a long time and everyone rejoiced at his good fortune.

Small mining camps opened up mines and floated stock all over the hills. Some stock sold for as low as ten cents per share with some not even worth the paper upon which it was printed. Some worthwhile ventures died for want of capital. The Homestake Company and other large companies soon gathered up the stock that was worth anything.

In those early days, generally a tunnel was first driven into the mountainside. As the earth was removed, timbers were placed to keep the earth and rocks from falling and crushing the workmen. The alternate method was to dig a hole straight down and a windlass* and bucket were used to bring up the dirt and rock as if dug from a well. Oscar Silver brought that first rope into the country. As in the case of the tunnel method, the men timbered the shaft walls as they worked down.

Sam McMaster was responsible for the original Homestake development. When he died, Thomas J. Grier became the Superintendent. A more efficient cage system soon replaced the windlass and bucket system. Meno Voight

---

*A windlass was a lifting machine consisting of a cylinder wound with rope and turned by a crank.

came from California to put into effect the first cages that raised the ore to the surface. He served as Head Blacksmith until his age deemed it time to retire. Mr. Voight designed cages run from hoists. Eventually, certain cages carried only men while others carried cars loaded with ore.

Free milling ore was the simplest process used to extract gold in the early days. The ore was dumped from the mines into great crushers, similar to old-fashioned coffee mills. The grinders crushed the rock into small pieces that then passed under the stamps to be crushed into powder. This powder was washed through a trough lined with copper plates covered with quicksilver. The quicksilver sucked the golden grains onto the plates and became known as amalgam. The amalgam, when removed from the plates, could easily be slipped into a worker's pocket and smuggled out of the mill or the assay office. This happened once or twice, but the pilferers were caught. In one case, the man was a very trusted mill hand. The case was very quietly settled, with few knowing anything about the affair, and the man quickly departed Lead. A few years later, he drowned in the Belle Fourche River and Papa buried him.

The tailings that passed over the amalgam plates were later run through the blanket house. In the blanket house, strips of Brussels carpet bound with canvas on the ends lay on incline tables. Teams of two men held the carpet while water and the tailings passed over and through the carpet depositing and collecting much more of the fine golden particles into a concentrate. I understand that this process has long since passed into discard. The carpets were eventually burned and the gold collected from the ashes more than paid for labor and other expenses.

The thump-thump of the mill stamps lulled me to sleep as a child. They fell without a break, day and night, year in and year out. I remember well one afternoon when something went wrong and the stamps at the mills ceased to fall. People stopped in the street, rushed from their houses and businesses with one cry, "What's happened?" The trouble was soon adjusted and the stamps once again began to fall. A sigh of relief went up from the whole community as though the dead had come to life again.

In studying the lives of men like T. J. Grier and Meno Voight, I realize the power over life and death that was placed in their hands. A broken or weakly formed cable or a hasty, false movement of the cage could mean workers' deaths. It was no wonder why the superintendent of the mines studied the men he placed in key positions. Foremen in the mines, mills, machine shops, hoists, and even out in the mountains collecting timber all had to know and do their work well. No drunkards could be found in any of those vital positions. Life was too precious to be trusted to a befuddled brain.

The forest around Lead was used for timbering the mines as well as fuel for the great boilers of the mills and heating people's homes. In those early days, continual trains of flat cars loaded with cordwood came into Lead. The wood was dumped into a huge pile between the Star Mill and Mill Street until the great wood fire occurred that burned for weeks and threatened the town's very existence. This fire revealed to the company the danger of their method and led to the development of other plans.

In the early days, the men worked by candlelight in the underground chambers twenty-four hours a day. At first, they worked twelve-hour shifts but later the shifts were broken into three eight-hour shifts. The surface workers received less pay, for as their name implied, they worked above ground out in the open-cut or at the opening of a tunnel, and thus were in less danger.

The three classes of underground workers included pick and shovel men, gunners, and timber men. Pick and shovel men were unskilled positions and as a general rule given to newcomers. The gunners were the men who did the blasting, handled the dynamite, and cleared away the walls of granite that blocked the way. They worked in pairs or sometimes in teams of three. One held a great steel drill or bar sharpened at the end somewhat like a chisel or screwdriver. He chose the optimal location in the rock where the dynamite would work best. Then his partner or partners, with huge malls, would swing and strike the head of the drill. The men worked in measured strokes: first one mall would strike, then the other, in perfect rhythm, and often to the tune of some song. They kept a bucket of water at hand, and poured water into the hole as the work went on to keep it from heating up. But drilling was not the only part of that work. From time to time the gunner would test the depth of the drilled hole. If he determined the depth was satisfactory, the hole was dried out and usually left to cool until the change of shifts or, if cold enough, the gunner would place the dynamite caps and a timed fuse. All the men would then leave that part of the mine and the gunner would touch off the fuse and leave after the others were safe.

Sometimes the blast did not go off, implying a danger that it might go off later. The gunner always inspected the dynamite before the workmen were allowed to return. Many a gunner was injured by a delayed blast going off.

After the blast, the pick and shovelers cleared out the fallen rock and earth putting it into the cars that were then pushed to the cage, hoisted to the surface, and on to the crushers in the mill. Working in the mills was not considered dangerous with the exception of potential deafness from the constant pounding of the stamps.

After the space was cleared sufficiently, the third group of miners, called "timbermen," took their places and erected large timbers, formed like inverted U's to support the ceiling of the drift.* Sometimes these drifts were short and connected to other drifts. The long, main passageway with its connecting drifts was called a "stope."

The men worked much like ants in a great ant hill—click of pick, scrape of shovel, a blast, and tumbling rock crashed down; then click of pick and scrape of shovel and thump of rock and dirt into a small car, pushed on to the cage; a gong sounded and the cage rose to the surface, then pushed to the crusher, dumped, and the huge coffee mill ground on and on in its mighty jaws; then under the stamps—thump, thump. The fine powder fell into the water and over the amalgam plates, and then washed for the quicksilver to pick up the golden grains. Come cleanup day, the plates were scraped and the amalgam taken to where it was tried in the furnace. The final result, although not large, consisted of very heavy bricks of pure unpolished gold, ready for the mint.

After high-grade ores began to give out in the 1890's, workmen resorted to chlorination. A chlorination smelter was built just outside of Deadwood

---

* A drift is a horizontal passageway running through or parallel to a vein.

and narrow-gauge roads were built to bring the ore down to Deadwood for treatment. Different treatments of the ores were tried. In 1901, Charles Merrill arrived at Homestake and developed a cyanide process for extracting 98% of the gold from the ore.

The Homestake Mine

LIFE AS A MINER

One can never understand the character of a people until he knows how they live. The daily existence, the work and play of life make the character of the individual and so with the people of Lead. Work in the mines in those days spelled one word in capital letters—DANGER. The man who left home in perfect health in the morning was lowered into the mine, at first by the old bucket method and later by cable run platforms called "cages," or he walked into the tunnels to take up his day's work. Perhaps his family would never see him alive again.

Life was a hazard, and children never knew when their fathers might be the next man injured or killed in the mine. The sight of a stretcher carried from the hoist would cause every child on the street to demand, "Who is it?" That was the life of those early days—a delayed blast, a broken timber, or a cave-in meant injury or death for at least one, sometimes more. When one man was killed, the question was always asked, "Who shall be next?" And the same question was asked when the second death came, for it seemed death never stopped until the third man was taken. If a cave-in occurred, usually three men were trapped and many years passed before the "jinx" was broken.

I remember many instances of this coincidence and especially the time when the jinx was broken. An explosion had occurred in the mine where they were driving a tunnel. Two of the men were blown out of the tunnel in pieces and the third, a neighbor of ours, was thought to be buried by tons of earth and rock. The rescue band worked day and night to remove the earth that blocked the tunnel in the hope that John Johnson's body might be found or that he might have been blown backward into the mine and still be alive. Hope died hard in the hearts of those men.

Mrs. Johnson was very ill at that time and they dared not tell her but she knew. In her delirium, she would say, "Don't give up, John. Don't give up. You'll make it. Now, once more, don't you see that light? Come, Johnnie, try again. Come back to me..."

The night and day ended and then another night and day came and went. On the third day, word went out that rescue was hopeless. But toward dusk a grimy, bloody, seemingly drunken man staggered down the hillside. No one noticed him for they had been watching the mouth of the tunnel. As he turned up our street he broke into a staggering run. Inside the Johnson home, Hilda Johnson was sitting up in bed with her arms stretched toward the door and muttering, "I knew you'd make it, Johnnie. I knew you'd come." The door flew open and Johnnie Johnson stumbled into the room.

Johnson and his partners had been working in the back of the tunnel. Two of them had gone forward just around the bend when the explosion took place. Johnson had gone back to pick up his coat and put up the tools. Although they were killed, he was trapped in a chamber of the mine. The blast had also opened a crevice in the side of the hill so that a thin streak of light filtered through. Surface water dripping into the mine gave him drink and with the mining tools he worked toward that little point of light until exhausted. Dropping off to sleep for a short time, he would rouse to work again until by the third day he dug a hole large enough to crawl out the side of the hill. Although far from the mouth of the tunnel, the opening was nearer to his home. Unfortunately, despite his earlier escape, Mr. Johnson was killed in the mine on July 26, 1903, and was buried in the South Lead Cemetery.

Gradually the Homestake Mine became known for its modern equipment and enormous passages. From a few hundred-foot-levels, as the main or horizontal passages of the mines were called, they have grown to the thousand-foot-levels. As of 1945, it is now three thousand feet below the surface of Lead and the whole city rests upon timbered chambers.

Life as a Miner

(EDITOR'S NOTE: The mine operation depth at the time of closing was 8,000 feet below the surface making it the largest and deepest gold mine in North America. The mine permanently closed on December 21, 2002. Currently, the Sanford Underground Science and Engineering Laboratory conducts experiments pertaining to neutrinos and black matter at the 4,850-foot level of the mine.)

In the early days, few safety devices were implemented in the mines. Surface water seeped into them and underground streams were encountered, so the water had to be pumped out. At first the men were only a few hundred feet underground and the air could be kept clear by ventilating shafts, but soon fresh air had to be forced in.

Safety devices have now taken into account any potential danger. The Homestake Mine is the safest in all the world. The company deserves a tribute for the manner in which it always treated its workers. Company doctors and surgeons guarded their health and provided hospital care for miners and their families. Baths, amusements, and library facilities for the older people and free kindergarten for their children were also available due to Mrs. Phoebe Hearst.

The home life of Lead miners was high quality and his occupation was held in high regard. The community offered every advantage to miners' children, and a miner's home was as well-furnished as any merchant's or professional man's home.

Looking at a miner's livelihood during the 1800's, one realizes the terrific nerve-racking strain they endured. After South Dakota was admitted to the Union in 1889, not surprisingly, fifty percent of the inmates of the State Hospital for the Insane in Yankton came from our mining district and over fifty percent of those were women. Many of the miners' children had a bluffing, daredevil air about them as a way to hide their innermost fear. Even in the later years when I taught in Lead, if someone noticed a stretcher being carried from the mines to the hospital, a boy was customarily sent from the classroom to find out who had been injured. The teachers knew that no work could be accomplished until their pupils knew that their fathers were safe.

One can hardly realize the mining industry's impact upon the lives of the children unless they have lived in the community day in and day out. I remember hearing the father of one of my playmates say to his wife: "Ellen, we shall be blasting today and I may be late." He was a foreman who went into any danger along with his men. I did not then understand the sudden rush of my playmate to her father's arms, but learned later what it meant to those left at home.

In my day in the Hills, the Homestake Company paid the highest wages with the shortest hours. Only one long strike was chalked up against the Company that occurred when followers of Thomas Mooney found a spark in the emotions of men to stir up strife. The strike began in the fall of 1909, brought about by radical labor organizers who tried to force the Homestake Company to hire only union men. The company refused by saying that every man had a right to earn a living if he gave honest labor for the money he received.

In spite of the insurrectionists, the honored legion stayed true, composed of forty-nine men who continued to work in the mines. Mine Superintendent Grier, with the help of Lead businessmen, formed a bodyguard for the workers who remained loyal and kept the mine going.

Due to labor trouble, Mr. Grier temporarily closed the mine from November 24, 1909, until January 18, 1910. The union finally succumbed and most of the men went back to work. I have not heard of any labor troubles since. Many of those men who remained loyal to the company have now passed to the other side, but those who remain, point with pride to the button they wear to indicate their rating with the company.

T.J. Grier did not have an easy job for he had many varied responsibilities. Most important was to keep the men healthy and happy in their everyday life. Grier's responsibilities included providing homes for men to live in and rear their families, clean water supply, pure air in the mines, timber to keep the roofs of those stopes from caving in, and care of broken bodies when accidents happened.

The prevalence of kidnapping was high at the time, with even Mr. Grier having his own experience. In October of 1907, he was notified to place

$10,000 at a certain location at a given time or his children would be taken from him. He placed a guard with his children wherever they went, and, as my own children associated with them, we too were protected. The case ended very quickly when the gang was caught, made up of numerous Italian Black Handers* who used a young Italian girl to pick up the money. She was followed and the men were then captured.

Most men were toilers in those early days, and honesty and good citizenship gave them their rank in the community. Among the prospectors and miners, life was more or less a gambler's existence. One day a man would be almost begging for his bread and the next he would make a strike and in his dreams become a millionaire. In reality, he may have only found a gold pocket where he would take out a few thousand with no more to be discovered. Such was the case of Patsy McCarthy, a poor Irishman, and his brother-in-law.

The two men had worked in the Homestake mine and prospected for gold on the side while Mrs. McCarthy washed and cleaned, making the "bread and butter." One day Patsy struck gold in Strawberry Gulch, and while the mine did not prove to be a bonanza it did provide a nice little competency.

Homestake employees were for the most part quiet men who did their duty and reared their families to be honest American citizens. Most moved away, but they left their imprint on the community: Meno Voight; the Treweek brothers, loved by their men; John Spargo; James Steele; Ole Danielson; William Frackelton; Nels Lund and the Lundin brothers; three English friends - Jim Honey, John Blatchford, and Sydney Staple; John Commiskey who ran the trains over the road to Piedmont for so many years and showed his quick resourcefulness when bandits held up the pay train; Richard Blackstone, the builder of Lead's water supply, railroad, and fill-in man when vacancies occurred in high places, yet preferring, apparently, a less conspicuous life, always helping others and giving credit where credit was due.

* Italian gangs who extorted money, precursors to organized crime such as the mafia.

Had it not been for foremen like Joe and Nick Treweek and their brother-in-law, Billy O'Brien, who went into those workings and stood the shifts and dangers alongside the common miners who trusted them, that work could not have progressed. Homestake miners were not slaves but rather free men whose bosses were also their friends. Foremen had a little more expertise on the work that needed to be done and were willing to take the hand of any workman as man-to-man in their efforts.

For many years, Ed Fry was one of the engineers who raised and lowered the cages into the mines. I went up the hoist many times and watched him sitting in his seat built like a huge chair high up above the floor with a great steel lever on each side and a star suspended in front of him. A gong would sound and according to the number of rings he would know whether ore cars or men were in the cage. If ore cars, the cage dropped quickly but if men, it was lowered slowly and very carefully. Otherwise, if a man lost his balance it might mean a fall of several hundred feet down the shaft to certain death.

I well remember one accident where a false signal caused Mr. Fry to lower the cage rapidly and a man was thrown down the shaft. An arm was located on one landing; a leg on another; and the dismembered trunk was brought up from the pit of the shaft. Mr. Fry was so shocked by the accident that for days he could not go back to work. He was entirely exonerated and eventually placed at the new Ellison hoist where he took charge of the cages that only raised and lowered men. He worked for many years in that capacity until age and failing health called for his retirement.

For many years Mrs. Ed (Frances) Fry was the only graduate nurse in Lead outside of a hospital nurse. She had taken her training in Ireland and was awarded the Queens Cross for her work during a riot. Mr. Fry's people were Church of England ministers, so naturally he became one of the backbones of the Episcopal Church in Lead. He completely abstained from liquor and lived a clean life. He often said, "One could not drink and handle a cage for it needed a clear head and quick thinking at all times." One could never go to sleep on that job.

Are these the only men upon whom T.J. Grier could depend? No. Many more made up that great chain of success, including Alex Ballantyne, S.S. Green, Con Green, Albert Steele, and a hundred others. Each man had his job, and they all contributed to the success of the Homestake Mines and mills.

At one point, Lead lost some of its glamour. Many of the restless souls who composed Lead's male population learned of a discovery of a new gold field in Johannesburg, South Africa. This new field called the gold-hungry souls of men to leave their homes and families and head for Africa.

Some men collected their belongings and followed that golden lure. Some deserted wife and children and were never heard from again. Others went to try their luck but returned to take up life wherever they could get a job. None were the better for it. Those who returned said very little of their wild adventure and the money that they threw away.

Thus the golden lure still worked. Homes broke up and lives of little children were wrecked as men worshiped the golden calf. Life in Lead was prosaic. Real poverty or want was rare in the Black Hills, and work was available to those willing to earn their pay. Furthermore, the shadows of the pine trees gave health and peace to those who dwelt there. Never was there a break in the thump, thump, thump of the stamps in the mills or the click of the picks and shovels while the pumps kept pumping water out of the mines, twenty-four hours a day, seven days a week, fifty-two weeks a year; year after year.

In the mining world, the word Homestake has beautiful significance, symbolic of security and protection. It is said that mines carry the promise of gold output for one hundred years thereafter. Even at the present time of the Second World War, when the mines have been shut down by government order, shares of its stock are hard to come by.

(EDITOR's NOTE: The War Production Board lifted Order L-208 on July 1, 1945, and the Homestake mine reopened in December 1946 as cited by Gary L. Buffington, Mining Homestake, The America Society of Safety Engineers, accessed August 17 2016, http://www.asse.org/practicespecialties/mining-homestake/)

IN MEMORY OF T.J. GRIER
by Mrs. S.R. Smith

**"Greater love hath no man than this;
that a man lay down his life for his friends"**

YOU ask, - Does the sun shine warm thru the pines?
Do the whistles blow as in olden times?
Do the men respond with heartfelt cheer?
Are the homes now safe for the children dear?
Do man and maid pledge troth today
And stroll to the church in the same old way?
Are the great black clouds of the strike all gone:
Is the battle for life and freedom won?

Well, yes, - thru the trees the sun glints bright
And pine boughs bend neath snow-flake white;
The whistles blow, the schoolbells ring,
With glad voices the children sing;
The good wife stands with smiles at the door,
The thump of stamps make the old mills roar;
And in the cages glad greetings abound
As they bear the men to the underground.

You see the man with nerve of steel
And eyes far-seeing, grasped the wheel;
The shadows gathered, clouds hung low,
While on the hillsides deep with snow
The men on guard made shadows grim
That reached and touched and thrilled the man
Till every pulse of heart and brain
Of a mighty chief arose to the strain,

Thru battle smoke of passions dire,
With face, stern set, he met the fire
That threatened all his heart held dear.
The ties that bind, the loves that cheer,
The mills, the mines, his home, his life,
All, all were touched in the fearful strife
That surged and swayed from side to side
Till the gulf grew deep and dark and wide.

The mines, the mills, and shops are manned;
Today contentment reigns in the land;
The toiler sings, for his hopes run high,
For maids, the wedding bells bring joy.
For this he fought, for this he won -
The battle of strife that saved his men.
Yes - peace to the camp has come to stay,
But the price, alas! We had to pay.

Bend low, - Dost hear thru whispering pines
His voice ring true in memory's chimes?
A voice to soothe, to lift, to lead,
And nerve the weak to nobler deed?
No greater love hath mortal shown,
For - for our lives he gave his own;
And o'er his grave where shadows lie
Methinks the pines bend low to sigh,
While hearts sore pressed still question - "Why?"

(Editor's Note: Thomas J. Grier died on September 22, 1914 in Los Angeles, California at the age of 64. He is buried in the West Lead Cemetery. On July 31, 1916, in front of the Christ Episcopal Church in Lead a statue of Thomas J. Grier, sculpted by Allan G. Newman and cast in bronze, was erected by the Homestake Employees, Homestake Mining Company, Hearst Merceantile Co. and friends and business acquaintances of Lead and the Black Hills.)

PART III
Pioneer Personalities

EARLY SETTLERS

The character of early settlers was a vital point in the development of the Black Hills, with men and women often the hardy pioneer type. Their one desire was to view new sights and penetrate the seemingly wild Indian haunts still unknown to the white man. The Indian legend that the Black Hills wore a curse upon all who entered roused the desire to explore, but one needed a stout heart indeed to enter.

Suffice it to say, after gold was discovered, Lead became famous outside the Hills and began to draw a following unto herself. The mines needed workmen and Homestake miners were given good pay every month. Steady paychecks developed greater appeal than prospecting.

In those days, ox teams generally brought in freight. These ox, or mule 'trains' as they were called, experienced many trials and adventures well worth recording. I remember one train that came in from Sidney and unloaded in Lead in 1879. The boss received his pay from the merchants, mostly in gold dust and nuggets, a common means of exchange at that time. They left Lead late that afternoon and never returned.

When a later train came in, its passengers reported having come upon the remains of wagons and the charred bones of men; whether freighters or emigrants, they could not tell. These may have been the remains of the Sidney freight outfit. Most likely waylaid by Indians and their stock driven off, the men were killed and their remains buried in one great funeral pyre. Their identities were never known.

WILD BILL HICKOK

As mentioned earlier, Uncle Jack witnessed the killing of Wild Bill Hickok. The morning of his death, Hickok turned to his friend Charlie Utter and made the statement that he was 'going west' that day. In those days, that term implied that he would die that very day. Upon his remark, Hickok sat down and wrote a letter to his wife, Agnes Lake Thatcher, gave it to Charlie, and asked him to see that she got it. Hickok's friends tried to laugh off the premonition and finally persuaded him to play a game of cards.

When playing cards in a saloon, Hickok always sat in a chair facing the door so that he could see the bar mirror and everyone who came in. On that fateful day, Charlie took Hickok's accustomed seat, forcing him to a seat with his back to the door. Utter never forgave himself for taking Hickok's usual chair, claiming that Jack McCall never would have done the deed if he had faced Hickok on equal terms. To him, McCall was a shiftless drifter in search of notoriety.

McCall rode into town with his cronies, boasting that he would kill Hickok. He walked into the saloon, went to the counter, got a drink, turned, pulled his gun, and shot Hickok in the back, never giving Hickok a chance to defend himself. Hickok was considered the fastest two-gun man in the country and McCall wanted above all else to be known as the man who killed him.

The town was bustling but at the first pop of the gun the street emptied out. P. A. Gushurst was the first person to enter the saloon after Hickok was shot. McCall escaped but Hickok's friends trailed the murderer. McCall was arrested and tried in a hastily formed court inside a primitive butcher shop, stump meat block and all. McCall was brought into this cramped room. One man stepped up claiming he was a legally appointed lawyer and would defend McCall. He called for a jury and saw to it that McCall's men were chosen. He then began his defense by declaring that Hickok had killed McCall's younger brother in Kansas without provocation and that McCall was simply avenging his brother's death. The jury returned a verdict of justifiable homicide and McCall was spirited out of town by his friends.

Later in Yankton, while drinking in the saloon, McCall boasted that he had never had a brother, and that the lawyer was not legitimate, having simply concocted the story to save him. McCall was then arrested by a U. S. Marshall, tried in a regularly established court, sentenced and hanged for Hickok's murder.

Contrary to present day portrayal, Uncle Jack shared that Hickok was not a desperado, but a law-abiding, law-enforcing official sent out to Deadwood to locate a criminal on behalf of the government. Aspiring to a peaceful life, Hickok was not a lover of Calamity Jane but rather, a respecter of womanhood, whose last thoughts were probably of his wife.

Hickok was buried by his friends in a little cemetery on the bank of the creek. Years later, when his body was moved to Mount Moriah Cemetery, it was found to be partially petrified from the silica in the water. A copy of the letter Wild Bill wrote to his wife the morning he was killed is on display at the Adams Museum in Deadwood.

A copy of the Thursday, August 10th, 1876, edition of The Black Hills Pioneer reads:

"Hickok's Assassin Ecquitted (sic);
Wild Bill is Buried"

"On Tuesday Wild Bill Hickok was buried by citizens of Deadwood, who, although they had known him but a few days, were shocked and grieved by his brutal assassination by Jack

McCall, the cowardly killer who was set free by a drunken and irresponsible group of men assembled as a jury for his trial.

Probably Hickok was the only man we have yet had in our midst who had the courage and other qualifications to bring some semblance of order to the lawless element in our camp. The fact that he was killed by one of the sorriest specimens of humanity to be found in the Hills is significant. This editor feels that the true reason for this cowardly killing is to be found in that fact.

The facts of the killings are as follows: Hickok was in the Saloon No. 10 engaged in a pocker (sic) game with three other men. For some unexplained reason he was not sitting with his back to a wall. This has been his ruel (sic) for many years, since his career of law enforcement had developed a long list of men who swore they would shoot him at the first opportunity. After they had been playing for some time, among the men in the saloon, Jack McCall appeared and approached the table from a point behind Hickok. No one paid any attention to him and when he was directly behind Hickok's chair, McCall drew his gun and shot Hickok in the back of the head. In the confusion which followed he made his escape out the front door and down our Main Street, disappearing in the backs of the store buildings across the street. He was found a short time later and the trial immediately originated with he (sic) disgraceful ending which we have noted."

"COLORADO CHARLIE" UTTER

In 1879, Charlie Utter became the hero of my childhood days. When in Lead, he often stayed at Mrs. Baldwin's place next door to Aunty's. One morning, my mother let me play on the walk-in front of Aunty's store. Before long, a striking man with long, silky hair and piercing eyes stood at the bottom of the steps and watched my antics. When my mother came to the door to see if I was all right, he spoke to her. "Madam, would you object to my amusing the little girl with some cards? I promise you no harm will ever come to her through me." We both turned and looked at the man known as Colorado Charlie. My mother looked him over, gave her consent, and never had cause for regret. I spent many a bright afternoon sitting on the second step, with my hands clasped in my lap, trying to sit still while Charlie sat on the step below and built card houses on the top step. His long, slender fingers fascinated me as he manipulated the cards into wonderful Chinese pagodas, temples, towers, and dollhouses. With his knife, he cut out furniture, animals, and trees.

I never heard an oath or unclean word pass through his lips but once. That day I was playing on top of a large dry goods box when the town bully, well under the influence of liquor, came toward me, flourishing his knife and saying: "Now I've got you, I'll cut off your ears." I screamed and crouched on the far side of the box, for I could not get down. At that moment Charlie appeared, and, with an oath, grabbed the fellow by the coat collar and threw him into the street with the injunction never to show up there again. He then lifted me into his arms soothingly and handed me over to my mother who, hearing my screams, had just reached the door.

I last saw Charlie Utter during the black diphtheria epidemic later that year. That same illness kept me in bed for weeks, and he left Lead before I was well again. For years, I kept the box of card toys he made for me, and to this day I can shut my eyes and see his fascinating hands and kindly smile.

From my child's perspective, Colorado Charlie was to me an ideal, with a halo of romance and glamour that settled around him and his long hair, his finely ornamented boots, and his trim muscular physique, lithe as a panther and straight as an arrow. He instilled confidence in me, and I felt safe. I will always remember him in his scouting outfit of coonskin cap, leather jacket, leggings, and moccasins, and his long-barreled gun.

The town bully never bothered me again, whether owing to Charlie's threats or because he died shortly after I recovered from my illness. He was a painter by trade and died in a fit of delirium tremens one night trying to chase the snakes from his paint, the men said. I never could see how the snakes entered his shop, when my mother assured me that snakes were not found in Lead.

"CALAMITY JANE"

That first summer in Lead, Calamity Jane was a character that stood out. I was standing in front of Aunty's store when she came into town riding the lead mule of a freighter's outfit. She jumped off with a "hip, hip, hurrah," and rushed into the house next door. Later a child called to me: "Come quick! She's hanging up clothes and hasn't her pants on." The rarity of seeing her in a dress and not her leather chaps really made her appearance that day a sensation.

She was in the Baldwins' backyard, and I rushed there, but on the way, ran into a two-by-four a carpenter had sawed off for the roof of a building. To this day, I carry the scar, for I almost put my eye out. Needless to say, I failed to see Calamity Jane, and when I asked my mother who she was, she told me not to worry my head, that she was just a naughty girl I would never know. She also said that Calamity Jane just wanted notoriety and to pay no attention to her.

Legend had it that Calamity Jane was so called because her father, a discharged private by the name of "Dalton," was killed by Indians when she was one year old and her mother Jane, wounded, lived long enough to get her to Fort Robinson, walking one hundred miles at night. Upon arriving at the fort, she gave the child into the army's protection before breathing her last. The soldiers adopted little Jane, calling her "Calamity Jane" due to the calamity that brought her to them.

She was everybody's child, yet nobody claimed responsibility for her. She grew up as a weed into a kindhearted but immoral woman whose language was of the vilest. Yet, like most of her kind, she had a heart that took in everyone in trouble. When smallpox broke out, who took that poor, frail boy into her cabin and shut herself in until she had nursed him back to life - the boy no one would even approach to offer a drink of cold water? The only person to offer help was Calamity Jane, our "Black Hills Calamity." She started out as a poor, drunken girl who worshiped Hickok, because he was a gentleman and he was kind to her because she was a woman.

For all of her vices, Calamity Jane cared for the underdog. One time in broad daylight, a cry rang out, "a fight, a fight," and men gathered around the contending parties. No one cared to interfere until, finally, that notorious kid of the army camp came along with her bullwhip and stepped into the ring, lashed the bully and pulled the weakling out of his grasp. She then dragged him to her cabin to sober him up and be brought back to life as noted in the Thursday, July 13, 1876, edition of The Black Hills Pioneer:

"Calamity Jane is Nurse"
"The man Warren, who was stabbed on lower Main street Wednesday night, is doing quite well under the care of Calamity Jane, who has kindly undertaken the job of nursing him. There's lots of humanity in Calamity, and she is deserving of much praise for the part she has taken in this particular case."

The notorious Calamity Jane had her part in developing the beautiful Black Hills. No one is all bad, and in pioneer days, the beauty of the soul and Christian humanity shone through the most ragged covering. Who was there to pick up that broken body stabbed and bleeding to death? Where were the nurses and doctors in those days? Calamity, the poor, debased woman of the town, took Warren to her own cabin and nursed him back to life. Read her story in the annals of 1876 and you will see the Bible story of the Good Samaritan. In Calamity Jane, gold sparkled under the surface of mud and rubble.

Calamity Jane died in 1903 and is buried in Mt. Moriah Cemetery in Deadwood near her friend Wild Bill Hickock.

BILLY HAYES

Billy Hayes

Billy Hayes, Uncle Jack's traveling companion and fellow shoemaker, was killed shortly after mother and I arrived in Lead. He went to Paul Jentges' saloon to complain about a nuisance from his saloon that contaminated the produce in his wife Eliza's store cellar. He met only harsh words and, as he left, Jentges hurled a heavy whiskey glass at him, crushing his skull. He died a few days later. The murderer never served a day for his crime.

As the case of Bill Hickok's trial demonstrates, law courts in those early days were more or less a farce. I happen to have the evidence and complete account of one of the first murder trials in Lead, as written by one of the trial witnesses:

> "On the 6th day of August, 1879, the little town of Lead City was stirred into indignation by the report that William Hayes, a shoemaker, had been struck on the head by a saloon keeper, which was likely to end in death for the unfortunate victim.
>
> The weapon used was a whiskey glass, but it proved a deadly one, crushing the skull and causing concussion of the brain that resulted in death on August 13th, seven days after the blow.
>
> At the post-mortem examination it was shown that the skull had been shattered and two splinters of the bone had pierced the brain, causing death.
>
> The case was then turned over to the court. The verdict of the coroner's jury was: 'William Hayes met his death by a blow from a whiskey glass thrown by one Paul Jentges on August 6, 1879.'
>
> Two days after, the funeral took place at the home of the deceased, which was next door to the saloon of Paul Jentges, the widow being the only relative in the large following which accompanied the body to its last resting place.
>
> The preliminary hearing took place immediately after the funeral. The best legal talent of the Hills was engaged by the defendant, but, after two days hard work, the defendant was bound under a $10,000 bond to appear before the District Court to answer the charge of manslaughter in the first degree.
>
> To avoid repetition, I have refrained from giving any testimony offered. In September, the witnesses for the prosecution were summoned to appear before the grand jury, and the result of the case of the Territory vs. Paul Jentges was an indictment of manslaughter in the first degree.

September 26th found Deadwood in ashes. The courthouse and all the county records had gone up in flames, and again Paul Jentges was put under bond, this time for $7000, as a new trial was ordered.

January found a new grand jury empaneled, the witnesses again summoned, and again the result was an indictment for manslaughter in the first degree.

The strain upon the widow had been so great that she was prostrated and for two months small hope was entertained for her recovery. This caused the case to be laid over and, with first one delay and then another, it was August of 1880 before the case was tried in the District Court. Everything had conspired to the advantage of the accused man. Even the only witness for the prosecution who had witnessed the throwing of the fatal glass had been laid away in his last resting place.

Trouble was experienced in obtaining a jury but, after hours of challenging and excusing, twelve men swore that they would deal justly according to evidence in the case of the Territory vs. Paul Jentges on indictment by the grand jury of manslaughter in the first degree.

The first witness for the prosecution testified that his attention had been called to the saloon by loud words which had reached him in his room across the street and, as he put his head out of the window, he saw Mr. Hayes coming out of Jentges' saloon, his face turned towards his home, one foot, if not both, on the sidewalk, when a glass struck him on the breast and rolled on the walk. Picking up the glass, Hayes turned to the saloon with it, and was again struck from within with another glass on the head. He did not see who threw the glasses.

The next witness was the Constable who testified that he saw Hayes pick up the glass and go toward the saloon, whereupon he, the Constable, tried to reach him in time to prevent him from throwing it back; but after reaching him, he heard something *crash through a picture or mirror behind the bar. Just then Jentges ordered the man to jail.*

    He started with Hayes, as Jentges ordered, but suddenly became conscious that something was wrong, and, looking more closely at Hayes, found that blood was gushing from a wound upon the head and the man was staggering. He, the Constable, then asked, 'Who done this?' 'I did, Jentges replied, 'and I don't care a damn who knows it. Take him to the cooler.' 'I'll take him to a doctor before I take him anywhere else,' I replied. 'The glass had struck him before I reached him; I think the crash I heard was caused by the glass thrown by Hayes. I think those glasses were thrown together.'

    The third witness furnished only the deathbed evidence of Hayes, first showing clearly that it was deathbed evidence and that Hayes was perfectly sane while giving it. The evidence was as follows:

    'Paul struck me first; I'd swear it on my dying bed.'

    'Do you know you are dying now?'

    'Yes, I know it.'

    'Did you strike Paul at all?' 'I don't know. If I did, it was after I was struck on the head. I don't know what I done after that.' This evidence was corroborated by four other witnesses who were present when it was taken down. The court then adjourned until nine the next morning when the witnesses for the defense were heard, and as it was understood that this was the only witness who had been present during the altercation, everyone waited impatiently for what he had to say. After being sworn, he became suddenly sick and had to leave the witness box. It was strange to see the man overcome, and many were the whispered comments made upon his strange nervousness, but it was accounted for when he took his place on the witness box.

    Do you think me partial in not being able to give the evidence as he gave it? He wound and entangled himself so much that it caused many a titter of suppressed laughter in the room. He said he was a brewer and was talking to Jentges on business when Hayes came up to Jentges and began talking insultingly to him, telling him he wanted him to remove something that Hayes deemed a nuisance. Jentges refused to remove it, and Hayes walked up and down the place for half an hour, using vile language and finally ended in striking Jentges and then started for the door, whereupon Jentges threw a glass at him, which struck Hayes.

The judge here called the man's attention to the fact that his evidence proved that Hayes was then upon the point of leaving the place and Jentges was no longer in danger when Hayes' back was turned. That evidence was quickly drawn back and something introduced instead, until the witness became so badly tangled up that he was finally excused with a feeling of pity for his weakness from all who heard him.

Jentges was the next witness and he corroborated the testimony of his first witness as near as it was safe, but acknowledging that he threw those glasses. This man was testifying for his own life or liberty and, if his testimony could save him, he was justified in swearing accordingly.

The last witness was the bartender. Every eye in the room was upon this man as he stood with his hand raised while the clerk administered the oath and, as the words, 'I will' was heard from the man's lips, I believe everyone felt that he would hear the truth, the whole truth and nothing but the truth when told to tell all he knew in the case.

He began: 'On the 6th day of August, 1879, I was tending bar for Paul Jentges. About 4 o'clock in the afternoon Mr. Hayes sat down with me. We were talking in a pleasant way and he was telling me his prospects, etc. He said he was working at shoemaking in Deadwood and was getting $100 per month. His wife kept the little grocery store next here and he had stayed up a day or two to help her as it was payday and there was some heavy lifting to *do which he did not think her able to do. He said he was going to work another year at his trade and then he would be able to help her put in a good stock of groceries and would then stay up in Lead with her. He now asked me if I wouldn't take something to drink. We then started to the bar together, and I asked him what he would take. He said, 'a glass of lemonade.' I took a glass of beer. Hayes paid for the drinks. All the time we had been talking, Mr. Jentges and the brewer had been talking in German. I did not understand what about, but it was something rather loud. As I came from behind the bar, I stepped out of the back door. I had not been out more than five minutes when I heard the fuss, and when I got in, it was all over. Mr. Hayes was not quarrelsome; no, he was not intoxicated. I never saw him intoxicated. I am sure I was not gone over seven minutes.'*

Now the evidence was all in; the arguments on both sides had been heard and the district attorney was telling the jury:

'Gentlemen, you are all liquor dealers; you know what a whiskey glass is and, even admitting the man, Hayes, to have been quarrelsome, you know that if you threw a glass at every man's head who became quarrelsome in your saloon, you might throw several every day, but I feel you are men who will do your duty.'

Then came the charge from the Judge to the jury, and at last the jury retired.

The verdict was manslaughter in the second degree and the people considered they had done nobly and no one feared the judge would not do his part, but he was not ready to pass sentence upon the prisoner; so he was allowed to go until the judge should think proper and, in the meantime, petitions for mercy were circulated and plenty who knew nothing of the case signed them, and at last the judge passed sentence: forty days in the county jail and a fine sufficient to pay the costs in the case."

What would your community think of that sentence? This sentence was an insult to the jury: they had not asked mercy, and it had been considered that because they were liquor men, they would be partial. They had done their duty, and accordingly believed the judge would do his, and he probably thought he did; but did Jentges serve his forty days? Not at all. He did not sleep even three nights in jail and never missed a day in his saloon, where he still prospered while Billy's widow struggled to support herself in her little grocery store next door.

(EDITOR'S NOTE: Billy Hayes is buried in the Mount Moriah Cemetery in Deadwood. His widow, Eliza, appeared in the 1880 census as a proprietor of a fruit and grocery store, and caring for an adopted daughter, Della Montine, age 12. In the 1900 census, Eliza Hayes is listed as an inmate in the Lawrence County Poorhouse in Gayville, a mining town between Deadwood and Lead.)

THE LARIMER FAMILY

Sarah Larimer

Frank Larimer

Mrs. Larimer was our friend and family photographer in Humboldt, Kansas. She told us of the hardships and dangers she and her son encountered as they made their way into the Black Hills in those first early days.

Like my uncle, Judge William Jackson Larimer had followed the

Union Pacific trail to Fort Laramie, Territory of Wyoming, and then into the Black Hills by horseback and pack mule. He was a lawyer by profession and education, and a prospector by desire. He left Mrs. Larimer and son, Frank, in Humboldt, Kansas. Learning that Mr. Larimer was ill, she determined to join him. When she arrived at Fort Laramie, she discovered he had recovered and had gone into the Hills. With nothing daunting her, she started after him. She and their son joined a small party of travelers, and went forward without fear.

The group had not traveled very far when they realized that a party of Indians was trailing them, and on the third day, they attacked. They took Mrs. Larimer and Frank as prisoners, and what became of the rest of the party was never known. Although they were not separated or badly mistreated, they were prisoners in every sense of the term. Frank, a stalwart lad, was allowed to mingle with the Indian boys and learned much of the language and ways of the Sioux. His mother was guarded more closely. Mrs. Larimer worked with the women, and the outdoor life hardened her for later experiences after they escaped.

For months, they had been with the band and had only a general idea of their location. Not having made any attempt to get away, they were gradually given more liberties. Finally, the men went on a hunting trip to the north. Mrs. Larimer determined that the time had arrived to make their long hoped-for escape. She had been berry picking with the women and had learned about the different roots that were edible, what berries to pick, and the general flow of streams. Though young, Frank had gained endurance and worthwhile knowledge from the boys. The men were not expected back for several days so Mrs. Larimer decided that when they had been gone two days it was time to make their move.

The moon did not come up until late making for a dark night. After everyone was asleep, Mrs. Larimer loosened the earth under her brush bed and rolled out the back of the tepee and crept to where Frank usually slept. However, he had already crawled over the other boys and was out standing in the shadows, waiting.

Together they made their way among the dogs and tepees to the edge of the camp that was near a stream. Taking off their moccasins they stepped into the water and went upstream along the bank for a ways. Then, crossing to the opposite bank where a small rivulet trickled down to another stream, they waded into the main waterway. Even after the moon rose they never left their watery road but traveled with greater urgency. Motherly love prodded them on.

By morning, they were miles away but they dared not stop. They took advantage of every bit of shelter. Mrs. Larimer had secured some jerked meat before she left camp which sustained them as they kept on their way. The sun came out hot. Thinking only to protect her son, Mrs. Larimer took off her white petticoat and tied it over his head. Frank snatched it off saying, "White could be seen farther than anything else." When he could not go any further she found a thicket and they hid themselves. Frank dropped off asleep at once but she continued to watch. When the moon rose, she roused the boy and they started again, always heading south.

For days and days, they wandered on, living on berries and roots and even tree bark. Finally, they reached the Platte River where they fell in with some trappers. These men took care of them and finally got them on a stagecoach back to Humboldt. They never reached the Black Hills for Mrs. Larimer was satisfied with the more quiet life of Kansas. Mr. Larimer, I believe, died in the Hills. At one time, he was Justice of the Peace in Lead but he never succeeded in his prospecting. He refused to go home without his stake so he followed that long, lonely trail of the unsuccessful to the end. He was no drinker or dissipater, just unlucky.

(EDITOR'S NOTE: Frank became an attorney at law and died in 1891 at the age of 34, William died in 1894 at the age of 68, and Sarah died in 1913 at the age of 77. All three are buried in the Oakland Cemetery in Centerville, Iowa.)

THE ALEXANDER FAMILY

Grand noble men and women made up the permanent solid society of those early days. One such family, the Alexanders, developed the hack line from Deadwood to Lead. Mr. Alexander had three buggies and ten horses, and employed ten men to drive people to and from Deadwood.

As I remember, Wesley Alexander was a Virginian by birth and very wealthy prior to the war, owning large plantations with blooded horses and many slaves in Kentucky. The war swept him of almost everything. So, in 1877, loading what little was left into hacks, he brought his family consisting of his wife, his daughter, Florence and her husband, John Corum, their household goods, a fine string of horses, and boys to handle them to the new gold fields.

The Alexanders settled in Lead, and this fine southern family became numbered among the most influential members of the community. As I grew up, I spent many happy hours in their delightful home and garden. Mrs. Sarah Alexander, as mentioned earlier, was the person who nursed Papa back to health after he contracted mountain typhoid. She loved flowers and birds, and in the summer months her tall hollyhocks and sweet peas and stately larkspur were a joy to behold. In the winter, the low rambling rooms of the house served as perfect bowers of flowers with singing birds. She had canaries and redbirds so tame - they hopped from plant to plant in the living room. They would light on Mrs. Alexander's shoulder and pour out a volume of song while she chirped in her loving way and fed them tiny tidbits.

Shortly after coming to the Hills, Florence's husband was thrown from his horse and killed. This caused the family, if it were possible, to become even more focused on one another. Many prominent men of the Hills made advances, but several years passed before Florence finally consented to marry again. Richard D. Millet, an Englishman and Chief Engineer for the Homestake Company, was the fortunate man. He married with the understanding that he was never to take her away from her parents.

Shortly after their marriage he was sent to South America. On his return, Florence met him in New Orleans and they enjoyed a long-delayed honeymoon trip through the old South and New England. On their return, they found Mr. Alexander ailing. A dreaded epidemic of typhoid was taking its toll and soon both father and daughter were laid to rest. Mr. Millet sold the hack-line, reserving only his wife's and Mr. Alexander's saddle horses which he then shipped to Salt Lake City with their household goods. There Mr. Millet made a home for his grief-stricken mother-in-law. A better son never could have been found than R.D. Millet.

(EDITOR'S NOTE: An obelisk in Mount Olivet Cemetery in Salt Lake City, Utah, marks the deaths of Wesley Alexander, December 26, 1890; Florence Alexander Millet, December 29, 1890; Richard D. Millet, September 6, 1914; and Sarah Alexander, June 30, 1924.)

THE HILL FAMILY

Across the street from the Alexanders lived another southern family, the Hills. Judge Henry Hill was the first Justice of the Peace in Lead. He was elected in 1878 and held his first criminal case on June 25 of that year. He died less than a year later on March 23, 1879, leaving a wife, Mary, two daughters, and a mulatto girl named Lettie Cole.

Mrs. Hill earned a livelihood by knitting stockings and sewing. The youngest daughter never married but moved to Los Angeles with the exodus of Black Hills people that took place years later. The eldest daughter married the noted evangelist B. Fay Mills and left Lead in the early 1880s. In reality, Lettie Cole was the family member who left the deepest imprint on the community, she who was thought to be the daughter of an old slave who belonged to Mrs. Hill's family.

Lettie Cole was the personification of patience to all the children of those early days. We brought magazines to her from which she cut out pictures and pasted them on paper cambric, forming scrapbooks. The children cherished her handiwork, and her scrapbooks were passed around from bedside to bedside for much-needed amusement.

Lettie Cole's example gave me my philosophy of life. Lettie was a paralytic, chained to a well-padded wooden chair all day long. Her hands were always moving and a bright smile masked the constant suffering she endured. She was one of the first persons I visited when I recovered from my broken back. Noticing my suffering, Lettie said "Keep the corners of

your mouth turned up, Miss Sadie, and it won't hurt half so bad." Through
my life her remark became a refrain:

> "Keep the corners of your mouth turned up,
> Keep the corners of your mouth turned up,
> Though the aches and pains may come
> And your steps lag slowly home,
> Yet your smile will make them glad,
> Where a frown would make them sad,
> And the pain won't be so bad.
> If the corners of your mouth turn up."

P.A. GUSHURST

The first person to enter the saloon after Hickok was shot was P.A. Gushurst. His life and experience, as told by him, would form an interesting book in themselves.

Gushurst's childhood home was in Rochester, Minnesota. As a young man, he went to Omaha, Nebraska, and worked for Lucus Brothers Groceries. After a business college course, he worked for William Connors of the Union Pacific shops. He started as a timekeeper but later went into the lathe shop whereby he learned that he was not a mechanic. He was ambitious and wanted to be independent. Mr. Connors and Mr. Gushurst became fast friends and when the gold rush to the Hills began, they planned on making the venture together. Gushurst had his mind set on opening a grocery store.

Mr. Connors was an older man with a great deal of business experience so they took only their money with them. Mr. Connors said, "We can buy our goods in the west and save the freight charge."

They left Omaha in February and traveled to Cheyenne. Discovering that it was not safe to go into the Hills unaccompanied by soldiers or a party, after a delay they joined Judge Dudley's outfit of twenty-two men. Together the group rode or walked to Fort Laramie, Custer, and into Deadwood.

Connors was a little man whose push and perseverance few could tolerate. At Custer, they found a man who had a lot of potatoes and who wanted to go back home. Gushurst and Connors bought them up for fifteen dollars per hundred, along with dried apples and horses. They engaged a man named Sweeney to haul their purchases to Deadwood. Sweeney tried to give them the slip but Connors was a match for him. When Sweeney was ready to leave, Connors was sitting on the seat beside him and Sweeney was thus compelled to keep his agreement. The men later learned that their outfit had narrowly missed the seven or eight hundred Indians who waylaid the residents of Custer shortly after their departure.

Mr. Gushurst used his tent to set up his first store. He kept his potatoes hidden under his camp equipment and sold them by the bucket, twenty dollars per bucket.

Judge Dudley brought equipment to establish the first sawmill in Deadwood. He did not have sufficient money to pay the freight so Mr. Gushurst loaned him the money. When Mr. Gushurst put up his first building, he sawed part of the lumber himself at Dudley's mill, including fourteen thousand shingles. When he came to pay Dudley for the lumber, Dudley charged him the price of the cheapest lumber although he had used the best. Gushurst joked that he should have built a better building as it would not have cost him anymore!

The early businesses of Deadwood were not always as legitimate as Mr. Gushurst's but Deadwood was not all bad. While Lead later attracted several good businessmen from Deadwood, many remained to overcome the evil influence engendered by such dives as The Gem, The Green Front, and the death dealing dives of Chinatown located just inside the gates of the city.

Gushurst sold out his store in Deadwood and helped to survey claims and the towns of Washington and Central. Along with others, he organized and laid out the town site of Lead proper. He gave his rifle and seventy-five dollars for his lot and put up his building. He was the first to buy a miner's claim on July 10, 1876, that was a one-fourth interest in the Pierce Claim. He later sold it to the Homestake Mining Company at a good price.

Mr. Gushurst never lost an opportunity to study ores and became one of the best judges of mine prospects in the Hills. This knowledge meant money not only in his own pocket, for he was always willing to share his knowledge that often saved or made money for his friends.

P.A. Gushurst

Mr. Gushurst met his wife, the niece of the Manuel brothers, in Lead, experiencing love at first sight. From that time on he could see no other woman. They were the first couple to marry in Lead. They were unfortunate in the loss of their oldest children by the epidemics of those early days. Their daughter Florence stands out vividly in my childhood memory as a brilliant little girl. She died at the age of four during the 1883 diphtheria epidemic in Lead. The Gushursts later moved to Denver, Colorado. But the family lot in the Lead cemetery speaks to their wounded hearts, of the days when doctors were not dependable and quarantine regulations unknown. His family was one of Lead's finest and we counted them among our truest friends.

Mr. Gushurst's story of how he broke his boy of smoking always delighted me. He saw his son when quite small, slipping behind a building and later returning, smelling of tobacco. He told his son that he was not a man until he learned to smoke and gave him a great old stogie of the strongest kind, insisting that the boy smoke it in the store. The boy was brave enough and became "white around the gills" as the saying goes, but he finished smoking it. He then handed him another until the boy became so ill that Mr. Gushurst became frightened. He spent the night pacing the floor and calling himself a fool. Fortunately, the boy recovered. As long as I knew him, he never smoked again.

Smoking in those days was a common pastime of even very small boys of the rougher families, and today it seems to have extended into all circles. I regret to say not only boys but girls also have acquired the habit even in our best families, until it is rare to find a child of fortune who does not smoke.

NELLIE STORMAN

Few of the present generation have felt Professor Darling's explicit influence but the schools of Lead continue the work he started. Mother urged education all those years. Several young people went to the young, promising Normal* schools in Fremont, Nebraska and Spearfish, South Dakota. Lead drew many of her finest teachers from Spearfish.

From my perspective, Cornelia "Nellie" Storman, a little fair-haired Scandinavian girl brought to the Hills by her father and mother, played the greatest part in the development of public schooling in Lead. My Mother took a great interest in the child for she seemed to have no outlet in life but books. At the age of thirteen, Nellie taught in a little school at the foot of Pennington Hill near Uncle Moore's cabin.

In summer, I visited her school and listened to Nellie teach. I played with her and her pupils at recess, and at noon we ate our lunch out of our pails (formerly lard pails). In the fall, Mother drove us down to Spearfish and Nellie made plans to enter the Spearfish Normal School to receive her formal education and a teaching degree.

Nellie Storman was one of the first, if not the first, to continue her education beyond the Lead school. She paid the town and state back in rich golden coin for the education they provided. She gave the credit to Mr. Gushurst for the final push that sent her to Spearfish Normal. Billy Fawcett

---

* Normal Schools were created to train high school graduates to be teachers.

once called me "Lead's little golden nugget" but to me, Nellie Storman is the grandest pine tree the Hills produced in Lead's rocky soil. She was the true forester, nurturing the pinecones placed in her hands to develop into sturdy trees. She was a teacher in the primary room, teaching first the children of those early days, then their children and grandchildren.

Nellie stood out as a leader in the community, a force to be reckoned with in the daily life around her. She saw broader horizons than most people but returned to the soil that nourished her to a noble womanhood. Nellie was born a teacher for the souls of those placed in her care and rejoiced in their glory, forgetting self. She had immeasurable influence in bringing Lead to its standing as a community. Always a clean Christian woman, she continually held up a high standard in life before her pupils.

Was she loved? Yes... by every man, woman, and child of that community. We sink into insignificance when we realize what she meant for the growth and development of Lead.

(EDITOR'S NOTE: Cornelia "Nellie" Storman was the first teacher of the South Lead School and later became the school principal. She served the Lead School district for over 60 years and is buried in the South Lead Cemetery.)

HIDDEN IDENTITIES &
UNKNOWN PERSONALITIES

Lead and Deadwood were similar in having questionable characters, but I believe Deadwood was really the lodestone with the greater number. Many of these individuals could lose themselves more easily in Deadwood when necessity demanded. Since the businesses of Lead were more strictly a legitimate work-a-day world, chances were fewer for those of a questionable nature to develop. Then, too, Homestake managers frowned upon distractions that would diminish their employees' usefulness. Lead was the treadmill of the mining industry, the small camps around, questing grounds for the fortunes all hoped to find. Deadwood held a more glamorous life for all who came to the Hills whether as visitors, permanent dwellers, or pure adventurers.

As business interests drew men into close relationships, their inborn characteristics emerged. The honest, hard-working plodder went about his daily tasks with little thought of what his neighbor was doing, except to rejoice, perhaps, in his success. The thief watched with a sly eye for a chance to gyp a poor, unsuspecting chap, and get away without being caught. In the Black Hills, we found all types and personalities. The true names of some I shall use, while the names of others are best passed into oblivion.

In Deadwood, one man made periodical trips to mid-western cities, putting out such ads as:

WANTED:

Talented young ladies to take small parts in theatricals.
Expenses and good salary paid.

Many young, innocent girls might tell the same story as Agnes. Agnes was a young rural teacher, making twenty-five dollars a month. She had some training in music, having a very sweet voice, and was a talented reader in her high school associations. Her father and mother, staggering under a mortgage on the farm, gave their consent to her answering the ad. She was small, pretty, and talented. Our gentleman offered her expenses and on hundred dollars a month, and, a wardrobe if she would go with him. Six girls went. When they arrived in Deadwood, they were taken to the theater and assigned their rooms. Agnes was honest and pure. After three days, she realized what she had stepped into, but made up her mind to act in the plays until she could make enough money to get away. Refusing to sell her body to the lusts of her employer, she was drugged and debauched, and a bullet from her own revolver ended her existence when she became conscious of what had happened. While this specific tragedy happened in Deadwood, the same or worse may have happened in Lead, for vice was everywhere.

A Presbyterian minister's son from the east became infatuated with cards and a girl from one of the Lead City dives. He pleaded for her to give up the life and marry him and he, too, would go straight. She refused, and two graves told the tale a few days later.

One afternoon, an English gentleman alighted from his fine horse before the Express Office in Deadwood. He presented letters of credit, looked around for property, bought a nice home, and became interested in a mining property. He advertised for a housekeeper. About the same time, a petite, quiet English woman and her little girl came to the Hills. She applied for the job and got it.

Life went on for several years. He became known as a wealthy bachelor who shunned women, but was a great socialite. He climbed high up in lodge, business, and social circles. His housekeeper was a quiet little body that attended to her own business, and her daughter was generously, yet very modestly, educated by the master of the house.

Upon his sudden death elaborate funeral preparations were made and carried out. A lodge of sorrow* was held. The stores closed and many of the

---

*A lodge of sorrow is a ceremony conducted by Masonic or Elks Lodge members at the funeral of a member.

townspeople attended his funeral.

Three months later a young man, the perfect image of the English gentleman, left the stage and asked the way to the office of a prominent lawyer. Then the story came out. Our gentleman had left his wife and young son in England to hide himself, the gardener's daughter and their little girl in the Black Hills. His own younger brother, whom he had not seen for several years, had followed him and lived in an adjoining town. Desiring to see justice done to the legitimate wife and child, the brother sent the word home.

The brother generously provided for the woman and girl, but claimed the bulk of the property for his sister-in-law. Needless to say, the whole affair was quickly hushed and the gentleman's name was seldom spoken in Black Hills social circles after that.

Another case of lost identity came into Lead one evening in the shape of a fine looking young couple with a beautiful curly-headed little boy of about five years. Arriving late in the fall, they rented a house for the winter. They had plenty of money, kept quite to themselves, but were pleasant with everyone who met them. They rode horseback a great deal over the mountain trails. One day, late in spring, a big backed up delivery of mail and express came in. The sheriff in Deadwood received a large packet and proceeded to tack up some posters in the Post Office. One poster was a very good likeness of our quiet friend that stated, "WANTED" for holding up the US Express. Everyone expected an arrest, but "the birds had flown." I do not know whether they were ever caught, but certainly not in Deadwood. They departed as silently as they had arrived - from the unknown into the unknown they vanished.

LESTER

Another character arriving in Lead in the early days was a black man named Lester. He was a slave as a boy before the Civil War and ran away from his master to join the Navy. After the war, he drifted west to the Hills. He was always conspicuous on the fourth of July, for he did like to parade, especially in his old Navy uniform. Having been reared as a houseboy in the south, Lester was a handy man around town. Whenever he saw me as a little child, picking my way across a muddy street, he would rush up and tote me across. Years later, on a visit to Lead with my 4-year old daughter, Marie, I met old Lester on that same old muddy crossing. Lester immediately picked up the little tot and carried her across the street. He was the first colored person she had ever seen and, being dressed in white and very conscious of her clothes, she looked up at his hands, and then at her dress, and brushed her clothes carefully. I did not want to hurt Lester's feelings, so I said: "She has never seen a colored person before, Lester." He threw back his head with a hearty laugh, saying: "That's all right Little Missie. I used to tote your mother across that same hole when she was little like you, but her curls were black and yours are gold." I added in my mind, "Yours were black and now are white." I smiled and he smiled back and passed on.

(EDITOR'S NOTE: Ambrose Lester died on April 17, 1906, and is buried in the South Lead Cemetery.)

THE OLD MISER

About this time another character loomed upon the horizon of Lead. In the mad race of civilization to the new gold field, a shriveled up old man whom we all called "Uncle Moore" was carried along, by no one in particular, but the crowd in general, until he finally landed in Lead.

His outfit consisted of a dilapidated spring wagon drawn by two aged white horses, and his old sun-yellowed water spaniel trudging along under the wagon that bespoke a long journey with no fat wallet in the old man's pocket. A mutual understanding seemed to exist between the four - that they would share alike, good or evil, as fate decreed.

The old man immediately began to work as a drayman; a long felt want in the little settlement for no store delivered its merchandise in those days. As his smallest charge was a quarter, he made several dollars during the day and was never idle. If not groceries, there was always wood to haul and cut. He did not care what the work was, as long as he was busy.

As weeks sped into months people began to wonder what manner of man he was. The roughs were met with a cold stare from a pair of deep set eyes of quiet blue, shaded by heavy gray eyebrows. The inquisitive neighbor met the same cold look, and the old man remained unknown except in the present. The past was a blank, the future unknown, and the world was never asked to enter any part of it. He arrived in the morning, and at night he camped by a little stream on the hills in Strawberry Gulch, a mile from the busy hum of our town. There, after the six o'clock whistle blew, he wound his way back to the hill and, after caring for his horses; he entered the small cabin that he had built. Walled in at the back by the steepest mountainside, shaded at the sides by leafy mountain pines, birch, and a tangled thicket of wild raspberries, there he dwelt. A clear mountain brook ran in front of the cabin, providing water for beast and man.

His cabin had but one window over which he pasted a piece of greased paper to let in light, but through which no one could see. His plank door was never found open. He sought no companionship above that of his horses and dog and trusted no one. Everyone but children and animals mistrusted him, and behind his back people whispered strange tales. His dog, always by his side, shared his every bite, and his horses nickered when he came near.

For five years he toiled, with no outward sign of financial success. Where did his money go?

Winter came on, deep and snowy, the gulches were full, and wood was difficult to find. The old folk called the old man "the Miser." That winter the children grew joyous over long sleigh rides on their homemade sleds down the hills with "Uncle Moore's" bobsled at the foot of the hill, ready for them to hook onto for the long climb back up. The shy little boy or rosy faced girl never saw him as they hooked on behind, but the mischief-maker, or bully, who threw a snowball at his dog, old Towser, or pushed a weaker child into a snow-bank, caught view of him immediately. They never received favors from "Uncle Moore," and they even felt the flick of his long whip when they attempted to "hook a ride."

One severe winter the snow banked high, closing the roads. Even in town people tunneled through the snow from their homes to the streets. The children could not go to school on their own but Uncle Moore brought his old wood sleigh to the houses and rapped on the door with his whip handle, then put the children on his sled and towed them to the schoolhouse. At four o'clock, he brought them home safely and never took a dime for his work. The children needed schooling and he saw that they got it. He loved children and they in return, and he gave to them what he could.

One day, thinking to visit his spite on the Miser, a cowardly giant kicked Uncle Moore's dog. With cat-like agility, the old man struck him in the face with his fists, hissing between clenched teeth, "You will, will you?" But it was too late; his dog had a broken leg, and although Uncle Moore cared for the dog like a baby, poor old Towser passed away during the winter.

Winter wore on, and instead of going home for dinner, the old man found a corner near a stove in some store and ate his meager lunch of crackers and cheese. Several times he returned home to find his cabin broken into and ransacked; once, he even found planks of the floor torn up, but he said nothing about it.

One day the old man failed to appear; then another, and another day passed. A man passing his cabin heard the horses making a disturbance, and investigated. The old man had passed to his reward, alone, just as he had lived. The jury concluded, "natural causes" for his death and his body was turned over to the undertaker. In searching the cabin, it was discovered that he had been sending money regularly to a convent in Indiana, and a tracer was sent there.

Two young girls were found, daughters of an old Civil War buddy who had married the girl he loved. When his buddy was killed in action, Uncle Moore had assumed the support of the orphaned children, and shortly before his death he had placed sufficient means in the hands of the Sisters to complete their education. Trusting no one in Lead, he made weekly trips to a Deadwood bank, depositing his small earnings to be sent out each month to the Mother Superior. His horses were sold to pay his last expenses, and another chapter in the early history of Lead was closed without further investigation.

JACK HEMMINGWAY
& BOBBY BURNS

Lung trouble sent Jack Hemmingway to the Black Hills in the early 1880s. Born and reared in an eastern city, he knew nothing of roughing it in a western mining camp. However, the will to live is strong in every breast and if roughing it would make him well he would rough it.

He wandered over the hills around Deadwood and Lead and, after following several gulches, he spotted a rather scenic spot overlooking a beautiful little mountain creek a couple miles away from the hurly-burly mining camps. There he built his cabin and staked off a claim to give reason for living there. He did just enough work to hold his claim, and no one paid any attention to him.

When September came, he stocked his cabin with provisions so he would not have to go to town when the deep snows arrived. For a time, all went well. He had plenty of nice clear water to drink and food, for his purse was not empty. He also had books, especially his Bobby Burns, for he loved the old Scotch bard and read him by the hour over and over again.

Finally, the snow came and Jack was cut off from his fellowman. When one is alone one longs for companionship. So it was with Jack. As the winter evenings grew longer, Jack began having trouble with pack rats carrying off his supplies, especially his precious potatoes. He killed a pair and the depredations stopped for a while but soon they resumed.

One evening, Jack had been reading his beloved Bobby Burns. He laid down the book on his shelf, lit his pipe, and stretched himself out on his bunk to dream. Upon hearing a stealthy noise, Jack looked over to the shelf to see a young, hungry looking little pack rat gnawing at the leather corner of his precious book. His sympathy went out to the pack rat for he thought, I am like that poor, scrawny pest, just trying to hang on to life. The rat had chosen Bobby Burns as his resting place.

Jack moved slightly to watch the movements of the rat. As it scampered off, Jack got up and placed a piece of hardtack out for bait. Soon the rat returned, grabbed the hardtack and ran off again. For several nights Jack fed the little rodent. Gradually emboldened, it finally sat on the table while being fed. It had grown considerably since its first visit and soon became quite tame. Jack named him Bobby Burns.

One evening, Bobby appeared and as he sat on the book, his usual resting place, he dropped a pebble into Jack's tin-cup. Jack looked up: "Ho, ho, trying to pay for your supper? But I don't like stones in my coffee." Jack emptied his cup in his wash-basin as he did not want to go outside just then. As the pebble lay in the basin, it caught the gleam from the lamp and Jack, startled, picked it up and examined it, to discover a gold nugget. Jack looked around. Bobby was still there, expecting his food.

Evening after evening, Bobby presented Jack with a pebble and Jack examined his movements to find where he got them. He noticed he went out through a hole in the floor of the cabin. Finally, Jack took up the board and discovered Bobby's burrow. Then he followed it for he felt Bobby had more pebbles hidden away. Since the ground under the cabin was not yet frozen, digging was easy. One day an old prospector came around so Jack told him he was digging a pit for his potatoes.

Jack did not have to dig far until he broke into a gold pocket in a rocky fissure. He gathered up the golden nuggets in a flour sack, stored his provisions and covered up the mouth of the pit with the floorboards for fear of prying eyes. He then packed his grips and went to Denver with his gold. Upon his return, he continued to work his claim quietly. He took out about ten thousand dollars' worth before the pocket gave out. He never found the mother lode, but Bobby and his gold nugget cache along with the air from the pines had given Jack his health and a neat little nest egg for the future.

PART IV

Pioneer Progress

OUR TRIP TO MINNESOTA

Sadie, age 8, while visiting Minnesota
(1882)

We made many trips in and out of the Black Hills, but one
that really continues to send shivers down my back was
taken in late June of 1882. Mother's health had been weak that winter and
the doctor ordered a change. As a result, the folks decided it was time for us
to visit Papa's folks in Minnesota.

An Indian uprising was feared during our travel, so we chose to leave when the bullion from the Homestake Mine went out, a time when the stage was always well guarded. The passengers consisted of Mother and myself, Captain C.V. Gardner, Mr. Wardner, and Mrs. McDonald and her thirteen-year-old niece.

When we left Deadwood, the warm Chinook winds brought the first spring downpour of rain. The rain continued all the way to the stage station on the bank of the Cheyenne River near the Indian Reservation. We pulled into the station to find the river, which was usually forded at that point, running a raging torrent and impossible to cross. It was deemed best to stay all night at the station and wait for the "up" stage to reach the opposite bank. The plan was to transfer the passengers and luggage from one stage to the other.

The men built a large raft of logs to transport the luggage. The women were to go across in a boat. When we sat down to supper that evening, Indians were thronging about the house, peering into the windows and speaking amongst each other. We were advised to ignore them and especially to show no fear. The station house consisted of a kitchen, a dining room, a bedroom for the agent and his wife, and a large office room. The bunkhouse and barn housed the men and horses near the corral.

That night, Mrs. McDonald and Mother slept in the bed in the bedroom, while we two girls slept in a straw tick on the floor. Mother insisted that this tick be placed next to the wall behind the bed so that she could be in front of me if Indians broke into the room. For our safety, armed with six-shooters, the men slept under blankets on the floor of the office.

The next morning, the men fastened ropes to the horses to attach them to the raft. The horses swam across the river and pulled the raft ashore while men, standing on it and armed with long poles, kept drifting trees and debris from swamping it. I could not understand why they initiated the raft way up the stream when they wanted it to land straight across. Mother said, "Watch and you will see." The current was so swift that I soon understood. The raft was finally drawn up the road at the ford. The men unloaded our trunks and we waited for the other stage to drive up.

Next, a flat-bottomed boat was brought to the bank and the treasure chest placed in the center on the floor. I was seated on top of this chest, Mother sat in front of me, and Mr. Wardner, who could not swim, sat in the prow of the boat. Mrs. McDonald and her niece sat on the backseat. A one-armed young man holding a double-bladed paddle then stepped into the boat. When Mother saw that he was going to take us across, she asked for a pair of oars but none were available. Her upbringing near the Lackawanna River in Pennsylvania had made her a good oarswoman.

We started across, dip of paddle on one side, then dip on the other. With each dip, the heavily loaded boat shipped some water. Mother and Mr. Wardner bailed out the water as best they could but as we came within three or four feet of the shore the boat settled and we had to wade the rest of the way soaked to our waists. We opened our trunks and took out dry clothing. The ladies changed behind the drawn curtains of the other stage while the men changed out in the bushes. We hung wet items on the outside of the stage to dry and when all was again loaded, we drove on, hoping to make the train in Pierre, Dakota Territory.

Our hopes were in vain, for the train pulled out of the depot just as the stage topped the hill at the outskirts of the city. Captain Gardner took charge of Mother and me and piloted us to the hotel near the depot, a frame building. The rooms were small and bare, furnished with a bed and a washstand holding a white bowl and pitcher. A tin bucket stood on the floor, ready to receive the slops. The door did not have a lock, so that night, Mother moved the washstand against it to be sure no one would enter.

We slept very little; at least, Mother did not. Four men were evidently playing poker in the next room and we could hear loud talking all night. Sometime after midnight, a row began, and ultimately, shots were fired. We heard a rush from and to the room, and soon learned that a man had been killed.

As soon as daylight came, Mother got up and dressed, then got me up. Repacking her grip, she prepared to find less harrowing quarters. After breakfast, we spent the rest of the day in the depot or walking the streets of the city. Only one who has gone through such experiences can realize the relief we both felt when we settled into our sleeper for the last leg of our journey to Minneapolis. When the train pulled out, we felt that we had really reached civilization once again, and we relaxed and looked forward to a summer of pleasure.

That summer proved a foretaste of many years of petty persecution for my poor Mother. She took it with her chin up and the dignity of a thoroughbred that could not be downed. When we reached Minneapolis, my Great Uncle Dan Elliott met us at the train station. He took us to his beautiful cement block home on Portland Avenue, a wonderful house in my eyes. Great large rooms were beautifully furnished with a wonderful porch, itself as large as our three rooms at home. The house was in the center of a whole block of level ground, a sight I had never seen. It included a garden, a tennis court, a croquet court, and such wonderful shade trees, heaven to me. Uncle Dan and Aunt Ett were grand, and their daughter Dora was nice, too; however, since she was a teacher, I saw very little of her. Aunty was not well, so she had to be kept very quiet. She seemed to fall in love with Mother at once and Mother with her.

Aunt Ett was Papa's father's sister, as was also Aunt Jennie Shaw who lived across the street in a much smaller house with her husband, Freeman. We soon learned they were not at all like their brother, my Grandpa Benjamin Smith. He seemed to hate Mother and me and looked upon us as usurpers of his inherent rights. Aunt Jennie had a daughter, Lillie, and a son, John. John was a medical student at the University of Minnesota and was taking summer classes. He became a hero in my eyes because he could "talk bones."

On the Fourth of July, Aunt Jennie and Mother went into the city to see about our trunk and do some necessary shopping, so I stayed with Lillie. John discovered that I did not know anything about fireworks, and decided that I must have some for that night. Without saying anything to Lillie, he took me with him to get them. On the way, I stumbled and bumped my head. John picked me up saying, "Oh! Oh, did you bump your noggin?"

"No, my cranium," I answered.

"Your what?"

"My cranium, my frontal bone really."

At that moment, we arrived at the drugstore, where he filled my arms with bundles of fireworks, rockets, Roman candles, and pinwheels, etc., until I was unable to carry any more.

John put me on a streetcar, telling the conductor where to drop me off, and hurried on to his classes. I was eight years old, but not as large as my four-year-old cousin. You can imagine my mother's horror and consternation when upon crossing a downtown street, she saw me all alone waving from a streetcar window.

Mother and Aunt Jennie caught the next car home where they found me safe. Lillie had not missed me. She was reading an interesting novel and thought John was looking after me. That was a red-letter day in my life, for John brought some of his medical chums to see the child wonder perform. But fireworks were even more wonderful to me that evening than "talking bones." To Mother, however, it was a fright she never forgot, for no one could convince her after that to leave me with anyone except my Aunt Sarah Bragg.

It was a hot summer. I well remember how we sweltered in the heat, but Mother grew well and strong. Everywhere we went, I heard Papa's sisters and aunts say to Mother: "Now, Lizzie, watch out for Hat and don't let her saddle the old man onto you." Hat was Papa's older sister. She had taken charge of affairs when Grandmother Smith died.

We finally went to visit Aunt Hattie in Monticello expecting to see Grandpa, but we never got to meet him. We did not stay very long, as Mother realized we were not very welcome. We met Uncle Wendell, Papa's youngest brother, who was seven years older than me. Wendell asked to return to the Black Hills with us, a trip that Aunt Hattie favored very much. As none of them had the money to pay for his expenses, Mother would have to pay them if he went. All the rest of the family told Mother not to do it. The day before we were to return to Lead, Uncle Wendell turned up in Minneapolis. Aunt Hattie had given him the money to reach Minneapolis.

That night was one never-to-be-forgotten. Mother took us to the theatre to see Shakespeare's OTHELLO. Wendell had never been to the theatre before and got so frightened he crouched down between the seats and hid. I laughed at him and he became very angry. He was a great big, overgrown boy of sixteen and afraid of a play. I had never known fear and to be afraid of a story was truly funny to me. My Mother had read aloud almost all the plays of Shakespeare and talked of them for she had seen many performances in Philadelphia. As a result, the play was not a surprise to me.

I have no recollection of the trip home except that we returned by way of Pierre with Uncle Wendell accompanying us. Uncle Wendell never forgave me for laughing at him during the play. The next winter, in 1883, I slipped off the path and hung over a hundred-foot mineshaft clutching a small evergreen. He walked on and left a couple of small boys to pull me to safety. I never told of his treachery but the boys told the scholars and he became tabooed by all the school.

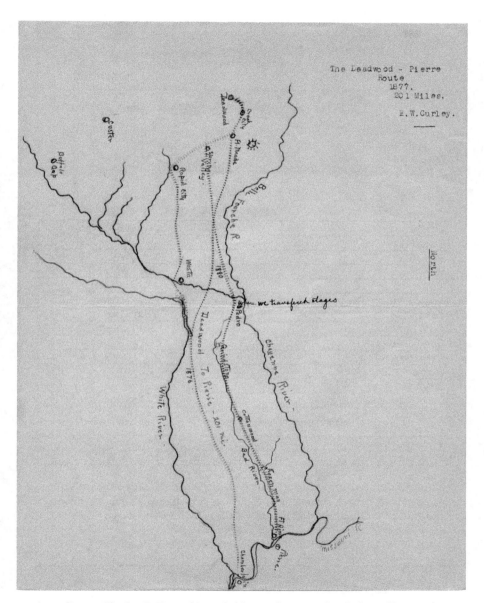

According to Charles C. Haas, this probably was the route that Sadie and her mother traveled in 1882 when they went to Minnesota.

The DEADWOOD-FT. PIERRE Route - 1876

E.W. Curley

The table of distances and conditions along the route.

Stations	Miles	TL Miles	Water
Deadwood	0		(Thru Red Valley)
Rapid City	40	40	
Box Elder	8	48	Good water. No wood.
Washtay (Wasta)	7	55	Good water. No wood.
Holes	18	73	Alkali water.
No. Cheyenne River	5	78	Alkali water.
Lakes	8	86	Alkali water.
Pino Springs	9	95	Good water. No wood.
Dead Mans Creek	16	111	
Grindstone Butte	4	115	
Buzzard Creek	12	127	
Mitchell	15	142	
Cottonwood Creek	14	156	
Frozen Man Fork	12	168	
Lance Creek	10	178	
Willow Creek	15	193	
Ft. Pierre	10	203	Dry. No wood.

Deadwood to Pierre, via 1880 Route via Ft. Meade and Spring Valley. (Apparently no detail routing of the route was made. This is apparently the route that you traveled in 1882.-CCH). It was considered the "best all weather" route.

THE HOUSE IN SOUTH LEAD

When we returned to Lead after our trip to Minnesota, Papa had moved our things to the house in South Lead. This house was Papa's original cabin, built of large twelve-inch hewn logs, and a story and a half high. The outside of the logs had been sided. The north side of the cabin had a lean-to built in and a porch ran across the whole front. A second lean-to on the backside of the cabin originally contained a cozy little bedroom and the old kitchen.

While we were in Minnesota, Papa had built a large new kitchen with an 18-foot ceiling, located on the south side of the cabin and constructed with a large, stone-walled cave cellar that extended into the mountainside. A long flight of stairs from the kitchen led up to the backyard on the little hillside above the house where we had a chicken coop. He turned the old kitchen into a big dining room with two high windows opening onto the hillside, while the original cabin became the parlor. The north side lean-to turned into Mother and Papa's bedroom, and a stairway went up to the loft above the parlor that served as my bedroom.

We stored our winter supply of food in the hillside cellar, and there the pack rats also found their food. The rats were big fellows and would carry away our provisions, especially our potatoes. They always left some worthless thing like bright pebbles or pieces of tin in exchange. Eventually, Papa killed the rats and they ceased to bother us. The parlor had wallpaper with great big red roses and contained a big stove and fine furniture, including a great big wonderful armchair that allowed you to lower the back down and then lift up the seat. Upon doing this, you could turn it over onto the floor with the arms for legs, making a fine single bed where I loved to sleep.

When winter arrived, Papa cut a hole in the ceiling of the parlor to run the stovepipe up through it and into a drum, out through the roof, thus warming the attic that served as my playroom and bedroom. What a grand playroom, for I could have it all to myself, as the grown folks, who were over five feet tall, could not stand up in it, except in the very center. Then, too, I could also climb out the end window onto the roof of the dining room and onto the hillside without bothering anyone.

With the attic mine and that wonderful parlor chair, Papa often brought someone home to stay all night. Among those overnight guests was an old prospector friend from Crook who told stories of the early days before the government opened the Hills for settlement, for he had slipped in before Custer was even sent by the government.

He told of traveling the Missouri River on a boat and then dodging Indians into the Black Hills. I sat and listened with ears and eyes open to his weird and often gruesome tales. Before the legal opening of the Black Hills, many trappers and adventurers filtered their way into the pine-covered heights, leaving sad records of their boldness.

The old prospector shared how he had crawled into a clump or thicket of pine looking for a place to set up camp, near what is now known as Spearfish, when he found four decomposed bodies with their camping equipment. I asked him, "Were they killed by Indians?" He replied, "Hell no, they had crawled in there in a storm and froze to death or starved. There was no food left but wild beasts had not devoured the bodies. My buddy and I dug a hole and pushed them into it and covered them with dirt and rocks and then we placed their frying pan and kettle on top. We then left and looked for another campsite."

He repeated this story many times, for he spent many nights in our home and told wild tales from 1874 and 1875 before Custer's entry into the picture. He lived at the settlement in Crook for many years, a little old wizen figure that would suddenly appear with a pack on his back, stay a few days, and then trudge back to his home in Crook. He seemed to prefer trading in

The House in South Lead

Lead instead of Deadwood.

The nights that he would arrive in our home, Mother would have Papa roll out our big bathtub. This bathtub was a unique affair, a regular tub with an 18-inch flange like a platform attached to its top edge and which sloped toward the inside of the tub, all built of galvanized steel. This platform was supported at one side by heavy wooden legs so that one could sit on the rim and put his feet down into the tub. This design prevented water splashing when taking a bath. Thus, the old prospector enjoyed a good hot water bath before he crawled into the bed made from the old armchair.

I have completely forgotten his name, but I can still see him as I saw him then, and his little house as I saw it several years later when Crook transformed into one of those ghost towns from the mining center it once was. He was one of the first to enter and he never left the Hills, nor did he ever find his stake, for he was as poor at the last as when I first knew him. However, he was rich with the stories of his tramps from Minnesota down into Nebraska and up the "Old Missouri" in a paddleboat.

He started one story like this: "Do you know how so many Indians got slant eyes? Wall you see there war a Chink cook on the old tug that came up the river to Yankton and he would marry a young squaw nearly every trip, and their kids had slant eyes." To me, that tale was fantastic but a few years ago I found that there were Indians among those in northern Nebraska who really did have slanted eyes. This story was partially confirmed at one of the agencies by the wife of an agent. She was of Indian blood herself. She was a finely educated woman and one who did a great work among her people.

I gathered and accumulated stories of the frontier until I could visualize a picture of men and women tramping along on foot, on horseback, or in wagons; some drifting off from the group to lose themselves in that unknown region, some dropping by the wayside exhausted, and some died and were buried by their fellow travelers. I could imagine Father DeSmet leading his band, in his effort to Christianize Indians. Next, I envisioned the trappers following the trails of wild animals for their pelts, and lastly, the seekers after the precious gold in scattered trains leading to settlement and the development of that beautiful paradise - the Alps of America in miniature.

Thus, through the use of that old armchair/folding bed, I learned much of the early history of the Black Hills. As the years went on, the old chair became such a nest of bedbugs brought in by its many poor old prospectors that Mother demanded its removal, and the old chair and its many occupants ceased to be. However, that armchair became a symbol of the history of those old early days and my first attempt as a writer was printed out while curled up in that chair.

In the South Lead house, I spent most of my evenings alone with my dolls in the little room with a kettle of mush cooking on top of the Round Oak wood stove. Although alone, I was far safer than watching that kettle of vice and degradation when we lived above the store. No evil sites were available to watch and darken my child mind. I was not afraid for I had always been alone in my play. My imaginary friends Sally, or Maggie, or Dolly would spend the evening with me and we never got into any trouble.

Now that the last bank note was finally paid, we were able to have a quiet home life in the little house on the hill. Papa expanded his business and devoted his whole time to it. The store closed at 10 o'clock with no work on Sunday unless there was a funeral.

In those early years, Mother spent most of her time in the store, and I would stop there on my way from school and wait for her to go home. While waiting for customers, Mr. Gurney, Papa, and I would sit around the Charter Oak stove, while mother would read aloud Mark Twain's <u>Tramp Abroad</u>, or Charles Dicken's <u>Little Dorrit</u> or <u>Dombey and Son</u>. Often, after supper, Mother returned with Papa and I would be left alone to study my lessons and read.

I had one very naughty trick at that time. I hid when I heard them coming and made them find me. I had done it so many times making quite a game of it. A large wood box sat by the side of the stove with a lid that closed with a spring catch. One night, when I thought it was about time for the folks to return, I climbed into the box, as it was almost empty. I planned to play "Jack in the Box," but the lid snapped shut and, trapped as I was, I fell asleep and did not hear their arrival. After searching the house, they aroused the neighborhood, but no one knew where I was. They were starting out with a lantern when the neighbors' daughter said: "Did you look in the wood box? She sometimes hides there when we play 'Hide and Seek'?" They found me just in time, for I was already unconscious from poor air. I never again tried to hide after that. I had learned my lesson. I think Mother learned one too, for if she expected to be very late she seldom left me alone.

About this time, I received my last switching with Mother's riding quirt. I had been accused of doing a certain thing that a playmate had done. As I had been forbidden to play with the girl, I simply said I had not done the deed. Mother thought I was lying. No matter how you tried to prove you were telling the truth, once she had made up her mind, there was no use trying to change it.

After the whipping when mother left the house, I took the beautiful little ivory handled whip and threw it down Albert and Minnie Eveleth's cistern, never to be found. Mother was thrown from our buggy in a runaway a short time after. As a result of that accident she didn't need her riding quirt for she never went horseback riding again. She never whipped me after that time.

Shortly after our chicken coop was built, someone gave me a black Polish hen that became quite a pet, and Nip, my dog, and Black Rosie, my hen, became very devoted friends. Nip carried crusts of bread for Rosie to eat and they often drank together from the water pan.

The Bender family lived down by the creek and they kept hogs that ran all over town and were an awful nuisance. The Benders kept entirely to themselves and everyone seemed to shun them. The terrible "Bender Killings" committed in Cherryvale, Kansas, were still on people's minds, and, as the "Cherryvale" Benders escaped, townspeople often whispered and speculated about where the "Lead" Benders came from. This family and the townspeople mutually left each other alone, but their pigs roamed the town.

One day, a big hog came into our backyard and caught poor Rosie as she dusted herself. In spite of poor little Nip's frantic barking, the hog tore off Rosie's head and, grabbing the body in his jaws, beat it for home with Nip at his heels. From that day, as long as Nip lived, he would chase a Bender hog clear home, no matter what part of town he found it. Mr. Bender demonstrated his loathing of my dog in a trial held a few months later.

Papa was on a deer hunt and Mother had taken ill, so about ten o'clock at night I was sent to get my Aunt and the doctor. Nip accompanied me and on the way, unfortunately, we encountered a Bender hog and Mr. Bender. Nip jumped and barked at the hog and then dashed back to me with Mr. Bender after him. As the dog took shelter at my feet, Mr. Bender gave a vicious kick meant for the dog, but struck me instead, badly bruising my leg and knocking me down to the ground. Nip defended me and Mr. Bender ran away. I managed to reach Aunty and returned home crying. I was still limping from the kick when Papa returned home the next evening. He then found Mr. Bender on the main corner in town and called him to account. When Mr. Bender became abusive, Papa gave him a bad thrashing. Papa had a bad temper when given the opportunity, and consequently, Mr. Bender had Papa arrested.

I ended up making my first and only appearance in a court of justice and was frightened out of my wits. The Judge lifted me up onto the table before the jury, held my hand, and encouraged me to tell the story of how Mr. Bender had kicked me. Of course, I did not realize until years later that he had intended to kick the dog, since I was the one he kicked and the judge put it to the jury. The jury never left the room and I remember a man shouted, "Why didn't you lay him out, S.R.?" The judge assessed Mr. Bender a $10.00 fine as well as court costs and told him to "watch his step next time." Some told Papa he ought to have been fined for not giving Mr. Bender more.

Poor old Nip was later poisoned, but caught in time to be saved. As long as he lived, he continued to chase Bender's hogs home from all parts of the town in spite of efforts to stop him.

GRANDFATHER SMITH

Shortly after Wendell Smith came back with us from Minnesota, Aunt Hattie began writing that Papa must take care of their father. For a while, Papa sent money to support him, but that did not satisfy his sister, and finally Grandpa came to live with us.

Mother still worked at the store in the afternoons and evenings and kept her house going. I went to school with Wendell for a time, but he was so large and had so little schooling that he was ashamed to attend class with the smaller boys—so he would often play hooky.

When the folks discovered what he was doing, Mother told him that he had to go to school or work and pay his own way, and he could not live with us if he did not go to school. He left us, but Grandfather stayed on and made life miserable for all of us by his continual interference in the management of the home. He continually found fault with everything Mother or I did. Mother did not do things right; she wasted his son's money; she "kept those d_____ birds that wouldn't let him sleep in the morning." If we had pancakes for breakfast, Mother had to stand and fry his "just so," no matter when he wanted to eat them, and we "should eat bacon fat instead of so much butter." So the nagging would go on until Mother and Papa could not stand it any longer and sent the old man to live in the hotel. However, then he spent a majority of his time at the store and interfering with business affairs. He stood guard over the cash register so Mother could not even make change for a customer. After four years of his petty persecutions, Papa finally sent him away from Lead and always paid his expenses wherever he was and gave him the best.

At this time, Mother raised canaries as a hobby, with a pair of German rollers, Bernie and Bessie, and a yellow female, Goldie. From these birds, she raised many young ones and sold them for $5 apiece, allowing her to raise her own spending money independent of the Smith family. The birds angered Papa's father, but gave us all a great deal of pleasure, for when the sun shone through those big dining room windows in the mornings, Bernie's beautiful warbles would lead a wonderful woodland chorus and often start Mother singing about her work.

Father Rosen, a local Catholic missionary, often visited on a sunny day to sit and listen to the birds. He called them the angel voices that lifted his heart from the sordidness of life to the gates of heaven. Mother gave him a young singer but it never sang like Bernie.

One cold winter's night, we were sitting around our big heating stove in the parlor when we heard the very weak mew of a cat and went to the door. Outside, a tiny little Maltese kitten was almost frozen. I cuddled it in my arms until it was warm and begged Mother to let me keep it - "No, it would kill my birds," was Mother's decided answer, but she did let me take it to bed and allowed me to feed it some warm milk with a medicine dropper. The next day she did not take it away for it was so small that it could do no harm for a while. She thought it would die anyway.

Mother also had a pet mockingbird in addition to the canaries that flew freely about the house. Owing to Mother's working in the store I was home alone a great deal, so I took my kitten with me about the house. I often sat on the floor with the cat in my lap and coaxed Dick, the mockingbird, over to me. Flossy, my kitten, learned to be quite friendly and watched him closely. Dick pecked at Flossy's toenails and she would draw her feet up under her but never tried to catch the bird or hurt him. Finally, I let the canaries out of their cages also and trained Flossy not to harm them. Mother knew nothing of this training but she became used to the cat and so I was able to keep it.

When spring came, Dick managed to get outdoors one day and Flossy began to stalk him. We noticed a big yellow cat was also stalking Dick, and I became thoroughly frightened. We soon realized the other cat was also the source of Flossy's worry.

Finally after much maneuvering, Flossy coaxed Dick near to his cage, which we had placed on the porch floor. When Dick finally went into it, Flossy laid down in front of the cage door and yowled for us to shut the cage door. Mother knew then that Flossy would not harm Dick, but she never really trusted her. One evening when we went to church, we left Flossy asleep in the front room but closed the door into the dining room where the birds were kept. We burned a center draft oil lamp for light in the dining room and left it on the table turned down quite low. On returning, when we reached the gate we heard Flossy howling terribly and hurried inside to see what was the matter.

When we opened the door, Flossy dashed towards the dining room door and we could smell smoke. Opening the door to the dining room, we were almost stifled and all we could see was a tiny red flame coming out of the lamp. The entire room was black. Throwing the doors and windows open and retrieving another lamp, we found the birds had suffocated. Mother laid the birds on the table and Flossy climbed up and laid her head against the little birds and mewed in the most mournful manner. That sound made us all cry and Mother even took the kitten in her arms to soothe it. Grandfather Smith said, "Well, those d_____ birds won't keep us awake now." He was certainly glad the birds had died, but no one else was and Mother never raised another bird.

(EDITOR'S NOTE: Benjamin Smith died in 1907 at the age of 90 and is buried beside his wife, Eunice, in Riverside Cemetery in Monticello, Minnesota.)

MURIELLA FRY'S WEDDING

Muriella Fry

I will always remember attending my first church wedding. My friends and I went out on the hill and gathered wildflowers to decorate the church for the wedding of Muriella Fry, my Godmother. Mother was responsible for decorating the church for her wedding. That morning, Mother was busy with plans and arrangements and left me to do the dishes. I never wore slippers out of the house except once in a great while to an evening party, but that morning I had my toe slippers on and played with my cat. As she lay under the stove, I gently kicked her to make her move while I poured the boiling water out of the big kettle to rinse my dishes. But woe to me, kitty and I both jumped at the same time, the dipper turned in my hand and that kicking foot received the full benefit of the spilled boiling water. I did not dare yell, for that would cause Mother to discover what I had done, so I gritted my teeth and finished washing the dishes. As the girls lingered outside, I did not wait for Mother to tell me to put on my shoes, but opened the door to the parlor where Mother was talking to some ladies. I yelled, "I'm going, Mother," and dashed out of the back door to the girls outside and off we went. My foot and leg were very uncomfortable, especially after I had stepped on a sharp stone and cut a gash on the instep. We returned with our arms loaded with the beautiful wild alyssum, roses, larkspur, and foxgloves and trooped down to the church to watch the ladies put the blossoms into the evergreen arch that formed the back of the altar before which Miss Fry was to stand. Then home we went for supper and to get dressed for the wedding.

It had turned a bit chilly when the sun went down and Mother was mortally afraid I would take cold. She told me to pull on my white stockings over my others and to hurry to dress, as we would have to be early. Papa was out of town that week, so we dressed and rushed down to the church. That was a beautiful wedding to me. The decorations and altar were a wonder to my child eyes. Miss Fry married David Hunter, the foreman of the Pluma Mine. The Frys seemed to belong to me, for her brother, Edward, was my Godfather too. What a day to be remembered and chatter about, as Mother and I trudged up the hill after the reception or the "party" as I called it.

Bedtime arrived and I knew the truth had to come out at last, for I had put it off as long as I could. Mother said, "undress" and I did as slowly as I could while talking as fast as I could, but when Mother was ready to put out the light, one stocking was still on. Mother snatched hold of the top of it and off it came as well as all of the skin from my leg. Mother nearly fainted but when I told her the truth she said nothing. She found clean linen and fresh lard and bound up my foot and leg and put me to bed. I never said a word either, for I knew that it was time for me to turn over and go to sleep. My leg healed and never left a scar except for the stone cut on my instep. In those days, children and grown folk all kept most of their aches and pains to themselves.

That cat was my playmate and never seemed to resent anything I did to her. One day, Mother pierced my ears so I could wear the dainty Black Hills gold earrings that Mr. Barclay had made for me. When Mother left me alone to go to the store, I pierced kitty's ears and put straws in the holes. Kitty did not like it and gave me a scratch or two, but we were good friends and when the operation was over I gave her some butter that she liked dearly.

So, through hurts and pranks and jolly times, child life passed in those early days. Childhood friends and companions came and went just as life changes today.

CHURCHES & SUNDAY PASTIMES

The church was a vital element in the life of the community. Sunday was "church" day to Mother and we went wherever religious services were being held, no matter the denomination. Even though we were Episcopalians, mother took me several times to the Roman Catholic Church. This church influenced many social activities in community life. Eventually, the congregation outgrew the church on Sunnyside and built a larger one near the public school.

The first priest I remember was Father Peter Rosen from Deadwood. Father Rosen was a fine, fatherly, broad-minded man loved by the whole community. Whether Catholic or Protestant, all of the children were considered his, and they loved him. Father Bernard Makin preceded Father Rosen. As I mentioned earlier, Mr. & Mrs. P.A. Gushurst were the first couple married in Lead and were married by Father Makin at St. Patrick's Catholic Church.

Protestant churches were also soon established. Papa and a few of the Protestant men built the Congregational church in the evenings and on Sundays. It was smaller than the Methodist church but more centrally located at the junction of Main Street and the Deadwood Road in back of the First National Bank.

The Methodist church dedicated their building in 1881. For a few years, disaster seemed to follow it. For example, shortly after completion, a windstorm nearly demolished it. The Christmas fire was another near catastrophe. The Christmas committee had built a ship-form, covered with cotton batting, muslin, and evergreens. Strung with colored paper chains and lit with small candles fastened in place with wire holders, the ship was on rollers and loaded with gifts for everyone. As it was pushed from behind the curtains to the front of the church, the swaying branches and decorations caught fire from the tapers. There was little chance to save anything. The church, fortunately, had large front doors and windows on both sides so the building emptied quickly. Several received severe burns and the interior of the church was badly scorched before the fire was extinguished.

The same people seemed to support both Protestant churches. For example, I attended both Sabbath Schools, and Mother sang in the Congregational choir in the morning and in the Methodist choir in the evening. When the Congregational Church outgrew their first building, they built a larger building on South Wall Street. Papa bought the original building to use as a warehouse for his store.

Among the first Protestant preachers were Reverend Oliver E. Murray and Reverend B. Fay Mills. Reverend Murray went from Lead to fill the pulpit at the noted Wabash Avenue Methodist Church in Chicago. Reverend Mills was just beginning his ministry while in Lead. He was married to Mary Russell Hill, the daughter of Lead's first Justice of the Peace, the Honorable Henry Hill. Reverend Mills left Lead to continue his evangelistic work throughout the country following Dwight L. Moody as his ideal.

The Congregational church housed the Children's Loyal Temperance Legion and the older folks' Temperance Lodge. The Y.W.C.T.U., the W.C.T.U. and Temperance League met at the Methodist church. Members of these groups worked together for the same end...to abolish alcohol.

I made my first appearance as an entertainer when the Sunday School gave an evening program and the primary class opened with a song, "When He Cometh to Make Up His Jewels." The children were to speak pieces and I appeared in both roles.

Owing to a spell of tonsillitis, I had not practiced with the rest of the children, but mother had drilled me at home, and I was on the stage when the curtain went up. Mother had trained me by striking a chord and then singing with me. When the song practice was over, she drilled me on my piece, "Grandpa's Story of the Wicked Bear."

As I said before, that night I was on the stage when the curtain went up, and the organist started to play the song and I started to sing - off key, of course - and the other children followed me. The organist stopped, but we sang it through to the end and marched off the stage.

My speaking piece should have come toward the last of the program, but without waiting to be announced, I marched right back on the stage and gave my piece in a very precise manner until I came to the last line which ended: "And that used to frighten me." I could not think of the word "frighten" and started, "And that used..." I stopped, gasped, and then screamed: "Oh, that used to scare me," and ran off the stage to hide my face in shame in my mother's lap as she sat in the audience. Needless to say, it brought a good laugh and applause from the audience, but shame to my mother.

Later that evening a gentleman friend of my mother's took me on his lap and remarked that, "That is a pretty dress." I immediately raised my dainty dress, saying: "Yes, but I've got a dirty one under it." Mother had put a slightly soiled white wool dress under the sheer white Swiss for fear I would take more cold after my recent illness. Mother often said that was the climax of the evening, and she took me home as soon as she could. Needless to say, it was some time before I was permitted to again perform in public.

Another story is quite amusing. At one of the early evening meetings at the Congregational church, my little dog, Nip, caused quite a disturbance. We had gone to church leaving the dog shut in the house as no one ever locked a door in those days. Uncle opened the door, not knowing we were away and let the dog out.

Nip came at once to the church and made for the rostrum where he expected to find me, then took his place in front of the pulpit. The minister, a rather stout little Welshman, made a dive to get him just as Nip spied me in the pew a few rows from the front. He jumped on the front pew, then over to the next just as the minister made a grab for him. By the time the minister had recovered, Nip had reached me and settled down at my feet to be seen no more.

There was a roar of laughter from the boys in the back of the church and the minister made the remark, on regaining the pulpit, "The dog seemed to have better manners than some humans after all."

A few days after, when calling on my mother, he recognized our dog, came up to him and, stroked his head, saying: "You little devil you made a fool out of me but you were better behaved in church than any of us."

Sometime before June 1879, a gentleman came to Lead, bringing many boxes of books, all classics, and started the first library. He freely loaned these books to the people and when he left, gave most, if not all, of them to start the Congregational Sunday School library. I do not remember the man's name, but he lived near J. K. Searle on North Bleeker Street. I borrowed many books for my mother from him. These books started the circulating library that filled a great need in those days, helping to keep the children off the streets. Later, Mrs. Phoebe Hearst opened a fine library for the town with reading rooms and a paid librarian who not only cared for the books but also planned weekly musical and literary programs. The library was first opened on upper Main Street until a building was provided near the Homestake store on Mill Street.

Most of the stores were open seven days a week but Papa and Mother decided that their store must be closed on Sunday. So to church we went— Sunday morning to the Congregational church and Sunday School. In the afternoon, I went to the Methodist Sunday School and in the evening we went to the Methodist Church.

Uncle never worked on Sunday, so he often took long walks through the hills during the day if the weather was pleasant. We had one of the few organs in town. About four o'clock a group of friends gathered in Aunty's big dining room and, with mother at the organ, they sang songs, visited, had their tea, and then sang songs again until church time. After church, they would return to Aunty's to continue singing. On winter nights, usually at about ten o'clock, everyone would enjoy bowls of hot oyster stew, and then, to home and bed.

Music held a large place in the homes of Lead. Of course, the dance halls and saloons were occupied by old square pianos, but Mrs. Samuel S.

Green's Steinway Grand, brought all the way from Racine, Wisconsin, was the first piano in a private home. Mrs. Green and her sister, Nellie Bogart, were graduates of the New England Conservatory, and were very fine musicians for that day.

Mrs. Jennie Birdsell owned a melodeon - the only one in the country except in one of the oldest saloons - and when the Birdsells left the Hills, Mother bought it and sold our organ to Henry James.

For years, I practiced on the old melodeon that, to outward appearances, was a grand piano. I took lessons first from Mrs. Green and then from Professor John Baptiste Favario, an Italian musician and composer who had drifted into Lead after the 1886 Haymarket riots in Chicago. Favario had been playing in a music hall just off Haymarket Square when the riot took place. He composed a piece of music interpreting the sounds as they came to him at that time. He gave the original manuscript to me and I still have it in my possession.

Episcopal Bishop William Hare came to establish St. John's Mission in Deadwood on October 2, 1881, and Christ's Church Mission in Lead the next day. That meeting was held in the Congregational Church. Bishop Hare had been actively working to organize the Episcopal Church since the beginnings of the two towns. Three years earlier, on July 1, 1878, he had appointed E. K. Lessel as a missionary to the Black Hills. Unfortunately, due to failing health, Rev. Lessel returned to New York in May of 1879, where he died nine months later.

As I remember it, when Bishop Hare came to Lead in 1882, he baptized six children including myself, and two adults, at the home of Richard Blackstone on South Lead Hill. Services were held in the Opera House over Jacob's Saloon. Reverend Potter of New York was the priest sent to the Hills. He lived in Deadwood, holding services there in the morning, and evening services at the Opera House in Lead.

I will never forget one service that was rather startling. The choir was finishing an anthem, when a drunken man staggered through the door and intoned, "...and the Angels of heaven are - hic - singing above - hic - while the demons of hell - hic - ply their trade below." About that time, two men in the congregation reached the poor fellow and piloted him away.

The preacher, Reverend Potter, turned to the drunkard's hymn for his text, and my mother often said it was one of the finest sermons she had ever heard. Rev. Potter was a heavy drinker himself and realized his own misfortune. He tried to lead others away from drink. Reverend Potter and his family realized that they did not fit into western life, however, and soon returned east.

The name of the young minister who prepared me for confirmation escapes me. When the Bishop arrived for my confirmation, I had a bad case of tonsillitis and was unable to be confirmed at that time. In 1888, Bishop Thomas confirmed me at St. John's Episcopal Church in Wichita, Kansas.

Bishop Hare promised the people that when they had a lot and could raise four hundred dollars, he would give them four hundred more to build a church. Finally, in 1887, they began to build Christ Episcopal Church at Wall and Addie Streets. The building was completed in 1888 but no minister was found to take charge. The church was a little frame structure, but we were proud of it, and George G. Ware was sent to take charge of Lead jointly with Deadwood, while living in Deadwood.

Ware was very successful in building up both churches. During his time, a fine red brick church and parish house was built on upper Main Street. The Episcopal Church eventually became the largest Protestant congregation in Lead.

My first year teaching school in Lead, I also taught the younger children's Sunday School with Lottie Webster Beemer. On Easter Monday of that year, our classes gave a sacred program in the church entitled "The Building of the Cross." Mrs. Thomas Uren sang the songs. One hundred thirty-four dollars was collected and with it the congregation purchased the baptismal font still in use today.

Years later after I was married, all of our children were baptized at Christ Episcopal Church. On Bishop Hare's last visit to Lead, he baptized my youngest son, John. Too feeble to hold the baby, Rev. Montgomery helped Bishop Hare and my godfather, Edward Fry with his wife (Frances), stood for the child as he had stood for me twenty-four years before.

The Presbyterian Church and manse were built on South Wall Street near the schoolhouse. Reverend W.S. Peterson from Philadelphia was the first minister and served from 1894-1899. I recall that Mr. Peterson did not have any children. The Baptist Church began around the same time and Reverend Joseph A. Archibald led that congregation. As an accomplished architect, Reverend Archibald was instrumental in helping build the First Baptist church. He had two sons and two talented daughters, Pearl and Alleyne.

Thus, you see, the wild and woolly Black Hills pioneer days in Lead had religious centers from its earliest beginnings. Admittedly, lawless characters participated in gambling, drinking, and loose living. At one time, forty- two saloons existed along with forty-three legitimate business houses. We did not have motion picture houses or places of amusement for the first few years, but the lonely unattached man could seek relaxation among the old pine trees that rose from the prehistoric swamps. The rocky hills surrounding Lead were a place of grandeur and health for mankind.

YOUNG LADIES THAT
MY MOTHER HELPED

In those early days when the snow was heavy on the hill and the temperature was way below zero degrees Fahrenheit, my favorite play place was behind the old sofa in the corner of the front room. The back of the sofa was high and, while I sat on the floor with my dolls and my little sewing kit, it hid me completely from those in the room and so I often heard strange stories. One day, a young woman came to see my mother. She had led a rather questionable life, but had fallen in love with a young man who wanted her to reform and marry him. Mother told her to do it, but she said, "It would do no good for I would only drag him down. People know what I have been and no one would ever have anything to do with us, and he would only be unhappy and what chance would I have of going straight?"

My mother replied, "Remember, few in a frontier town like this are without skeletons in their closets, and people who live in glass houses hardly dare to throw stones. If you do what is right, people will learn to respect you. For a few years, you and John will be all either of you need in companionship and, by the time you do need more, you will have proven yourself. The best people will respect your efforts and help you." I heard the young woman say, "But I will always be an outcast and our children will be outcasts." My Mother said, "You will not be an outcast in God's sight and you can go to church and John will be with you."

At that time, my cat gave my presence away and I was sent out of the room, but later I learned that John and the girl had married and mother helped them get settled in their little home. A few years later, John took a job with another mining company and they moved away, building a new home in a community where her past was unknown. "Those who live in glass houses cannot throw stones" often comes to my memory, and, as the years go by, I realize more and more, how few of us do not live in a glass house.

Another time, a group of women were gossiping at our house, and Mother spoke up saying, "Is there anyone here who hasn't a skeleton hidden away in her closet somewhere that we must parade someone else's skeleton?" Not a word was said, and it was not long before the group broke up. I noticed that some time had passed before the ringleader of that crowd called at our house again. But I heard that lady make the remark one evening, "Mrs. Smith is a woman with a past." I wondered if she did not have one, too.

A few years later, one young teacher, Miss "C" came from the East and being a stranger, she found a room at one house and boarded at the hotel. At the hotel, she met men and women from other walks of life, and formed a rather unrestricted circle. One evening, she was asked to go with the crowd for a sleigh ride around the Belt and accepted. She discovered that she was paired off with a very dashing young businessman whom she had never met, but since she was with the crowd, why not. In the course of the evening he stopped at a hotel in Deadwood for refreshments and, while the others asked for wine, she asked for lemonade. That was the last she remembered when she woke up the next morning in her room with a violently sick headache. Later on in the day, a Sunday, her landlady came to her room and told her that since she disapproved of drinking, she had rented her the room, thinking that they shared the same convictions. She told Miss "C" that she would have to move at once.

At the time, Papa was on the school board. Miss "C" came to Mother and the facts of the case became clear. The girl had joined a wild crowd, had been taken to Deadwood and given knockout drops, and was used by her escort. He was a married man with a wife and child.

Mother took the girl into our home for the rest of the year and the affair was hushed up. When school year finished, Miss "C" returned to her home in the East a much sadder and wiser woman.

Young Ladies that My Mother Helped

About that time, an epidemic of peritonitis arose among the younger women of the town and several found resting places in the cemetery on the hill. One of that crowd left to visit a sister out on the coast and committed suicide a short time after. All of the girls had been very friendly with a certain well-to-do young man about town, and rumor said he owned one of the swanky houses of the underworld. So, for a time at least, Lead followed in the footsteps of her sister, Deadwood. That young man eventually married one of our nice quiet girls and reared his family on a fat pocketbook. Thus, the skeletons rattle in many closets in Lead and elsewhere.

SOCIAL LIFE IN LEAD

Sadie, her dog Nip, Lizzie & Seth
(mid 1880's)

D ances will live long in my memory, though I preferred more
sedate affairs. Socials, oyster suppers, and dances were the
amusements of the older people but the whole family attended. Even tiny
babies in arms were taken, and laid to sleep on a bundle of wraps in the
corner of the hall while their parents waltzed, galloped, or danced to "Old

Dan Tucker" or "Turkey in the Straw" until long after midnight. The dances began at eight and at midnight oyster suppers were served, then on with the dance until three or four in the morning, when the men would go to work.

The Miners Union Hall was a building 34 feet wide, two stories high covering half the block on Bleeker Street facing Main. The Hall had a large, bare room with long benches placed in the center of the room in front of the stage for entertainment. When a ball was in order, the benches and chairs were placed along the walls and the center of the room left clear for dancing. Along one wall was a long table on which was piled food of all descriptions for the midnight lunch. When the winter months developed, with deep snows and blizzard winds, hot oyster soup at $.75 a bowl was the favored repast.

Printed programs were handed to the ladies as they came onto the dance floor from the cloakroom. The men filled their names in the blank spaces after the names of the dances, thus claiming the privilege of that dance with the lady of their choice.

Mother was considered a very fine dancer, but Papa could dance only the square dances. When the waltzes, especially, came, he could hardly stand to see mother go on the dance floor with someone else. Finally, one evening he sat down beside her and quietly maneuvered a portion of her dress skirt under his seat. When she tried to stand up the skirt ripped from the belt and she was jerked violently back onto the bench. We went home at once and mother refused to go to another dance for some time, and then only with the understanding that she danced with whom she pleased and what dances she pleased. Papa never interfered again.

Two of the largest social affairs of the year were the St. Patrick's Ball and the Catholic Fair. The patron saint of the church was St. Patrick and St. Patrick's Day was a feast day. Though it coincided with Lent, a grand ball took place where everyone congregated from all over the area. People arrived in sleighs of all descriptions and danced all night.

The Catholic Fair was held in the Miners Union Hall. The fair lasted for three afternoons and evenings each year. Booths were built around the walls of the hall, leaving the center space for dancing and the stage for those taking part in the program. Items such as fancy work, candy, lemonade, and so on were sold at the booths, along with a fortune-telling booth and booths where quilts, pieces of furniture, pictures, and other articles were raffled off.

This fair was the old historic fair equivalent on a smaller scale. In the evening from eight to nine, performers put on a program of musical numbers, readings, and skits. There, Charity Martin, known on the New York stage as the Black Hills Nightingale, made her first appearance. Another young singer, who later became known as one of the most beautiful women of San Francisco and New York, Louisa "Lula" Beaupre, the daughter of Edmund and Mary Beaupre, also participated in those programs.

Billy Lang sang his comic impersonations of Irish and German songs. The Treweek brothers, Joe and Nick, with my mother and others, made up quartets and home talent opera companies, singing "Martha," "Pinnafore," and "The Mikado." In later productions, J.M. Tegarty (a protégé of Mrs. Phoebe Hearst), Mrs. T. J. Grier, and many others, took on lead parts. Few received voice training in those days. Performers were mostly natural singers whose love of music gave pleasure to the whole community. They sang the classics of music and verse that everyone enjoyed.

After the programs, the floor was cleared for dancing, beginning at ten and continuing until midnight. During the dance, votes were cast for the two great events that would occur at the end of the evening...awarding a big doll to a little girl and a diamond ring to a young lady.

Two leading little girls were chosen to compete as the most popular child for the doll, and votes were sold at ten cents apiece. The child receiving the highest number of votes won the doll. In other words, the one whose friends put up the most money received the doll.

The most popular young lady received the ring in the same way, but these votes were sold for twenty-five cents per vote. Each night between dances, the votes were announced. On the last night, the hall was crowded and it was almost impossible to dance. Every ten minutes, the priest would post results on the board, and then each minute starting ten minutes before midnight.

Parents and sweethearts put up their last penny for the sake of their candidate, and I well remember one contest when over fifteen hundred dollars was reportedly raised on the doll alone.

The two contestants were Alice and Annie. Alice's father was a boss in the mines and he had forced his men to put up money for his child. This angered his men and, on the quiet, they made up a purse and gave it to Annie's brother with the understanding that he was to purchase enough votes to put Annie in the lead at the last moment.

At eleven-thirty, it seemed that Alice had won and Annie's friends had given up. Alice was several hundred votes in the lead. At eleven-forty, a few scattered votes for Annie were added; eleven-fifty, Annie gained a few more but Alice's father covered them. To all appearances, Annie had lost and Alice was carried to the platform. At eleven fifty-seven...fifty-eight, and fifty-nine; the hammer was raised. Annie's brother stepped forward, putting down the money for one hundred more votes than Alice had, and Alice's side did not have time to counter the raise. The hammer fell and pandemonium ensued. Annie Abt won the doll!

I became so excited over the announcement that my folks took me home before the contest ended. Alice's screams still ring in my ears for they were audible three blocks away as we turned into our gate.

I believe that was the last time the event took place, for the people of the town felt it was unjust to put children in that position. In reality, Annie was the more popular child of the two, loved by everyone who knew her. Alice was considered spoiled. Her parents thought her the beauty of the town and taught her to consider herself as such. Winning the doll never seemed to affect Annie, but Alice became bitter. A feud emerged between her small following and the other children of the town.

Mollie Herlihy won the ring that year, but I cannot remember who the other contestant was.

(EDITOR'S NOTE: Annie Abt lived in Lead, SD, her entire life. She was one of five children and her father, Frank Abt, was a hotelkeeper and also served as town mayor from 1900 - 1902. She married Richard Purcell on Oct. 11, 1899, and died just over a year later on November 11, 1900, at the age of

24 years and 9 months due to complications from childbirth and Bright's disease. Mollie Herlihy was the second oldest of four children in her family. She lived in Lead her entire life and married George Parlin. On February 19, 1892, she gave birth to their son and died two months later on April 10, 1892. S.R. Smith handled her burial.)

The Knights of Pythias and Masons held other gala days each year, but unlike the other balls, they were by invitation and rather exclusive affairs. The Masked Ball, which ushered the Old Year out and the New Year in, was held by The Knights of Pythias and began around 9 p.m. At midnight, the masks were removed, and what fun and scrambling! A dainty maiden would prove to be one of Lead's young businessmen or your partner, with whom you had been cutting up all evening. The man whose identity you were certain of would prove to be a perfect stranger.

One time, a group came up from Deadwood and kept very much to themselves, or thought they did. One of the gentlemen, dressed as a big frog, monopolized the time and attention of "Miss America," whom he was confident was his partner. She, in her turn, led him on, realizing whom she was being taken for. Knowing the girl, she imitated her mannerisms but was unable to fathom his disguise. He maneuvered so that he was her partner when the masks were raised. As she raised her mask, his face changed and, with the exclamation, "Holy Gee, I don't know her from 'Adam's off ox'*!" He then quickly ducked into the crowd.

Years after, following the First World War, she met him again as her husband's buddy in the training camp at Fort Snelling. They recognized each other while dancing the Virginia reel on New Year's Eve after the Armistice and shared a good laugh. The Masonic Ball was an Easter Monday event and called for the finest, newest, and best in the way of dress. The ladies wore evening gowns, though not of today's style, for they very decidedly covered one's body. Occasionally a small open square or V might be in the front of the neck, but high in the back, with a long train skirt with linings of crinoline and silk. The waists were heavily boned, and under the dress were

---

*"Adam's off ox" was an expression used when a person was surprised by someone.

many petticoats and furbelows.* If the sleeves were short-elbow length, the remainder of the arm was covered with long gloves or mitts of fine lace. Feet were dressed in stockings to match the dress, and the lady carried her dainty dancing slippers with a fan in a fancy silk or velvet evening bag.

As soon as the ladies reached the ball, they headed straight to the dressing room and took off their high-buttoned street shoes and donned dancing slippers. Hair was dressed high and, if one was lacking hair in abundance, it was supplemented with puffs and switches from the store, and elaborately jeweled combs and flowers ornamented the whole. Powder consisted of simply the finest cornstarch, and was used only to take any shine off. Rouge was vulgar and used only by women of the street.

The men wore business suits or, if they were exceptionally well dressed, a Prince Albert coat, black trousers, and fine boots. These boots were often worn on the outside of the trousers, and generally custom-made of the finest leather and fit to the foot like a glove. Shirts were white and the ties, black, while the vests were made of rather fancy, rich material in white, if very refined, or fancy figured, if more dashing. My Uncle made boots that sold as high as fifty dollars a pair, with twenty-five a common price. Even ladies had their shoes made to order.

Uncle made my shoes for many, many years, as well as Mother's and my aunt's. After boots went out of style, men wore high shoes, for oxfords were still unknown in Lead. Gamblers and cowboys' boots were highly ornamented; many were thigh-high and carried finely wrought spurs at the heels. A saying in those days was, "You could tell a man by his boots."

Several card clubs in those days included most prominently the High Five Club, composed of married people, and the Whist Club of both young and old. In these later days, the community gathered more into smaller groups.

In 1883, when I was nine, a gentleman, Mr. Pearson, came from New York and settled near Pluma. He had heard that the Hills were helpful for lung trouble, so he arrived in the hope of prolonging his life as he was a consumptive (or a tubercular). Mr. Pearson had been interested in theatricals in New York, and each summer brought out some prominent actors and

---

* Furbelows are pleated pieces of material or ruffles on a garment.

actresses for a vacation. When I was ten, Grace Hawthorne with Mr. Chamberlain, her leading man, her understudy, and her friend, Miss Damon, came to Lead. To pay their expenses and to give a treat to the people, Mr. Pearson asked them to perform several plays. One was "Miss Multon" or the "New East Lynne," and I played the part of the child 'Paul' with Grace Hawthorne. Before she left Lead, she asked my mother to let her take me and train me for theatre, but Mother said, "No." We had seen enough of life "behind the scenes" to discourage any desire for it.

While in Lead, one of the actors had acquired a jug of whiskey unbeknownst to the rest and hid it in his dressing room. He played the part of Bill Sikes one night and when he came off the stage, grabbed a hatchet that one of the prop men had been using and went after another New York actor. He had suddenly become a madman and pandemonium resulted. He was finally overcome, tied up and taken to a hotel where he sobered up. The other actor received a gash in the arm, which was soon dressed, and all was peaceful when the group left Deadwood.

On their return east, that same madman drowned in the Missouri River. He had consumed some liquor before getting into the boat and, in trying to jump onboard, upset the boat and lost his own life.

Lead had its share of talented citizens, including Oscar Silver, a violinist. Although he had footed it into the Hills with only a pack on his back, he soon became a prominent businessman of Lead. While he always had his violin nearby, he never gave the impression that he knew much about it. He loved music and showed his interest by attending all musical entertainments. While he would tenderly play chords and scales on his violin, he consistently refused to play in public.

One day, a noted German violinist was making a concert tour and stopped in Chicago for a concert. There he learned that Oscar Silver, his favorite pupil in Germany, was living in Lead. He came out to visit him. Mr. Silver persuaded him to give a concert. After playing several pieces, the violinist turned towards Oscar Silver, placed his fine violin in his hands and demanded that he play a certain piece. Mr. Silver objected, but the master said: "I did this for you; now you play for me."

The audience sat for half an hour spellbound, with not a sound but that violin. It spoke. We could visualize the lonely boy going through the forest, and the rabbit scampering, and hear the birds chirping and singing, and the leaves rustling as the wind sighed through their boughs. I have heard the piece many, many times, but never like that. I was only a little child, but that performance has lived with me all my life. At the end of the performance, the old master cried happy tears and clapped him on the shoulder, saying: "My boy, you haven't forgotten."

Oscar Silver seldom played in public after that, but the few times he did he was always a big draw. Mr. Silver has long since passed to his reward. A Jewish dreamer, respected by everyone, he never piled up money, but his friends loved the quiet little man and honored him.

During the winters, home talent was used principally in concerts, as music was always popular and many good voices and a few talented readers were available. Mother was one of the most popular, and later she trained most of the younger generation in declamatory work. As for me, she wrote most of my pieces and drilled me in their delivery. Due to her writings, I am able to reconstruct most of the events herein narrated.

While my mother sang in all the musical programs, I never could. Although she spent a great deal of money on my musical education, I had no talent nor a great love for it. I liked to hear the old songs and later attended the Sickner Conservatory for a time in Wichita, Kansas. I eventually withdrew from the conservatory due to poor health, although I enjoyed public speaking and continued to develop that ability.

FOURTH OF JULY

Sadie dressed in her "Miss
Black Hills Costume" for the
July 4th 1883 parade

I n 1883, the morning awakened with bright sunshine, as fire carts
and hook-and-ladder trucks rolled in from adjacent towns. The
little mining town became a hive of red- and blue-shirted men, representing
different hose companies. This was the gala day of the year, the firemen's
tournament. Teams from all over the hills, with gaily decorated carts and

trucks, racing teams, individual competitors, and child representatives, all participated in the day's events. Flags floated and buntings flapped from the store buildings and dwellings.

Every man who could be spared from the mines walked the streets. Mining activities of Lead and the Belt towns were taken into consideration along with competitions with fire apparatus. Miners came from miles around to use the great boulder on Pine Street for the drilling contest, and bets on the winning team ran high. The prize translated into a month's extra pay for each of the miners.

To the children and their parents, the old "Car of States" where small girls represented states in the Union was the great attraction, and the outstanding feature of the parade. On that Fourth of July, the small number of little girls available to represent the states reminded us of diphtheria's terrible inroad in the juvenile population.

I was nine-years-old and July 4 was a gala day for me because I had been selected to represent the Black Hills as "Miss Black Hills." Most people were able to get off work that day for the grand parade held at one o'clock. The winning fire company team of 1882 led the parade, with all its regalia of red shirts, tin helmets, and gaily decorated cart. The mascot, usually a little girl beautifully dressed, or sometimes a boy, or a boy and a girl three or four years old sat on the cart, in a bower of artificial flowers. The winning company in 1881 came next, headed by its captain with his trumpet.

The "Car of States" was next to follow, a hayrack whose huge platform was raised in three levels. On the top level was the goddess of liberty in a flowing white robe, holding the American flag. On one side was an Indian girl, "Dakota;" on the other side, I stood as "Miss Black Hills." I wore a black net dress with stripes of gold braid all over and spangles and beads of gold, silver, copper, lead, and mica. A veil of golden yellow net covered me, while on my head my black crown spelled "Black Hills" in gilt beads. The veil represented gold dust; the braid, gold veins; and the beads, the nuggets of gold found in the hills. Around the three of us sat girls wearing gold crowns and white and blue shoulder sashes on which was printed the state they represented. Bunting and evergreen trees were on the uprights and covered the wheels of the rack. Men walked along each side to ensure the car did not tip or the children fall.

The other Hose Companies followed with their carts, with the different lodges in their regalia, along with the teams who were to compete in the different tournament events. Unfortunately, the parade was cut short when the temperature dropped suddenly and people rushed home for heavy wraps. I was heartbroken when a heavy old winter coat covered my beautiful dress, and we had to rush to the hotel to warm up and have our dinner. Shortly after we arrived at the hotel, hail began to fall. A snowstorm settled over the mountaintops and snow filled the gulches and blocked the roads.

At the Fireman's Ball that night, the men wore their uniforms. I remember Papa's red flannel shirt, black trousers, a patent leather belt with huge buckle, and his fireman's hat with red shield on the front. I was permitted to stay up until ten o'clock and watch the grand march. I even danced with an old bachelor friend before mother took me down the street a few doors to my aunt's and put me to bed.

The next day, the foot races and miner events were pulled off in the morning. In the afternoon, the drilling contests took place. These last events were among the best. Each mine sent its team of drillers consisting of three men. The great rock was chosen and the men worked as if drilling a hole to set a blast in the mine. The men who drove the deepest hole with their drill in the given length of time won money and honor for their mine. Hydraulic and electric drills have since displaced manpower. The machine age has taken over in the mines just as it has in the rest of the world.

Boxing and wrestling matches, not the scientific matches of today, but the "catch-as-catch-can" and rougher forms also occurred that day. But the last day was the greatest. Then, each Fire Company sent a selected team to race against time, including the nozzle man, who went ahead with the hydrant man, and the runners who pulled the cart loaded with the hose. As they reached the hydrant, a coupler attached the hose to the hydrant and turned on the water at the same time the nozzle man attached the nozzle ready for the water. Both couplings had to be made with at least three threads, and the team accessing water in the shortest time from the "pop of the gun" won the money.

Woe to the company that could not hold its hose or had its nozzle blown off when the water was turned on, and woe to the crowd in the path of that writhing, squirming hose that got out of control! I saw men and women bowled over like tenpins and drenched to the skin, but always with a laugh and, winning or losing, each team received its share of applause. This event capped the celebration except for the wild debauch and rivers of liquor that flowed freely everywhere to mark the victories. Aching heads usually resulted in absences in the mines the following day.

While at first organizations and churches carried on the social events of the community, small cliques and groups formed their own pastimes. National traits began to soften and tone down. The community became more "American" and democratic as education and high standards of living developed. The old pioneers demanded the best for their children, and the children raised their eyes to heights beyond the narrow horizon of Lead.

THE TEMPERANCE MOVEMENT

Time changes all things, and in Lead the changes came quickly. In the early 1880s, a "Clean-Up-Lead" movement began to grow. Quiet, persistent, and effectual, the movement bore fruit within the decade, and by the 1890s, Lead became a thriving little city of legitimate businesses and pleasant homes. Young people could walk the main streets in the evening without being considered dregs of humanity. That decade of moral struggle, however, demands a tale of its own, with its heroes and heroines who built a better foundation than they would ever know. God alone can look into the hearts of men and read the pages they have written.

The dens of the alley were swept away, the prostitutes were forced into houses off of the main streets, houses whose doors were closed and whose curtains were drawn to protect innocent childhood. Saloons were forced to put up swinging doors that hid the life inside, gambling dens were housed in second-story or back rooms and, eventually, most of the vicious devices were outlawed and left Lead for more favorable fields.

In the Black Hills, mining interests were uppermost in the minds of all, and moral interests were in the minds of only a few. Deadwood was noted for its Chinatown and opium joints. Lead kept fairly free from the opium menace but the other vices ran rampant. With saloons at almost every other door on the main streets, and houses of prostitution wide open, the devil certainly had an easy time. With the uncertainty of life, the wild hope of riches, life, and everything else was a gamble, a reckless uncertainty. Unfortunately, the gambling instinct was stamped into the characters of the smallest children.

Not surprisingly, some girls became mothers at thirteen and fourteen and some boys in the third, fourth, and fifth grades were confirmed drunkards. When I later became a fifth-grade teacher, two of my male students, 14 years old or younger, went on periodic drinking sprees. One would go into delirium tremens and the other would wander into an abandoned tunnel and sleep off his debauch.

I saw a judge in Lead place his two-year-old son on a saloon counter where everyone could see him from the street. The father placed a pipe in his son's mouth and a glass of whiskey in his hand so he could smoke and drink with the crowd.

One of our neighbors was an alcoholic. She was originally from California and had a very beautiful daughter by a former husband who still lived in California.

When her daughter was in her teens, she moved West for school and met her father and brother. She never returned to Lead to live but on a return visit she stayed at our home and I witnessed a heartbreaking scene. Weeping on my Mother's shoulder, the young lady sobbed, "Oh, if I could only be proud of my mother." Her mother was a good person except that she was never sober. Her current husband allowed her to drink one quart of whiskey a day.

On the other side, the people who withstood the liquor and gambling dens were outstanding representatives and had fine homes. The first move towards "cleaning up" the town was taken by the Homestake Company between 1879-1880 when it forbade anyone under the influence of liquor to work in the mines. Men had to be sober or they could not work.

A Temperance League was formed among the older people, who were known as "teetotalers," and were scoffed at by the liquor interests. In addition, the W.C.T.U., headed by Mrs. Emma Vickers and my mother, Mrs. S.R. Smith, the Good Templars Lodge and, among the children, the Band of Hope, formed other groups. The leaders of the men included S.R. Smith, Percy Vickers and George (Joseph G.) Inman. Papa was the President of the Temperance League for several years. They, too, were only a small group around which a considerable following gathered, but they were the officers.

Through that organization, such speakers as John B. Gough, Cyclone Jim, Susan B. Anthony, Anna Shaw and Frances Willard, with many lesser lights were brought to the Hills. Frances Willard gave a little pin to me at that time, a tiny picture of herself, and is a treasured possession of mine today. The little bundle of white ribbon is still tied to it. The Band of Hope, the Y.W.C.T.U., and the Temperance Union were the stepping-stones of temperance work for eight years of my life.

Frances Willard, Susan B. Anthony and Anna Shaw made several trips to the Hills and made their headquarters at our home during the fight to bring South Dakota into the union as a constitutionally dry state. While resting in the hotel after his lecture, John B. Gough was drugged and taken to a dive in Deadwood by the liquor friends. Papa spent three days looking for him. After that, never was a temperance speaker allowed out of the protection of his friends, and our home became the harbor of safety.

Reverend Murray became very active in the Temperance cause and, one day, shortly before he left for Chicago, he started out on a drive around "the belt," as Central, Terraville, Deadwood, and Lead together were called. He stepped into our store to speak to Papa and, then leaving, jumped into the buggy and drove off. He did not notice that during his absence a couple of practical jokers had tied a demijohn under the buggy and placed a beer keg in the back of it. Consequently, this caused quite a hilarious uproar along the way.

Cyclone Jim was sent by the Temperance Bureau to finish the campaign. He gave the final talk standing in the street in front of the First National Bank and facing three saloons with two more in full view. He was a small man with piercing eyes and a voice that could be heard for blocks away, above the roar of the mills and the catcalls of the liquorites.* He was a veritable cyclone in voice and body.

Papa stood where he could see every move of the milling crowd and saw someone place a stone in the hand of a drunken Irishman by the name of Patsy McCarthy.

---

* Liquorites were individuals who opposed prohibition.

In the nick of time, he sprang and struck Patsy's arm as he hurled the stone at Cyclone Jim's head, missing its mark. Two men took Patsy home to his wife, Mary, where he slept off his drink. The next day his wife made him promise to vote against the saloon, saying: "If it hadn't been for S.R., you would have this day been a murderer." "Me, a murtherer?," says Patsy. "Yes, a murtherer," and then she recounted the whole story to him.

Patsy worked in Pennington County. The evening of the vote, a mile long descent to the town awaited Patsy and his companion, a German. They sat down on a log at the top to rest a few minutes before the climb down into Lead to the voting place. As they sat there discussing the issues of the day, Patsy said: "If God spares me life, I'm going to vote for prohibition." The German swore an oath and replied: "And if God spares my life, I won't vote for prohibition," and then he immediately dropped dead. Patsy jumped and dashed for the polls. Grabbing a ballot from Papa as he went in, he cast the last vote in that precinct for the day, one for prohibition.

When Patsy exited, he made straight for Papa, saying, "There's a dead man up there," pointing to the hill. After a while the crowd heard the whole story and they moved up the hill with the coroner. Sure enough, there lay the German whom God had not permitted to vote. Temperance carried in that ward by one vote, and South Dakota was voted in dry although the law was later declared unconstitutional.

Among the would-be temperance children, one child stands out clearly. She was a frail, dainty little miss, the daughter of one of the leading mine officials. The doctor ordered her to drink brandy every day, but she begged to be a "Blue Ribbon" girl and refused to take it. Her mother and the doctor compelled her to drink it. Today she fills a drunkard's grave.

The Salvation Army came to town and meetings were held in the Miners' Union Hall on the corner of Main and Bleeker Streets. The Army was soon driven out, although they did some good work while there. Children were barred from the saloons, and the Russian Alices, in conspicuous garb, were moved off of the main streets.

Up to that time, the Homestake Store, under Alex McKenzie, sold liquor of all kinds, but Alex said that if liquor was voted out, he would dump every drop into the creek and never sell another drop, even though he was a heavy drinker himself. He kept his word. When the returns came in, he dumped all the liquor into the creek and became a total abstainer for as long as I knew him.

After the election, many of the saloons remained open despite an attempt to close them. Although Papa was president of the Anti-Saloon League, Mr. Inman insisted that since he was responsible to no one, he would sign the papers closing the saloons. Papa had his business and a wife and child. Mr. Inman then started the prosecution in the courts thereby winning the hatred of all the liquor men, and leading to an attempt on his life.

The Temperance workers of those days fought at the risk of their homes and their lives. As a child, I was given a revolver and taught how to defend myself when the injunctions closing the saloons were signed. Papa and Mr. Inman drove up the street with Winchesters in their hands, watching the crowds in front of the saloons. Attempts were made to set fire to our buildings. Mother was threatened with a rail-ride and we dared not leave the house at night for some time after.

That winter, we had an epidemic of black diphtheria. Mr. Gregory's wife and child and the doctor had it. Mr. Inman did Mr. Gregory's outside chores and slept in his woodshed for a time. One night, when Mr. Inman went home after a cold, wet day, he went into the shed, picked up a light piece of wood and the ax, held the stick-on end to split it, struck it lightly to gauge the next stroke, and it split open. With that stroke, he exposed a plugged hollow filled with enough dynamite caps and powder to blow up the whole neighborhood had he struck a blow hard enough.

The investigation grew too hot for a certain saloonkeeper who left town in the night and, although he owned considerable property, he did not return until after Mr. Inman's death a few years later.

With the success of the election, the temperance people thought they could rest on their laurels. Saloons closed and the houses of prostitution moved to side streets. Drugstores went in where Jentges and the Family Liquor Houses had been. However, only a short while passed before the terrible blow when the courts declared the law unconstitutional.

The saloons returned, but something had been gained. The company store and half the saloons had gone out of business and never reopened. Drugstores perhaps sold as much liquor, but behind a heavy screen and not by the glass or to minors. Lead became a much cleaner town to rear a family in and was never again that old, wide-open town of the early 1880s.

TRANSPORTATION

I well remember crossing the Badlands in those early days of stagecoach and covered wagon traffic. In dry weather, travel was tolerable in spite of the sun's glare and the great enveloping dust clouds. Rather, worse still were the swarms of buffalo gnats that drove beast and man wild with their pinpricking sting. The most abhorrent times were the wet rainy seasons. Men would sit for hours holding a shovel against the wheel rims to scrape the gumbo* off as we drove along. We took a respite now and then to dig out the gumbo collected between the wheel spokes.

Our journey was hardly a pleasant jaunt of twenty or thirty miles a day on horseback amid picturesque scenery. Rather, the sturdy pioneer stock of our Virginia Adventurers and Plymouth Rock ancestors was required to face the challenges of pioneer life in the Dakota Territory.

Railroads do not build themselves nor go from one place to another in a haphazard manner. The Union Pacific, completed in 1869, joined Sacramento, California, to Omaha, Nebraska, and thus opened up the West to expansion. Until then, other than Salt Lake City, appreciable-size communities were non-existent between the two cities. The Indian Reservations in Nebraska and Dakota territories were major obstacles to railroad building.

The Union Pacific Railroad to Sydney, Nebraska, or Cheyenne, Wyoming Territory, provided easier access for the earliest prospectors and

---

* Gumbo was a fine silty soil that formed an unusually sticky mud when wet.

businessmen to enter Custer and later Deadwood and Lead. Trails into the Dakota Territory were available from Cheyenne and Sydney, and from the north, the Montana or Laramie Trail offered a route. The latter was the least used due to its sparsely populated district. Over the Bismarck Trail, a vast amount of early freight was hauled in covered wagons, pulled mostly by oxen at the rate of ten to twenty miles a day.

Custer became the first established city in the Hills, thanks to General Custer making this area his headquarters when conducting his government survey. The first gold was also found there. But its importance did not last long. So little gold was found in that neighborhood that men drifted deeper into the mountain gulches, following the creek beds in search of the precious gold's source.

The Fremont, Elkhorn & Missouri Valley Railroad Company was organized in Fremont, Nebraska, in January of 1869 to construct a line up the Elkhorn Valley in Nebraska. A land grant from the state of Nebraska amounted to about 45,000 acres.

Finally, in 1881, the company extended its main line to Long Pine and then reached Valentine in 1883. In August 1884, the Chicago & Northwestern acquired the Fremont, Elkhorn & Missouri Valley and thereafter the work was pushed rapidly until in November 1885 it reached Buffalo Gap, Whitewood, in 1887, and Deadwood in 1890. A branch from the Gap to Hot Springs was also built the same year.

Due to Lead's altitude and the formation of the hills underlying it, broad gauge railroads did not attempt to enter Lead. Narrow gauge lines under separate private ownership tapped the main lines. The Chicago, Burlington & Quincy, referred to simply as the Burlington, eventually came within two miles of our thriving city.

A narrow-gauge line was built a year later up from Deadwood to the Bald Mountain and Ruby Basin Mines. Thus, the gold output of the Hills was the lodestone, pulling the steel rails across canyons and over mountain passes and through tunnels until the precious metal could be carried out into the hurly-burly of a world market. There it could be exchanged for necessities at first and later for luxuries.

Transportation

The branch line to Alliance and Newcastle was extended to a connection with the Northern Pacific in Billings, Montana, in 1894. This line came to Edgemont, at the edge of the Black Hills, and, from there to Deadwood, a branch line was built.

Many tales about railroad construction range from the laughable to the tragic and remarkable. Near Pringle, South Dakota, I believe, an expensive fill was initially needed but an accidental blast caused a landslide that did the necessary work instead.

The little Black Hills and Fort Pierre narrow-gauge road was built to bring the wood and timbers for the mines into Lead, and had many experiences and memories attached to it. When the rails were laid part of the way, Lead held its Labor Day Picnic at Horseshoe Grove beyond the big trestle. In the summer, women boarded the wood train with three-gallon pails to fill with the luscious red raspberries that grew so plentifully throughout the timber. They left in the morning and met the train at the water tank as it returned at five o'clock in the evening. They provided a rich harvest for the winter cupboard and enjoyed a day of pleasure.

One trip I shall never forget is when Mother, Muriella Fry (later Mrs. David Hunter), Bessie Treweek (later Mrs. William O'Brien), and I, along with two others whose names I have forgotten, went out on the morning train and expected to return by five o'clock that evening. Mother found a large patch of berries just before we were supposed to quit to meet the train. She told the others to go on and we would follow as soon as we filled our pails. Mother became so engrossed in filling her bucket that she did not realize the time or weather conditions. When she looked around, she did not know where we were but thought she did, and started for the train. Around in a circle we went. She tried again and again to find our way to the train but we kept returning to our starting point.

Clouds gathered and it was dark. I told Mother which way to go but she did not believe me. Finally, to prove me wrong, she went part of the way. When we heard the train whistling and bell-ringing, mother started to run with me towards the train.

We reached the trestle where the train was waiting and hoping we would arrive because it was the train's last trip into town for the day. When we reached Lead, Papa and a posse of men were waiting with lanterns to go back with a train to search for us. It was 11 o'clock at night. Mother never went on another berry picking expedition. That experience was enough. She purchased her berries after that.

An 1888 trip of that train will long be remembered. It was regarded as the "pay train" when it went out to pay the timber workers at Englewood and Brownsville. An article from The Lead Daily Call dated October 13, 1948, describes that experience better than I can, although I remember the time very clearly.

ATTEMPTED TRAIN ROBBERY
60 YEARS AGO RECALLED HERE

Deadwood and Lead residents recalled that it was just 60 years ago that the famous attempted Black Hills and Ft. Pierre train robbery took place in Reno Gulch between Englewood and Lead.

William A. Remer, later sheriff of Lawrence county, paymaster for the Homestake Mining Company, was on the train en route to Brownsville to pay off the wood workers. He had about $20,000 in his grip, according to the accounts published the day after the hold-up. With him was Richard Blackstone, superintendent of the road.

John Commiskey was engineer, Reese Morgan, fireman; Charles H. Crist, conductor, and Charles Lavier, brakeman. As the train neared a trestle and a curve the engineer discovered that the rails were spread and hastily reversed the engine. At about that time, the robbers raised up from the brush where they had been hiding and began shooting. Remer fired a shot from the train and Blackstone got out where he could do some shooting. One of the robbers was seen to mount a horse and ride swiftly away. The money was safe in a tool box in the engine.

The engine's whistle was blown and another engine soon came and with it several men and guns. A search was made for the robbers who had fled into the brush. Three of them, "Spud" Murphy, George Young and John Telford, were arrested the next day at Rapid City, and another one, Jack Doherty, was arrested later with John Wilson. The latter two broke jail before they were brought to trial and escaped to Canada.

The wood workers at Brownsville were an unhappy lot when word of the robbery reached them and when the train finally came in, they remarked that they were glad that no one had been killed but that it was too bad the money was gone. About that time Remer climbed down out of the cab with the yellow satchel with the money and their expressions changed rapidly. 'You couldn't take that money away from Buck Shot Remer,' they declared.

Joe Hilton of Deadwood remembered today that he had heard the shooting but thought some hunters were out after game. He was a schoolboy at the time living at Englewood and going to school in Lead. He said he was a little frightened when he came home that night because some of the robbers were believed still hiding in the brush."

Another train incident had more serious consequences. When the Black Hills and Fort Pierre road was completed, the railroad company did not clear the right-of-way of timber as much as it should have before running its celebration excursion train over the road. The day was beautiful and a long train of flat cars with planks for seats was hooked to the engine for a picnic at Piedmont, the end of the road. The train was scheduled to leave in the morning, with the picnic at Piedmont thirty-nine miles away, and return in the afternoon. Papa, Mother, and I intended to take the trip but just as the train was ready to pull out, the death of an old friend caused us to give up our seats to three others who were initially going to be left behind for lack of room.

The train pulled out with bands playing, whistles blowing, and shouts and laughter. Since the roadbed was new, the train moved rather slowly. Our seats were located on the last car. As the train moved along, the vibration of the train caused a huge pine tree close to the tracks to begin swaying. There was no way to communicate to the engineer to hasten. Most of the passengers were watching the scenery ahead or talking to one another. Few noticed what was about to happen when the tree suddenly crashed across the last flatcar killing two and injuring others including those who had taken our seats that morning.

A more pleasant tale was told about a railroad contractor, Mr. John Fitzgerald, who was especially fond of a good span of mules. He never could see a span of fine mules without coveting them. Working for the construction company was Joe, a man known to be half Indian. Joe was sent to Rapid City to acquire some construction materials, and drive a fine pair of mules there. When Mr. Fitzgerald stepped out on the street he caught sight of them standing nearby, and made a beeline for Joe and the mules.

"Nice mules," said Mr. Fitzgerald. "Yes," said Joe. "Will you sell?" and Mr. Fitzgerald began to dicker. Joe shook his head. "$200?" said Mr. Fitzgerald. Joe shook his head. "$300?" said Mr. Fitzgerald "No sell," said Joe. "$400?" The bid increased and Joe still shook his head. "Oh, now, here take this and you take the mules to the construction camp and leave them." Mr. Fitzgerald pushed $500 into Joe's hand and walked away.

The next day Mr. Fitzgerald asked the camp boss if a half-breed had left a team of fine mules at the camp. The boss knew nothing about it, but upon looking around, Mr. Fitzgerald spied the mules and called the attention of the boss to them, saying, "There is the team I bought from the Indian yesterday." The boss laughed: "Why Mr. Fitzgerald, that is your own team Indian Joe has been driving for months." When they looked for Indian Joe, he had left the job. Mr. Fitzgerald did not go after him. He had forced the money on Joe and he thought he had bought the mules. Later, when he ran across Indian Joe and knew that he was honest, he rehired him and put him in charge of his mule teams again.

Floods were a constant menace to the railroads in that part of the country. When the spring Chinooks began to blow, the snow began to melt. The snow-slides and thawing filled canyons and softened the overhanging banks. The fills fell away or were carried downstream, tunnels caved in, banks slid, and rocks blocked traffic until repairs were made.

My last experience was when a flood had swept through the gulches in 1904, washing out the roads between Lead and Deadwood. My husband and I, with our children, left Geneva, Nebraska, on the Northwestern to Fremont, then to Deadwood. On the way, the train had just passed over a fill, when the fill gave away and went down behind us. Near Rapid City, we were on another fill, twenty feet high, when the rails spread. Fortunately, the wheels went down between the rails and the coaches did not roll down the embankment. Boxcars were sent out from Rapid City and we packed into them for the rest of the trip. However, that was not the end. Just as the engine started to nose its way into the Deadwood tunnel, the tunnel caved in and left the train on the side of the mountain, with a raging creek between it and the wagon road into Deadwood, a few miles away.

The brakeman walked into town, and hacks were brought out and lined up along the road to take passengers into town. The children were carried across to the hacks, but the grown folks waded through mud and water up to their knees. The mud-covered men and women provided quite a sight as they entered the handsomely furnished Franklin Hotel that black night as the rain came down in torrents. Papa had waited for us in Deadwood until it began to get dark, and, believing the drive of four miles to Lead would be too dangerous after dark, he returned home, leaving word for us to stay all night at the hotel.

The next morning, we drove through the creek bed from Deadwood to Central, then over a badly washed-out road over the mountain to Lead. The regular road between Lead and Deadwood had been washed out and was impassable. Passengers found that trip to be a nightmare and the railroads lost thousands of dollars.

FARMING FAMILIES

Strangely, large families were rare, while families with two or three children were more the norm. Awful epidemics of diphtheria, scarlet fever, and meningitis that swept over the camps each spring often took little tots, so seldom were more than three living children in a home simultaneously. I only remember one outstanding family with five children.

Many families came to Lead, saved enough to start a farm in the valleys of the Hills, and then moved there to make a go of it. I recall one family had twin girls. As a child, I never could reconcile the fact that one of the twins had a birthday every year and the other only every four years. Such was the case, as one was born near midnight February 28th and the other one the morning of February 29th in Leap Year.

When the girls were about six, their parents moved out to a ranch in the country east of Rapid City. When the Sioux Indian uprising took place, this family's home was in their path, but the father had gone to Rapid City for provisions. The mother and girls hid in a cave when a group of Indians burned their home and passed on, continuing their wild raid. When the father returned, he found the mother a white-haired maniac wandering over the prairie with her children by the hands. I was told that she spent her remaining days in Yankton at the Dakota Hospital for the Insane, and I lost track of the girls.

Another family, the Whites, departed Lead and moved into the Spearfish Valley and developed a delightful ranch home, in spite of being hailed out nearly every year. One Fourth of July, we visited them. While sitting at the table, during the noon meal, it suddenly became dark. Before we could even get the windows closed, hail stones so large that they could not fit in a coffee cup (much larger than today's teacups) came down. The storm killed young horses in the fields and beat grain into the ground.

After the storm was over, Mr. White went to look after his stock while Mrs. White and the rest of us gathered up the wet, bedraggled chickens that had succeeded in finding protection, and brought them into the house. We put them in baskets and boxes around the stove to dry them and fed them mash filled with red pepper, but more than half of them died. Mr. White returned with the news that his finest calf and their young colt had been killed in the pasture. All of the windows on two sides of the house were broken.

THE CHINESE COMMUNITY

The Chinese community in Lead was unlike that of Deadwood in those early days. Deadwood's Chinatown contained opium dens and houses of prostitution. So-called "Flower girls" were sterilized prostitutes, for only wives were allowed to have children, and only high officials were allowed to have wives. The Chinamen living in Lead tended to be respectable business people.

Chinamen were allowed to stay in America ten years. If they died within the ten years, their bodies were returned by express to the Chinese officials in their native home. Any man who lost his queue* was debarred. I remember one case well. A good-natured old fellow ingested too much American "fire-water" in addition to some of his native concoction. When he fell asleep in the saloon, a practical joker cut off his queue and the poor fellow went wild upon awakening. Some Christian workers got his attention and eventually converted him to Christianity. He assumed American dress and habits, gave up drink and opium, and became one of the best cooks in Lead. But he never could return to China.

China was very strict about enforcing the ten-year rule of living in America. I was told a fantastic story about an old Chinaman who traveled to Honolulu, married, and reared a family. Becoming homesick for the tombs of his forefathers, he thought after so many years he could return and they would never know. He took a vessel for Canton. The moment he stepped

---

* A queue is a long braid of hair that hangs down the back of the neck.

on Chinese soil, he was arrested and taken to the salt mines, from which he never returned, although our Chinese and American Consuls did everything in their capacity. He was a Chinese citizen who had evaded the law.

In Deadwood, the Chinese Consul's male children were registered in China as soon as they were ten years old, while the girls were of no consequence. I well remember when the Consul's oldest boy set out for China the first time. He had attended Deadwood public schools, spoke English perfectly, and was to all appearances an American child. I saw him step into the stage with a wave of his hand to his mother and the rest of the family—a happy, carefree child. He made that long journey alone, and I never knew whether or not he returned.

In Lead, we had, in reality, only three Chinese houses: Sam Lee's, Old Ling's, and one on Pine Street for which I knew nothing. From the time we arrived in Lead until I left as a bride for Nebraska, our laundry was done at Sam Lee's on South Mill. I prize very highly the beautiful, white silk pillow tops embroidered by Sam's wife in China, along with the elaborate scroll written in English in the many colors of Chinese inks that Sam presented to me the morning of my wedding.

Sam was going to China, and I knew that I would be married the following summer. When he was leaving, I said: "Well Sam, I'll not see you again," and he answered quickly: "Oh, yes, Missie, I be back." "But, you know Sam, the new law has been passed and you cannot come back anymore." "I know, Miss Sadie, but you see I know my way, and I see you June."

Sure enough, two weeks before my wedding, Sam appeared at the door and asked for me. He held a bundle of sweetmeats,* nuts, and many papers which he explained held good wishes. He had brought them and the beautiful pillow tops all the way from China for me.

Sam's place was always very clean, and we children loved to stand in the doorway and watch him and his helpers iron the clothes so beautifully. The picture we saw was a long cabin room. On the right of the door were three-tier bunks end to end, six in number. At the foot of the bunks was a stove

---

* Sweetmeats were candy or confections originally made of candied or honeyed fruit.

with boilers of water always bubbling and old-fashioned irons. Beyond it, clothes hung from long lines of ropes. On the left of the door was a window and on a long table down the side of the room sat Chinese bowls filled with water.

Sam, or one of his helpers, would take a shirt off the line, pick up an iron from the stove, test it by holding it near his cheek, turn to the table, fill his mouth from a bowl of water, and spray the shirts by blowing the water out of his mouth in a fine spray over the clothes, then proceed to iron. When finished, he held the article up for inspection. If flawless, his eyes would sparkle as he laid it in the right basket for delivery; if not, back it went for a repeat process.

I well remember a little embroidered white flannel petticoat of mine he did not know how to wash, and spoiled it. He nearly cried when he presented it to my mother with the question, "How much? I fix right." And he paid the full price on the skirt.

Mother told him how to wash flannels, and he never spoiled another. When he had ironed an especially attractive little dress, he waited half an hour for Mother to come and inspect it, and his face shone like the sun after a few words of praise.

Mother would say: "Washing looks nice, Sam, shirts fine." Sam would grunt and hold up the special prize. "You think nice?" Generally it would be a little embroidered or be-ruffled dress. "You think little Missie look nice?" Mother would give the words of praise, and Sam would go away happy. Sam will always have a tender place in my memory, though I never saw him after my wedding day.

The other Chinese laundry was near the creek, back of Faust's on Bleeker Street. I never knew much about the place until one day, out sleigh-riding, the children said Old Ling was sick and the Chinamen had all left him but one. Knowing Ling was about to die, only one remained to push food through the door to the dying man. When Papa was called in to bury the man, he thought it would be quite an experience, so he went in high spirits. But no Chinaman could be found in the house. Papa was going to remove the body to the undertaking rooms when one popped up from the alley where he was scattering red papers covered with Chinese writing. "No take alay. No take alay." The command was so firm that Papa embalmed the body and sealed it in its metallic casket without further talk. He then went to Dr. Dickinson for the death certificate and learned he had been handling a case of leprosy.

As I mentioned, the body had to be shipped back to China, so when the funeral took place, the body was placed in the hearse and the Chinamen piled into all the available hacks with a retinue of "wailing women" following the hearse. As the funeral proceeded to the Express Office in Deadwood, the road was flooded with papers of all descriptions in Chinese writing. They believed that the "Sickness Devil" would pick up every paper and read it so he could not catch up and overtake the funeral party. That was the only case of leprosy I ever heard of in the Hills.

The body left on the stage that afternoon for San Francisco, but when it did not arrive in due course of time, a great disturbance ensued. Letters passed between China, Washington, and Lead. Tracers were sent out, but after the body had arrived in Omaha, all trace seemed lost. Five years later, Papa received a notice from a town in Florida stating they were holding a body for instructions. That was poor Old Ling's body, and it finally found its final resting place in China.

With the passing of Ling, the laundry and all it contained was burned. White women began to do the washing and later, white laundries sprung up. The Chinese, outside of those who had become Christians such as Sam Lee and the old cook, drifted out of the town.

Another Chinese business enterprise emerged in Lead unlike those of Deadwood. In the gulch across from the tollgate lived a thrifty old Chinaman who furnished Lead with the only green groceries obtainable in those early days. He had a queer looking little house with quite a cleared space on the bank of the creek at the base of an almost un-climbable hill. Here, he raised his neat rows of radishes, lettuce, young onions, cabbages, and even luscious strawberries. During the season, he picked wild raspberries and even chokeberries, and offered them for sale at very reasonable prices. He walked to Lead with a wooden yoke somewhat like one would put on an ox, and from the ends of the yoke were suspended two huge wicker baskets filled with his produce. He had his regular customers, and no amount of bribery from newcomers would obtain his products until all the regular customers had been satisfied. At the time of the flood, the little house and garden washed away. Whether the old Chinaman drowned or just left town, we never knew, but we never saw him after that.

The Chinamen loved chicken and paid enormous prices for them, especially at New Year's. I remember receiving an offer of $3 for my old pet hen, but I would not sell Rosie. She was old and had her toes frozen off one foot the prior winter. She could only hobble around but she was my pet. After Rosie was killed and eaten by one of the Bender's hogs, Papa told me that it would have been better if I had sold her to Sam, which did not soothe my grief. Chinese New Year was the gala day for the children of Lead. On that day, the Chinamen lavishly distributed their sweetmeats, nuts, and candies. Candies and nuts were shipped from China for this gala day. For a whole week, feasting and rejoicing took place in all the Chinese houses, especially in Deadwood. Candies were made from potatoes, like our potato chips but boiled in syrup. We ate slices of coconut, balls of ground up nuts cooked in fondant, candied ginger root, and best of all, fancy, prickly nuts. The shells were very thin, honey-colored, and reddish brown. When crushed between the fingers, the shells were almost empty except for a small layer of the sweetest, juiciest fruit around a large stony pit that could not be broken. Another dainty was similar to a thick strip of candied pineapple only far drier. We never learned its name, only that it was a fruit that grew in China.

Opium and "hop joints" were unknown in Lead. Deadwood had its dives and the Lead addicts satisfied their binges there. At one time, the old Pine Street Chinaman was accused of selling opium, but he left town and was never heard from again.

FOREIGN INFLUENCE

Among the better class of young people, very few drank in those days, and I only knew of one woman who smoked. She was an old Southern lady, and when she went to bed, her daughter would place a cigar on the table beside her bed so that she could smoke it if she could not sleep. She had two daughters who became drug addicts, so she was really better off than them. I understand, though, that both mastered their terrible habit and cured themselves later.

In the Hills, drinking was done primarily by the foreign element, both men and women. Almost all classes drank wine, and it was served at social gatherings for a few years. I remember a Masonic banquet where the three glasses belonging to Papa, Mother, and myself were the only ones turned down. The following year, it was not even served.

In the early days, the original settlement consisted principally of Italians, Austrians, Hungarians, Swedes, Norwegians, Danes, Fins, Germans, the Irish, Cornish, English, and Americans. The foreign element brought with them their native customs and many of them, their native secret organizations and feuds.

You may wonder why people allowed this immoral situation in the town. One would have to revisit those frontier days when so many first settlers were not without blemish to realize that everyone minded their own business and let their neighbors "look after their own backyards." It was much better to keep a whole skin then to have it punctured some night by a bullet from a dark stairway or alley. Even watching your own business too closely was not safe in those days. Tony was a little Austrian boy who landed in Lead just a few days after his father was killed in the mine. He took a great fancy to Papa and Papa to him. Papa saw that he stayed in school and later found a job for him suitable for his years and strength.

Tony saved his money as he clerked in a grocery store and Papa helped him start a little store of his own. Business in those days was conducted on a monthly charge basis and the Austrian-Hungarian people traded with Tony pretty generally.

One day Tony, with a very long face, came to Papa and said, "Mr. Smith, the wholesale man says he close me up unless I pay my bill next payday." Papa asked him, "Why, Tony, haven't you kept your bills paid? You have been doing a nice business and should not be behind."

Tony said, "Mr. Smith, you don't know my people. They don't pay but let the bill grow big and bigger and don-a like-a to be asked for money."

"Oh, pshaw... tell them you have to have it. If they don't pay tell the mining company to hold it out of their wages. That's the way here, Tony."

"But, Mr. Smith, they get mad."

"How much money do they owe you?"

"Jus four, five big bills. If I could get those money I could pay my bill."

"If they don't pay you tell them you'll attach their wages and they'll pay."

"Well, I'll try but you don't know my people. If anything go wrong Mr. Smith, you look after Rita? She going to have a little baby not long now." Rita was his little wife whom he had married a short year before. Papa smiled, "Yes, but you'll be alright Tony," and he turned to attend to a customer.

The month had nearly passed when Papa went on a business trip for a few days. One of the men was sweeping out the store before it was time to open up when Tony dashed in, saying, "Where Mr. Smith?"

"Why he's in the valley and will not be home until tonight."

"Tell him he keep his promise and I go home."

Shortly after seven the phone rang. Tony had been found dead in the alley near his home with thirteen stiletto marks in his back. He had tried to take care of his own business. It was never proven who did the deed, but one man was sent to the penitentiary for six years. The gang was against the individual, the old country vendetta.

One woman, a leader among the Italians, shocked my aunt terribly one day. Her husband had been killed in the mine the day before and she came into my Aunt's millinery shop to buy a black bonnet and veil "like American lady wear" to wear to the funeral. My aunt fitted her out in grand style. She then turned, "You take back Monday? Me buy nice hat, lots roses, I get married then." To my aunt, the woman appeared sacrilegious, but in her country, when a man went into the swamps to work, he provided for his family by picking out a successor who agreed to provide for his family at his death. The dead husband had arranged for a friend to marry his widow. Sometimes three or four prospective husbands lived in the same house in perfect harmony and in good fellowship. As they grew up, the children knew no difference in fathers other than they might carry different names.

The second husband, the dead man's friend, came into Papa's store and picked out the finest coffin available. The funeral was in their house, I believe, but I cannot be sure. As soon as the religious ceremonies were over, the procession formed for the graveyard. Three full bands led the procession, followed by the Italian Organization or Lodge members in full regalia. The Austrian-Hungarian Organization followed after the Lodge, trailed by what appeared to be all of the hacks from our town.

The procession extended from the extreme western boundary of town, down through Main Street, and almost to the cemetery on South Hill, a mile-long. With measured tread they marched, and I watched the grand parade from our doorway. On their return, instead of the Dead March, they came down the hill with rollicking music, and, at the bank, broke ranks and disbanded into the saloons where set-up drinks were served to everyone who wished to join the celebration.

True to her promise, the widow came into Aunty's shop the next day and bought the "So buful hat with roses" and said, when Aunty refused to take back the widow's bonnet, "Oh, well, me keep for next time."

The first of the month, the husband's friend paid the funeral bill to Papa, and seeing two comic chromos, pointed to them, demanding: "Give me wedding present." Papa said, "You just married?"

"Oh, yes... Me marry Mrs. R_____ Sunday."

Mrs. R_____ was his friend's widow. Papa gave him the pictures and he walked out of the store carrying one under each arm, as proud as if they had been great paintings.

These immigrants were simple folk and grew into fine American citizens. This particular group was from Corsica. For many years, the old feuds, old customs, secret organizations, vendettas, and even murders prevailed. Today their children and children's children are among the honored citizens of the communities in which they live. Parents who could neither read nor write now have grandchildren that are college graduates. Out of the swamps and the slums of the cities of Italy, in three generations, they have taken their places among the high defenders of their America.

This same lady married her third husband before we left the Hills. Her children became well-educated and outstanding citizens. They quickly assimilated American ways and married into English and American families, becoming truly American citizens.

Professor Jean Baptiste Favario's family was an outstanding Italian family. His wife was a street singer from Rome and, I understand, had a wonderfully sweet voice. His daughter sang in many early day entertainments. Professor Favario was highly respected and gave lessons to young people of all the Belt towns. His daughters' families now hold positions of trust in the city and county. They have lived the old saying, "When in Rome, do as Rome does." or "When in America, be truly American."

Each of the non-English speaking elements had their counsels, as they were called. These men met new arrivals or saw that someone met them when they got off the stage. They assisted in their finding a home and work and directed them in their general life until they were well established and could go it alone.

For the Italians, two other men who stand out distinctly in my memory were Tony Bertolero and Stephen Zerega, the Italian Counsel.

Early to settle in Lead were Austrian men who came usually in groups of six or more. Their counsels would meet them and usher them over to our store where they would buy a good spring mattress, a bedstead, pillows and blankets, a small kitchen stove, kitchen table and two chairs, a large kettle and long-handled spoon, and a large porcelain bowl. With this equipment, they set up housekeeping in one room somewhere in the Austrian neighborhood. One of the members of the Austrian Counsel I remember was Antone Jurich.

The Austrians were primarily Roman Catholics, and the church was the central feature of their community. They lived clustered together. The Italians likewise had their little group, but the Hungarians were mixed more or less with the Austrians. They were quite clannish in a way and each group had its own trading places, its own organizations, and customs.

The same could be said of the English-speaking groups who, in those days, attended the Methodist and Congregational churches and later the Episcopal.

Finnish elements settled mostly in the old Washington neighborhood and the Scandinavians, less segregated, mingled with the English-speaking peoples of the town and adopted their modes of life. The miners worked three shifts of eight hours each. There was always a job awaiting the newcomers, and two of them would go to work at night while two would see the sights and two go to bed. When the night workers came off work, they went to bed, and the two in bed woke up, did their chores, and saw the town while the other two went to their work. So the wheel went round, two in bed, two attending to home duties and town, and two at work. When the paycheck came, most of it was sent back to the old country, with the workers putting aside only enough for a meager existence.

When they saved sufficient money to bring the family over, they obtained a small house for their arrival. The men came into the store with such pride, and introduced their wives. I watched them draw out the old stocking, in lieu of a purse, and pay for the furnishings of their new home in America. The men worked as common laborers in the mine almost entirely, and one saw very little of them in a business way as the women handled most of the business end of family life.

The children started school at once and, as a rule, were excellent students. They quickly picked up the many languages spoken in the community. Later, when I was teaching in Lead, I had one student in the fifth grade who, at the age of 14, spoke twelve different languages. During World War I, he was used as an intelligence man by the government. Those who knew him told me that he perfectly spoke eighteen different languages. Today, I understand he holds a high position of trust within the government in the Secret Service department.

One summer I was ill and could not return until late fall to my studies in Wichita, so I arranged to study advanced algebra under the Lead Principal after school was dismissed. Quite often pupils were kept after school, and one boy named Steve saw me working over my lessons. One problem caused me some trouble. The Professor was doing the routine work, as multiplication, and so on, etc., and I could not solve it. Finally, I discovered a mistake in multiplication that the Professor had made. Steve was kept after school that night and saw the event.

Later, he wanted to quit school and his father would not let him. Steve said he could not learn anything from the professor, and his father came back with, "If Sadie Smith can, you can." Quick as a flash he came back with, "And she can teach him. He makes mistakes and she shows him." His father came to us for advice and we had quite a time straightening the young man out, but he continued his education.

In politics, these immigrants took an active part in the elections, the bosses, or consuls, voting the whole delegation whether they were naturalized or not. I remember well, Papa ran for mayor of Lead and the Austrian Consul came to him. "Mr. Smith, how much you give me Austrian vote?" Papa said, "Not a dime," and the answer came in a very humble voice, "I so sorry, I like you but so and so give $400. I guess I have to vote for he, but I like you, Mr. Smith. You can no make it more?" Papa lost by six votes.

The main issue, however, was to compel the mining company to bear its share in school taxes; it decided the vote by a very small majority. Papa was Treasurer of the School District for years and, having instigated that fight, he collected the first school taxes from the Homestake Company. Politics were naturally ruled by the Homestake Company for years and, as I have said before, the miners voted whether they were naturalized or not, and the mine bosses cast the votes of the foreigners.

I well remember the year women could vote on school matters. My mother took out her naturalization papers, for she was born in England, and I, a teacher then, had my watch taxed so I could vote. They had become a little more particular about naturalization by that time and were challenging votes.

One of the dominant features of those early days was the feud. Many of the Corsicans, Italians, Austrians, and Irish brought their feuds from the old country and had secret organizations including the Mafia, Facisti, Clanna Gael, Molly Maquires, and many others. Peace-loving people kept their tongues quiet and their noses out of their neighbor's business. We knew nothing and saw less and talked not at all if we valued our lives and our property. Many a murder went down in history as unsolved because one did not dare probe too closely into the facts, and many an accident or suicide was in reality a murder. The truth dared not be divulged by friends, or by undertaker, for fear of more deaths from the same source. Many men met death because they knew too much and could not keep their mouths shut.

The first secret organizations I became aware of were the Molly Maguires and Clanna Gael. These secret Irish organizations preyed upon English boys, especially on St. Patrick's Day. An Irish protestant who wore the orange ribbon on that day was hardly safe from molestation and at least two lost their lives.

One St. Patrick's Day, while I was playing in front of my Aunt's door, I noticed two men walking down the street on the opposite side. Just as they got to the Opera House stairway, they stopped. One man struck a match and dropped it, and stepped back by the wall. At that instant a shot was fired, and his companion dropped dead at his feet. The one was an Irishman and wore a shamrock, and the companion, a little Englishman, had an orange bow in his buttonhole. No one ever found out why it was done, or who did it, but I shut my eyes today and see again the crumpled body. The Englishman had been put on the spot and shot in the back. I was quickly brought inside the house by my mother, and was told that I must never tell what I saw. But I heard my uncle whisper under his breath, "Molly McGuire" as he closed the door behind me. The Irishman never served a day for his crime.

The Mafia was a Sicilian organization brought over by the Italians. Feuds of all kinds took place among the Austrian and Italian elements that they settled among themselves. Several murders could be traced to that source but only three brought court convictions.

The first case was in Deadwood about the time we arrived in the Hills but the murderers, an Italian and his wife, were never punished. Men were killed in crowded assemblies and no one ever heard a shot or saw the victim stabbed. They only knew that a man was killed and died in their midst. For instance, a man was shot in a boarding house with anywhere from sixteen to twenty people present. Yet, no one heard the shot or saw the deed done. The man was dead, and the rest of the world carried on.

The case of the young Austrian boy, which I related, brought a six year prison term to one man, though it was never proven that he was one of the murderers. Another case occurred openly in a saloon, but he too received a very short prison sentence. The final was the Black Hand attempt at kidnapping the Grier children, but was "nipped in the bud" by local officials and seemed to end the activities of the organizations.

Italians and Austrians brought their secret hates and life activities with them to this country in those early days, but American ideals and education won out as they learned what American freedom and life meant to a community. Today, none are more loyal to their America than the second generations of those once despised and really feared immigrants who found new homes in the Black Hills.

One day, a much-respected little Englishman was killed in the mine when he was sent in alone by his Irish boss to do a dangerous job. The boss's friend should have been with him. The next day, the Englishman's friend accused the boss of deliberately sending his friend into danger. When he got off work, the boss nerved himself with a revolver and several glasses of whiskey and tailed the English boy from place to place till he found him in a saloon surrounded by a crowd of would-be protectors. Reaching over the heads of the crowd, he shot the young fellow, and then dared them to arrest him. Everyone including the Sheriff left while he walked the main street brandishing his gun. Just as he passed Papa's store door, Papa made a leap for him from behind, got possession of his gun and pinned his arms behind him. Many were ready to help then and the sheriff arrested him and took him to Deadwood and put him in jail.

He was tried and sentenced to six years in the Pierre penitentiary. As he left the courtroom, he swore he would get Papa when he got out. He served his time and then planned to head to Lead with the boast that he was going to get his man. He went into a saloon while waiting for his train at Pierre, took several glasses of whiskey, got into a quarrel with the bartender and was killed.

OUR TRIP TO WICHITA

In 1885, at the age of eleven, I took my last overland ride by buckboard and a three-seated hack to Sydney, Nebraska. The Northwestern Railroad was in process of being built to Deadwood but was not yet finished that summer. Owing to a childhood injury, Mother was losing her sight in one eye. Mother and Papa talked of moving to Wichita, Kansas, where Aunt Sarah and Uncle Jack Bragg had settled two years before. Mother and I were to go ahead. She would have her eye operated on, and I would be put in school. Papa would sell the store and arrive later.

Dr. Elmore Munsell was Mother's doctor, and he had his office in the same building as Dr. John Terrill, a throat specialist. Since I had a bad throat due to accidentally drinking a solution of Lewis Lye when I was two years old, Dr. Terrill looked after me while Dr. Munsell looked after Mother.

The Munsell's home was a wonderful place for they had such delightful birds. Mrs. Addie Munsell's red birds and mockingbirds were so tame that they were allowed to fly around the glassed-in porch. One mockingbird would sit on top of the piano and warble the tunes that Mrs. Munsell played. When she was through she gave the bird some tidbits and it would fly out into the glass-enclosed porch among the oleanders that she had planted in tubs.

Mother's operation was a success. I was placed in school and we settled into life in Kansas with the pet mockingbird named "Dick" that Mrs. Munsell gave us. Dick became a great pet when we were in Wichita but never a singer because we did not know how to train him. Later, Papa said that he could not sell the store and told us to return to the Hills when school was out.

Business was very good that winter and one could hardly blame Papa for not wanting to leave Lead at that time. We went back expecting to move later. As a child, I thought that trip back to be really exciting; although, in reality it was very prosaic.

Papa had opened a branch store in Buffalo Gap and placed his father in charge. Papa was expected to meet us in Buffalo Gap. We bought our tickets in Wichita, and Mother and I started out, expecting to make the trip in comfort on the new rail line. Forty miles from the Gap, we were transferred to a construction train, still expecting to reach the end of the journey by railroad. We had not gone many miles when a friend of ours asked Mother if Papa was going to meet us at "the end of the line." For the first time, Mother learned that the "end of the line" was twenty miles from Buffalo Gap.

There was no going back until morning and no place to stay at the end of the line. By keeping her ears open, Mother heard a man say: "The boys will meet us at the end of the line and take us in." Mother immediately stepped up to them and asked if they were traveling to Buffalo Gap. They answered, "Yes, Ma'am," and Mother asked if they could make room for herself and her little girl. The men were quite taken aback, and stammered: "We'll ask the Boss."

A somewhat lengthy talk took place and finally the Boss came over to Mother, and, in a very gentlemanly manner, replied that some of his men were expected to meet them with a spring wagon and they would make room for us. Mother was delighted.

The arrangement had hardly been completed before we stopped at a siding. One of the head construction men whom we knew quite well got on the train. He was surprised to see Mother and asked immediately if S.R., as Papa was usually called, was going to meet us or if he knew we were on the train? Mother said, "No," and explained the plan of getting to "The Gap."

Our friend let out a whistle and said, "Do you know who you have engaged to take you there?" Mother shook her head. "Doc Middleton is a notorious outlaw and horse thief! Last night his young nephew was shot in one of the saloons at the Gap. It is reported he and his outlaws are on their way to shoot up the town. That's who you've engaged to take you."

Our Trip to Wichita

The next question was what to do? Our friend said: "Go with him and know nothing. Nothing will happen before you reach Buffalo Gap." We went and were never treated better. When we reached Buffalo Gap, Doc Middleton drove at once to the store and unloaded us. He then went to the undertaking room to see the body of his nephew. There, Doc Middleton told Papa, "Mr. Smith, I want no trouble, but I want to know how it happened. If it was a fair fight, that is all. I have a wife and a little boy and if the law will let me, I'm going straight." He got a straight answer. The boy was in the wrong. After the funeral the next morning, Doc Middleton paid the expenses, and he and his men went back to their ranch without making any trouble. That ride always stands out as a highlight in my life.

A few days later, we took the stage, a three-seated open hack from Buffalo Gap to Deadwood. As a storm came up on the way, we stayed at a ranch house all night. When we stopped at this house, the driver asked if they could give us supper and put us up for the night. They were Germans - an old man, his wife, his daughter, and son-in-law with their baby.

The house was a large, square-framed building with two stories, but without partitions except studding and only a ladder by which to reach the second floor. Homemade patchwork quilts were nailed up for partitions, and straw ticks were laid on the floor for beds. We stayed all night and had the best supper I ever ate, including ham, eggs, fried potatoes, the best creamed cabbage I ever tasted, salt rising bread, and dried applesauce. We ended late, and hardly touched the straw ticks before we were sound asleep.

The next morning, the horses were well-rested so we drove on to Deadwood and Lead. This turned out to be my last stagecoach ride. As I relate later, when I went back to school in Wichita in the fall of 1887, I went the whole way in a Pullman Coach to Kansas City, and, changing there, to Wichita. Thus the old frontier mode of travel was left behind.

Although Papa had promised to sell the store and move to Wichita to be with us, Mother learned that he never intended to leave Lead. Instead, he opened stores in Deadwood and Buffalo Gap against Mother's advice while we were away.

SMITH FURNITURE COMPANY REORGANIZED

W hen Mother found that Papa had no intention of leaving the Black Hills or selling out, she began to exert her influence about the store. Hutch Stevens, Peter Stevens, L. A. Fell, Joe Meade, and others were brought into the store. Papa hired a few girls but Mother demanded their dismissal at once, so they went.

About that time, Papa talked of a new and larger store building and decided to use some men who owed him money. Most of these men owed undertaking bills but were out of work. By hiring and paying them half of their wages, and applying the other half on their debt, the men could live and yet pay their bills. These men did not belong to the union and as they were really unskilled workmen, they were not paid union wages. As a result, the union objected.

Papa became angry at their interference and told them, "He'd see them in hell before he would let the men join their union." The result was a boycott against the store. Mother tried to get Papa to allow the men to join if they wished and to pay them union wages, but he swore that no man was going to tell him how to run his business. He said that he would lay the brick himself before hiring a union man. During the summer, the brick walls were gradually erected around the old frame structure and as one part of the new building finished the old part was torn down. So business went on in the original location.

At this time, Papa was having a hard time finding money to pay his bills. Union men were not paying him what they owed nor were they buying from him. He needed cash badly and the bank refused to loan him money. Mother finally stepped into the breach and borrowed the money from a friend on her own note, with the understanding that she was never to let it be known where the money came from. She never told anyone except Hutch Stevens, who helped her gradually collect the money to pay that note. He was her loyal supporter during those trying times.

When the union saw they could not force the issue and the women wanted things they could not get elsewhere, the boycott was gradually broken by the women, and they bought with cash. Thus, Mother had again saved the business. The S.R. Smith Furniture and Undertaking Company was incorporated with S.R. Smith President and Elizabeth Smith Vice President. The company was simply a subterfuge, for the stock was owned entirely by Papa. Mr. Stevens acted as Treasurer and Manager but Papa was always the boss. The arrangement did provide an "out" in handling the union question.

This transformation of business arrangements took place over several years, for Papa was not easily swayed from his own chosen plans. Affairs were not always pleasant at home in these years, but money was coming in in good shape. Papa belonged to almost all the lodges in the town, but I began to notice that he was excluded from the town's social life. While mother and I were invited to all the best homes, when men were included very few invitations were issued to Mother and Papa.

Mother endured all the hardships with her chin up. Eventually, Papa and Mother left Lead and spent their last years in California while some of Papa's family continued to bleed them financially.

The Stevens Brothers (left to right) Peter, Charles & Hutch

(EDITOR'S NOTE: Sadie was so fond of Hutch Stevens that she named her second son after him. Hutch Stevens died on December 6, 1907, from an accidental fall while hunting sage hens in Nevada where he was living at the time. He is buried in the Mount Olivet Cemetery in Salt Lake City, Utah.)

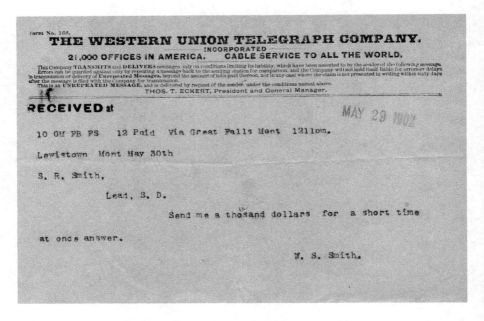

(EDITOR'S NOTE: Among Sadie's original manuscript and papers was a Western Union Telegram sent to S.R. Smith on May 30th, 1902, from Lewistown, Montana. The telegram reads, "S.R. Smith, Lead, S.D. 'Send me a thousand dollars for a short time at once answer.' W.S. Smith.")

PART V

Later Years

MY TEENAGE YEARS

Sarah Elizabeth's High School Graduation
picture taken in spring 1891

September 1887 found Mother and me heading back to Wichita so
I could enter high school. Mother bought a half fare ticket for me
but did not present it until we got to Newton, Kansas, for the conductor never
asked for it. At that time, a child rode without pay until she was seven. None
of the conductors had considered me older than seven because I was so small.

When I went to take my examinations for entrance to the high school, the teachers and principal smiled very knowingly until I passed the first-year test. Mother then asked to enter me in the second year and the mathematics teacher snapped, "That baby? Why she isn't over ten years old." Mother said, "Thirteen," and the teacher snapped back, "She don't look it."

Unfortunately, I had never taken Latin, commercial arithmetic, or bookkeeping, so I entered the first year of high school taking the first two subjects plus grammar, history, and physiology, in which I gloried and ended with a 100% grade. Latin was a different story, for I failed that flat.

During this same time, I attended the Sickner Conservatory where at the end of the first semester I had my lesson book slammed shut and was told to go home and practice. Unknown to my teacher, I could not see the notes. I told my mother what had happened. She took me at once to an oculist who fitted me with glasses. I was told I should have been wearing them all my life. Needless to say, glasses changed my whole outlook on life mentally as well as physically.

That year, due to my earlier back injury, a heavy back brace was added to my equipment. With no more eye or back strain, I became quite a normal child. Mother returned to Lead and I lived with my Aunt Sarah and Uncle Jack Bragg. I was a happy, healthy, carefree, young lady and grew like a weed. I became popular with my schoolmates, although I always played with the younger children in the grade school that was next to the high school, instead of walking sedately with the high school girls or chumming with the high school boys during the noon hour.

When I returned to Lead for the summer after my freshman year, I expected to find a large box that held my twenty-one dolls and other treasured playthings, with the lid nailed down, waiting where I had left it. The box was missing and the only thing that was left was the disfigured wax bride that had been the desire of all the children the Christmas I had received it. Papa had put it on the shelf behind the stove. When the fire was built, the heat melted the wax so that it ran down over her beautiful bridal costume making her a woebegone looking corpse. Heartbroken, I took her down and went into my room where I, a girl of fourteen, could cry my eyes out and no one would be the wiser. My childhood was destroyed that day for it taught me to put my trust in no one.

Despite my loss, my four years of high school were happy. Graduating in 1891, I returned to Lead to take my place as a third-grade teacher at the age of 17. I taught in the same schoolhouse building where I had begun school.

Before I finished at Wichita High School, our little old house on the hill had been replaced with a more pretentious house a few blocks away. In our new modern house on Addie Street, the young elite of the town gathered for their old-time parties after I returned to Lead. The group of young people was generally the same. Being the largest, our home seemed to be the headquarters.

Our group included the Hazen girls, the two Maudes (Faust and Miller), Harry and Josie Salmon, Charlie Coolidge, and Ed Trevaskis and always Hutch and Peter Stevens as well as me. Peter played the cornet and was in much demand in the bands. Most of the girls played the piano in a half-hearted way. Music filled many of the pauses between the old-time games.

Hutch Stevens, who worked with Papa, was my bodyguard at all times, for I was never allowed to go anywhere without someone to see that I got home safely. I was always chaperoned when I went out in the evening, either by my own folks or some married couple until I was eighteen. Mother always knew I was well looked after if Hutch took me. Hutch was one of the finest characters I ever met, and while much older than the rest of the crowd, he was always accepted.

When we were eighteen, Maude Miller and I gave our "Coming Out Party." Up to that time we had not gone with young men except as a group and chaperoned by some of our parents. The party was held at my home on Valentine's evening. Sixty invitations were issued, for thirty girls and thirty boys. Ruby and George (Maude's younger sister and brother) dressed as a fairy princess and prince, stood at the door to meet the guests and to give them rosettes of baby ribbon of different colors. Each boy found his partner by the rosette matching his own.

During the evening, we played "Change Cities" (also known as "Traveling,") "Spin the Plate," "Charades," and other party games. At midnight, we were served supper in the dining room. Then we all gathered around the piano for music, and the guests gradually left for home.

Another outstanding social time was at Dr. Freeman's. The Hazen sisters, cousins of Harriet Freeman, hosted a dance. Booths were fixed up representing different nationalities. Friends of the Hazen girls, dressed in appropriate costumes, served refreshments from the booths. They made a colorful and dashing appearance.

Wichita, Kansas
April 6th, 1891

Dear Papa,

I have received your welcome letter today also
the check but as I did not get through with my
Chemistry Examination till after three o'clock I did
not get it cashed today.

You asked what I needed for Commencement.
Well, I will need everything from slippers to the
ruche for my neck. I will see this week what the silk
for a dress would cost. I will get my gloves this week
so as to use them when I am confirmed too.

Hot! Oh it is so hot today. I am nearly melted
with all my heavy winter things on.

The violets and wild pansies are all in bloom
today and the south side of the walk is just purple
with buds and blossoms.

We are getting six and seven eggs a day.

Uncle Jack has his potatoes and corn in and the
ground is cracking all over the radish bed. We had
young onions for supper Saturday evening.

I got 93% in my final in Chemistry and it makes
me feel repaid for my hard work but I must not
crow too soon for I have four more to take in it and
day after tomorrow I have one of my finals in
Mental Philosophy.

I see by Mamma's letters that little Nora Gregory
is staying with you. How is her mama getting
along?

The peach and pear trees are all in bud and begin to look so pretty. The worst thing is the flies, bees and bugs are getting quite thick. There are about a half a dozen bees buzzing about in the yard.

Uncle Jack is making himself a pair of boots.

There are to be thirty confirmed a week from Sunday.

I have just gone through the drill with my Indian clubs and dumbbells and it makes me sweat. You will be surprised when you see what I can do with three pounds in each hand.

Aunt Sarah has just gotten back from the hot house and she has brought some lovely verbenas and a little rose bush. She is going to get out all the plants this week I think.

Mamma said she wrote on March the first but I got one dated April the first so she did not make the mistake.

Well, supper is ready so I will quit for this time. Thanks for your nice letter and the increase in my allowance.

Your loving daughter,
Sadie E. Smith

1745 N. Jackson Ave.
Wichita, Kansas

April 30, 1891

Dear Papa,

I am so tired tonight that I can hardly keep my eyes open. I got my Caesar grade today and they are 95, 96, 99 (85, 80)% making my final average in Caesar 87%.

That makes my grades about as follows Geometry 93, Cicero 91, Caesar 87, Chemistry 95, Mental Philosopy 85, Virgil I do not know anything about only that I have got 2 in it every month making between 90 and 95 but examinations always take me down for I get so excited I cannot do a thing anymore for I know so much depends on them although there is not near so much as there used to be.

O', Papa, please come and bring Mamma. If you are not here it will take half the pleasure from graduating away.

I cannot keep awake so I shall have to close now. With love to yourself and Mamma.

I am your loving daughter,
Sadie E. Smith

Sadie's Accounting for Allowance

Date		Debit	Deposit
April 1	Amount Moved		$13.25
April 6	By Cash		40.00
April 6	to Board	10.00	
April 6	to Interest	10.00	
April 6	to Borrowed Money	5.25	
April 6	to Shoes	4.00	
April 6	to Elocution books	.50	
April 6	to Stamps	.10	
April 6	to Car tickets	1.50	
April 9	to Autograph Album	.10	
April 9	to Pencil (.05) & book (.25)	.30	
April 9	to Muslin & buttons	.41	
April 10	to Class Flowers & Tree	.35	
April 10	to Ribbon	.35	
April 11	to Elocution & car fare	1.10	
April 12	to Church, car fare, paper & S.S.	.25	
April 13	to Linen	.69	
April 13	to Agnes support	.25	
April 14	to Under vests	1.25	
April 16	to Stamps & envelopes	.14	
April 18	to Dressmaker	.75	
April 18	to Gloves	1.00	
April 18	to Elocution 1/2 lesson	.50	
April 19	to Sunday School	.25	
April 30	to Oar	.50	
April 30	to Borrowed money	12.79	

TEACHING SCHOOL IN LEAD
& VASSAR COLLEGE

At the age of thirteen, I had taken my first county examination for teaching. Sue J. Neal issued my first certificate. Because of my age and size, Miss Neal did not know what to do with me. Finally, she issued my first-grade certificate with my grades, and wrote in after the word "qualified" "in all save age."

After I graduated from high school in Wichita, Kansas, in 1891, I returned to Lead as the third-grade teacher in the school that I had attended when it first opened. Lead had progressed to grades by that time and had acquired a high school. Beginning September 1, 1891, or at the expiration of their certificate held at that time, the Lead School Board required all school teachers to hold a first-grade certificate, with the intent to prevent hiring inexperienced teachers. While I had never taught under my old first-grade certificate, according to the law, that certificate permitted me to teach the third grade.

The average age of my students was nine years. I had one very large girl who had come in from a wood camp. She was a good student but had no previous opportunity to attend school. One of my male students that year, Alfred H. Ludin, later won a name for himself in law. He attended Lead High School and then the University of Nebraska. He was an outstanding young man and settled in Seattle. His university and his state have honored him and his name goes down in history as a Black Hills pinecone that developed into a sturdy tree casting its shadow into three states.

I look back with pride especially on the results of my work that first year. Of those forty-two children, most knew little of the better things in life, and some even were from the dregs of humanity. Yet today I feel that all were made better by our teacher-student relationship.

The second year, a larger percentage came from better homes but, strangely, did not have the outstanding development of individuals that characterized my first group. During the two years I taught the third grade, I saved fifty dollars each month out of my wages. Mother invested this money for me and said that at the end of the second year when school closed, funds were sufficient for my first year's tuition at Vassar College with an income of twenty-five dollars a month for expenses.

During my second year as a teacher, I had a difficult time writing my lesson plans and attending all the social functions given in my honor. By the end of that year, owing to a near nervous breakdown, the doctor ordered that I be sent to a lower altitude. Thus, I spent the summer in Wichita before entering college in Poughkeepsie, New York, where I paid my own way entirely.

I met Mother in Chicago for a week at the 1893 Exposition and then went on to Vassar College. At that point, storm clouds began to form on the horizon for Mother. Papa had become a prosperous businessman and some of his people back in Minnesota began to think him a millionaire. They were under the impression that he was sending me to college. They also noted that he had built the finest home in Lead and thus, it was time he did something for his poor relatives.

How all the information had filtered back to Minnesota no one knew, unless it came from Papa's father who was tinged with hate for the "china doll" that Papa had married. At the time, Papa's younger brother and an older brother along with his family had moved from Montana to Lead and were receiving support from Papa. They may have contributed to the insinuations and lies. Mother's life became almost unbearable.

Finally, Papa sent his brother back to Montana and set him up in business there. Another brother was embroiled in legal difficulties and Papa sent him the money to free himself. The younger brother was killed in Denver, and Papa settled his bills, at which point Mother thought she might have some peace. During this time, however, Papa's sister Hattie wanted assistance to send her twin daughters to college. She used the argument that since he was sending his wife's girl to college, he should also consider his own "blood."

But was he sending me? I had taught for two years and paid for all of my tuition and college expenses except for my room and board. Papa paid for that. I had worked Saturdays, evenings, and holidays in the store as a cashier, demonstrating pianos and clerking. Mother and I silenced the tongues of Papa's family on that score.

Due to my childhood back injury, I gradually developed a temporary paralysis of my motor nerves while at Vassar College which almost compelled me to return home before Christmas. With grit and persistent exercises in swimming, I stuck the year out. While at Vassar, I was not physically able to carry a full workload due to poor health.

After returning home from Vassar, social affairs reached a climax. A prominent couple hosted a large party, with all the elite of Deadwood and Lead invited. An invitation was issued to me and I was asked to attend with a certain gentleman and his wife, but Mother and Papa were not invited. They were the only couple left out in our group of friends. I refused the invitation, resenting the slight to Mother and Papa. But Papa insisted that I would go or not return to school in the fall. I did not go to the party, for I also had a stubborn streak.

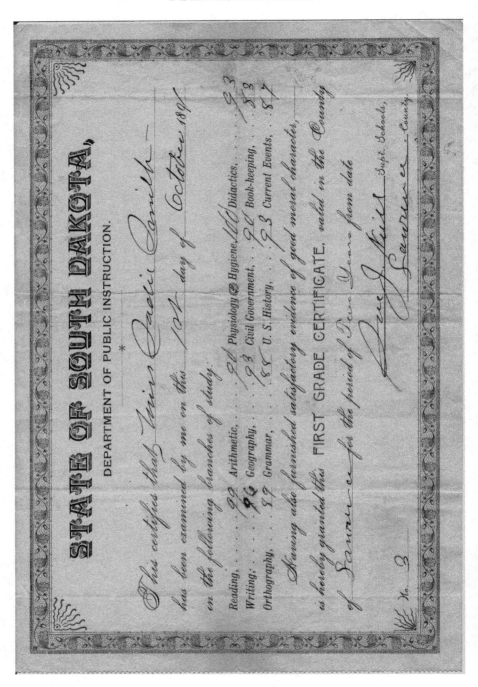

First Grade Certificate that allowed Sadie to teach upon graduation from high school. Her salary was $65 per month for 10 months. After two years, she enrolled in Vassar College in 1893.

VASSAR COLLEGE
Poughkeepsie, N.Y.

Wednesday, Oct. 18th, 1893

Dear Papa,

Your most welcome letter was received yesterday also the draft which the treasurer of the college cashed for me.

Yes, Mamma left for New York Monday and left there this morning at 9:30. She did not stop on her way back but went straight through. She ordered the font in New York and writes that it is very much nicer than she expected it would be from the cut we had of it. I only hope the folks in Lead will like it.

I was sorry to hear that Nip was dead and know you must miss him very much. When I came away I said I should never see him again, poor little fellow I am glad he is out of his pain and glad he died at home for I was so afraid that he would be on the street and we would never know what had become of him.

The college is five stories high and is built in three divisions connected by long arms in which are a row of bedrooms and a broad hallway. The central tower as it is called has the recitation rooms, parlors, dining room, chapel, President's rooms and library. The north and south towers are principally bedrooms but on the fourth floor, south tower is the Doctor's rooms and the Infirmary. To the south and a little back of the main building

are the Hot-house, and Art and Music Halls.
Directly south is the skating parlor and another
larger three-story building that I do not know the
name of. To the north and a little to the front is
Strong Hall where the girls room and have their
meals. This building has four floors and
accommodates one hundred and fifteen students.
North and back of the main building are the
Observatory, Gymnasium and Tennis Courts and
flower gardens.

The grounds are beautiful but I was greatly
disappointed in the buildings, they are of brick
with no decorations at all. The Library and
Entrance is very handsome but those are the only
parts of the college that are pretty.

The college employs seventy-four girls besides all
the male help they are compelled to have. They
have two small dining rooms holding from twelve
to sixteen and two large ones holding one hundred
and fifteen and four hundred. The chapel is
arranged much like a theater and has the main
floor and the gallery. All the regular students sit
downstairs but the Specials sit in the gallery. The
gallery is much pleasanter than where the
Freshman sit so the girls come up in the gallery as
often as they are able.

My seat is right in front of the stage but there is
one seat in front of me. Of course, I am in the
gallery and right near the large doors. The seats
on the main floor are all on a level but in the

gallery they are raised each row eight inches higher than the row in front. The chapel will hold several hundred I think: that is there are about seven hundred seats.

Everyone here seems very pleasant and friendly. One of the sophomores a Miss Florence Knight took me to a reception given by the Young Women's Christian Association and made it very pleasant. I got an invitation also from a Miss Childs but of course could not go with both.

I hope that business has brightened up this time for I know how you are when it is dull.

I shall close now with love to yourself and kind regards to the rest.

Your loving daughter,
Sadie E. Smith

UNIVERSITY OF NEBRASKA
& TEACHING IN LEAD

Photos of Sarah Elizabeth from the University of Nebraska (1894-1898)

W hen September 1894 came, I still had sufficient funds to enter the Midwestern college of my choice, the University of Nebraska in Lincoln. Vassar College had been Mother's choice, but I found no joy there as a wild, free, laughing, untamed, mining camp girl. Even my clothes were not like those of the other girls, and I had no business attending an Eastern college. I made my own formal out of silk wool for the outstanding party of the year. The art professor told me that it was the most artistic in its simplicity that evening.

I could not return to the pain and loneliness of another year. So, pleading my health, I persuaded Mother to let me parallel my course for one year at another college. This was the first time in my life that I stood up to my Mother and made my own decision. I had my twenty-five-dollar monthly income from Mother's investment, but I lacked the funds to pay for all of my expenses.

Papa even refused to pay the railroad fare to the University of Nebraska. A friend finally offered to loan me the money and I made my plans to leave. When Papa saw that I had outwitted him, he suggested a railway pass but I would not ask for it. Mother obtained passes for the two of us and accompanied me to the college from which I graduated.

With my time at the Eastern college behind me, I entered a new life at a Midwestern school. The first half of the year was still dictated. I had to study languages and I loved science and literature. I wanted to be a doctor but knew I must be a teacher. Mathematics came easily to me, so I wanted to specialize in that. Mathematics teachers were hard to find, thus assuring me of a position.

I mapped out my life, away from the daily surveillance of my every act by Mother. As the days and weeks and years rolled around, I became increasingly independent. Much of the student body considered me proud and haughty, yet for some reason, I was liked. I was liked for myself and I picked my own associates. The status of poor or rich made no difference to me. If I liked a person, I went with them, without anyone there to say, "No."

In the fall of 1895, my second year at the University of Nebraska, Papa was delivering some furniture after closing hours. On his return home, he was thrown from the delivery wagon seat and struck the back of his head on a stone along the side of the road, resulting in a brain concussion. For days, his life hung in the balance. His recovery, the doctors claimed, was due to the fact that he had never used alcohol or tobacco and his blood was free from disease.

After this accident, his disposition changed. He became suspicious of everyone and imagined injuries where injuries were not intended. He became very selfish and revengeful if his wishes were thwarted. As such, his business success began to diminish and Mother again had to step in and save the day. Papa began to resent my mother's watchfulness and that made life hard for her.

Had it not been for the clerks, Mother would not have been able to keep the business. The loyalty of Hutch Stevens and his brother Peter kept the business going in spite of Papa's eccentricities. I shall always think that injury caused almost a complete change of character in the man. He forgot how much he owed Mother. Had it not been for Hutch and me, at times he almost refused to support her. Instead, he would have turned everything over to the members of his family who had even refused him care when he was ill.

He was a man who wanted to be the only one in someone's life. Starved for love as a child, starved for the fulfillment of almost every ambition in life, he was unwilling to recognize that everyone must cooperate with, accept help from, and give help to others.

I experienced four happy years of freedom at the University of Nebraska. During that time, I struggled against physical handicaps that almost floored me at times. I also found my future mate.

College life was over at last and Mother looked with pride at my diploma. She had accomplished what she had set out to do and now I was hers, perfected, as she wanted me. Mother realized that it was by her untiring efforts that I received a college education. Her will had surmounted all difficulties and she was the one to whom credit was due. She was right, for I doubt if I would ever have endured the hardships.

My last four years of college were grueling for my mother. She spent as much of her time as possible at the store constantly watching the Smith family infiltrations, and the moral life of the community that was constantly threatening the homes around her. She knew not when it would strike her own.

While I was at school, she set up a teaching position for me in Lead upon my graduation. When I said that I would teach for a year and pay back what I had borrowed, and then get married, she did not worry. She could handle that as time went on. Young men with means were brought to our home, and Mother fussed when I refused their invitations, telling them plainly that I expected to be married the following summer.

Mother told me that I was a fool to be so narrow, and she was opposed to my marriage. She felt that my future husband offered nothing, while others could support me as I had been raised. Finally, I told her that if I was satisfied with a little that was my affair and not hers, and nothing she could do or say would alter my determination to marry the man I had chosen. At last Mother accepted the inevitable.

After five years of college work, I returned to Lead schools again, this time as a fifth-grade teacher. I presented the Lead School Board with the State Teachers Certificate I had earned at the University of Nebraska—the first Professional State Teachers Certificate that the School Board had ever seen. The members of the Board, however, demanded a regular certificate like the ones that other teachers had submitted. I sent my certificate to State Superintendent of Public Instruction Frank Crane in Pierre. With a joking comment, he sent me a state certificate that was good for five years. The Certificate was lost in the mail and not received until the day before school opened in the fall. As a result, until the last minute there was a question of whether or not I would be able to qualify.

Even in 1899, in that last year of teaching, Lead, to a great extent, was still in the throes of the Wild West. I taught the fifth grade in what was considered a well-graded school for those days. My oldest pupil in class was fourteen years old. I often wonder what has become of the fifty-two pupils from all walks of life that were enrolled in my class. I had twenty-five double seats in a second-story room in the old school building. The floor was so thin that one could see the studding in places. We had a large iron stove surrounded by a sheet iron shield, and the seats were arranged a row on each side and half a row down the middle. Windows were placed on three sides for light with blackboards on all four sides.

Alongside my own work, two pupils were seated at my teacher's table. As such, my hands were usually full during school hours, especially true as twelve of my pupils were considered the toughs of the town. Only one of them really met a bad end as far as I know.

We had readers, spelling was taken from the reading lesson of the day, and the teacher wrote the words on the blackboard each night after school for the next day. In the same way, number work was placed on the board. We had geography, writing, and language books. I introduced drawing that year as busywork.

Two of the toughs were habitual drinkers and had even, at that age, had attacks of delirium tremens. These children were not bad, but they knew the depths of vice in every form and had no home training to help them. On the other hand, other children came from the finest of homes, some of whom I have traced to positions of trust and power with the highest honors in civil life.

One family was so poor that the older children left school and worked to keep the younger ones in school. Of this family, the youngest child became a professor in an Eastern college, and another, with her husband, went down on the Titanic. I wish I knew where the other two were who were my pupils, for I had four from that family. I heard that Lydia, the youngest, went through high school with an average of ninety-eight percent in all her studies.

My last year in Lead was pretty much the humdrum life of an ordinary teacher. I taught using the old phonetic system that was first introduced in the Lead schools by Professor Kimmel. I introduced a new method of teaching geography that I believe became commonly used later. Teachers usually spent about two hours each day putting the lessons on the blackboard for their pupils to copy and study, and used corporal punishment when necessary.

My last year of college, Papa had loaned me three hundred dollars to complete my courses. After graduation, teaching in Lead allowed me to save enough money to repay him. The first Saturday night after finishing teaching that year, I paid Papa the last dollar of that loan and was married the following Monday. No one can ever realize the pride with which I paid the last dollar to the cashier at the store and took his receipt for "LOAN PAID IN FULL."

Lincoln, Neb.
April 1st, 1895

Dear Papa,

    I wish you could be here this evening for we have just a nice home evening. Outside it is snowing and inside it is so bright and warm.

    It has been so hot for the last week that we were getting out our summer clothes but Saturday it was cloudy and yesterday it rained but today it turned to snow and tonight it is quite cold.

    Today ends our vaction so tomorrow we begin school duties again for nine weeks steady work. We will get out the fifth of June if we do not stay to Commencement and I do not care to as I do not know any of the seniors very well so of course, am not even interested in them. Mamma has been singing all evening and seems so much better then when she first came down. Last night I worked until half past twelve on my notebook but finished it so I have it all ready to hand in tomorrow.

    I see by the papers that you have a new undertaking wagon. What is it like?

    Last week I went downtown on an errand and met a young lady who looked so much like one of the Wichita girls that I spoke about it to Mamma. The next day I met her again so went up and asked if it was Mary Randall and sure enough it was and she has been teaching here all year and attending the Uni. and both wishing to see some of the old girls and yet so near to each other and did not know it. She took dinner and spent the day with me last Friday as she too had vacation last week.

Tomorrow is Election Day here and they expect a great fight. The Republican candidate has come out openly in the papers and said that if he is elected the saloons, gambling dens and etc. shall run openly and tomorrow from ten to eleven and from three to four the W.C.T.U. and all Christian women are going to hold prayer meetings all over the city. Their main meeting is to be held in the town hall.

The Democrats are going to support the Republican candidate but the Populists have another, also the Prohibitionists but you see they are very few in number and there is little to show for either. The University boys have met and declared themselves opposed to the Republican candidate so you see they have taken a good stand.

Papa - please send me twenty-five dollars this week as I shall need it. I must stop now as it is after ten o'clock and I must go to bed.

Goodnight and love to yourself.

Ever your loving daughter,
Sadie E. Smith

Sketch of Sadie & Charlie from the 1898 University of Nebraska Yearbook "Sombrero"

Senior portraits of Sadie and Charlie from the 1898 University of Nebraska
Yearbook "Sombrero"

Yearbook quote from Sarah Elizabeth Smith - "I am so happy when I think
what a perfect husband you will make."
Yearbook quote from Charles William Taylor - "I burn, I pine, I perish, if I
achieve not this young modest girl."

Yearbook poem:

"There was a little girl
And she had a little curl
That hung in the middle of her face;
But she couldn't keep it there,
That little lock of hair,
For Taylor would muss it out of place."

It is Hereby Certified that

Sarah Elizabeth Smith

received the degree of *Bachelor of Arts*

from The University of Nebraska, in the year *1898* and in

addition thereto has successfully completed the requirements of

the University Teachers' Course, consisting of two years of

special and professional study; and is therefore qualified to

teach in the public schools of the State of Nebraska without

examination, in accordance with the provisions of an Act of

the Legislature approved April 12, 1897.

In Testimony Whereof we have hereunto set our hands

and caused the seal of the University

to be hereunto affixed, at Lincoln,

this *ninth* day of *June*

189*8*

Charles H. Morrill

President of the Board of Regents

George E. MacLean

Chancellor of the University

Certificate from the University of Nebraska qualifying Sadie to teach in the public schools of Nebraska without examination. The Lead school board did not accept this certificate until the Department of Public Instruction issued a five year certificate on August 1, 1898.

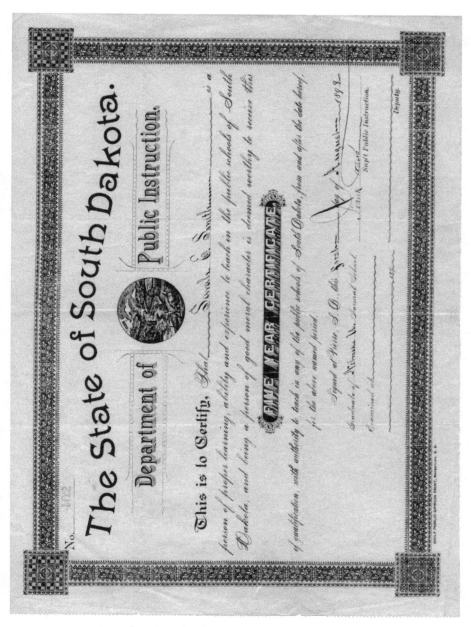

Five year certificate that allowed Sadie to teach school in Lead after graduating from the University of Nebraska.

MY WEDDING &
EARLY MARRIED LIFE

Sarah Elizabeth in her wedding gown

At the end of the school year, my wedding formed the crowning event of my life in the Hills. My wedding was a ceremonial church wedding. I bid my students goodbye, and one little girl put her arms around my neck and said, "My Momma says I must grow up to be like you and not like the bad girls who live at our house." Most parents of the town shared this sentiment, wanting a new life for their children.

In the early days of Lead, a wedding created the excuse for noise and practical jokes of all kinds. Usually the wedding occurred at the bride's home with no more invited guests than could sit down to a bountiful supper. Afterwards, the groom would take his bride to the home he had prepared.

Weddings almost always took place in the evening and the couple would barely be declared husband and wife before a hubbub would commence on tin cans, pots and pans, and even washtubs. Calls were made for the groom to present himself at the door and hand over at least a five-dollar gold piece for drinks and then pass cigars around. By the time my own wedding took place in 1899, some dignity had replaced the heckling sport of shivaree.* Most weddings were held in churches or quietly performed in the home.

My own wedding was quite elaborate, a church wedding with all the accompanying accouterments of today; the finest any girl could desire. I wore a traditional long train and veil, and my husband a tailcoat with striped trousers, for it was a morning wedding. Flower girls and three bridesmaids and ushers joined the five hundred guests in attendance. As the saying goes, it was a beautiful wedding and very churchly. As we left, my pupils of that year showered us with wild rose petals and rice. We received them after the wedding at my home in a very informal reception, where they and the immediate wedding party were the only guests present.

The sun gave promise of a happy life on the third of July 1899, but we pulled out of Lead at 2 o'clock that afternoon in a snowstorm. I stepped out into a life of my own, I thought, but there were always threads at first, then strings, then ropes, woven around me to draw me back to my Mother. She thought it cruel that my husband had taken me away from her when she could do so much more for me. Hard times and sickness brought us back to Lead, but one year working for Papa taught my husband and me that our road, if traveled together, must be independent of Mother.

I never knew my husband to say one unkind word to Mother. He was always a thoughtful son, grateful for every courtesy. I was the liaison between my side of the family and us as a couple, as he was for his side of the

* A shivaree is a variant of charivari, that is, a noisy mock serenade to newlyweds.

family. We were happy in our quiet life. We had a happiness no amount of money could buy.

After we left Lead, we made our home in Nebraska, returning for the summer months until 1907 when my husband took over the business for Papa for one year. Owing to heart trouble, I was compelled to leave Lead at that time. During that year, my one experience of Lead life was the threatened kidnapping of the Grier children and, incidentally, the danger to our own because of our friendship with the Griers. My husband and I wrestled with the depression of 1907-1908 when businesses of long standing went under. Labor unions tried to obtain control of every form of industry, indicative of a general unrest brewing all over the country.

Sarah Elizabeth and Charles William's Marriage License July 1, 1899

Mr. and Mrs. S. R. Smith
request the honor of your presence
at the marriage of their daughter,
Sarah Elizabeth,
to
Mr. Charles William Taylor,
Monday, July third,
Eighteen hundred and ninety nine,
at half after ten o'clock,
Christ Episcopal Church,
Lead, South Dakota.

Sarah Elizabeth and Charles William's Wedding Invitation

DEATHS OF PAPA & MOTHER

Eventually Papa and Mother moved to the Pacific Coast. Papa made considerable money in the Black Hills that he then took to their new home in California at 1608 Crenshaw Boulevard, Los Angeles, California. Papa died suddenly in his chicken yard when no one was around to give him any assistance. Sadly, I do not think that he realized that God alone could be the supreme head in all things so he died as he had really forced himself to be: alone. His influence died and his good died with him. When he passed away on March 28, 1921, the money that Mother had helped him make and save was left to Papa's brother and sister, who had bled him for their own interests all his life. Even Papa's clothing and personal effects were left to Papa's brother and sister, with the sister holding the keys to the safety deposit box.

As her sole income, Mother was left a life interest in the house that she had really built herself, and her legacy continued on in the lives of those she helped to see the sunlight above the treetops of those somber pines. Sadly, Mother lived as a nervous invalid for several years. At the end of her life, Mother's last words were, "Can you forgive me?" Poor Mother, she had never been happy herself but in the last six weeks of her life spent in our home, she had seen a happy home where love ruled. Could I forgive? Yes. Mother had lost everything in her worldly ambitions for her child while I, a little pinecone fostered in the Black Hills, had gained life's greatest blessing, true love. On May 1, 1926, she died at our home among all that love could give her and was buried as she wished, very quietly beside her grandchildren in our family lot at the Wyuka Cemetery in Lincoln, Nebraska.

MY RETURN TO LEAD

After almost forty years, I returned to Lead in July of 1945. I hoped to find old friends and landmarks to recall happy memories of childhood days.

On a steep and wide paved road, we drove down the hill into Deadwood. Not a sound greeted me; the town was silent. Asleep were the colorful Chinese women who once fluttered their fans in welcome. Asleep were the men in boots and Mackinaws. Even the saloons were silent, though it was early evening. The old creek murmured a lullaby, gliding along a narrow, high-banked bed as if walled in behind prison bars.

Up through town, we swung around on the highway that led to Lead. We left the sleeping city of Deadwood only to find a similar scene. Lead City was also asleep, put to sleep by the order of President Roosevelt. The mills were silent, the men were out of work, and the mines were shut down. Absent was the drowsy hum of a busy work-a-day life that I had witnessed from 1879 to 1908.

While some of the landmarks of my childhood were familiar, Lead had changed. Broad, paved highways led to her gates; even the Gateway was different. The scenes of my childhood had disappeared, including the homes where I had grown up. They were swallowed up by the subsidence of the earth beneath them. The great open mouth of what was known as the Open Cut devoured hoists and hills. Whole streets disappeared down its gigantic throat. In fear, the town moved up the gulch to get away from that ever-consuming hole. Homes now hung like small dovecotes high up on the mountainsides.

Ox teams and horses had given way to automobiles that now wound around the base of the hills. Gradually the autos rose to the top of the hill and then dashed down the steep, almost one-way street to meet the traffic at the base. Few seemed to attempt an upward climb directly.

I looked around for my old friends. I asked about different ones, and the answers came back, "Moved away" or "Oh, they died several years ago." The children who went to school with me were now grandparents with gray heads like mine. Lead's beautiful flowers and trees, as well as its children, seemed to be gone. I was told it was a clean town, and though it was clean, it was a town asleep.

As I experienced in the late 1870s, Lead developed from the discovery of the Homestake lode. The little scattered shanties of that first settlement of Washington became the thriving city of Lead in later years. The shanties, cabins, and tar-papered business houses gradually became well-built brick residences and business blocks. Streets were hewn out of the sides of mountains. Churches and schools replaced saloons and prostitution houses. Fine, outstanding characters, who came in with the scum and roly-poly of those first days of the mining camp, remained to build a fine community. Men and women fought for law, order, and good citizenship. Higher standards of living, as well as new buildings, began to tell the tale of those hardfought and won political battles of the 1880s that resulted in what Lead is today.

Many men, outstanding in those early days, have slipped from my memory; however, I did remember the business people, the merchants, and the boarding house managers. The first to come to mind was Mother Long and her boarding house on Mill Street. It had big front windows filled with growing plants and a long table set with good home cooking. Then there was the Springer House on Main Street. It was the "Ritz" of those early days, serving Sunday dinner every week as well as a grand feast in true hotel style on the Fourth of July. Coming later was Max Campbell's, or the Campbell House as it was called. The Blatts ran the Homestake Hotel that served as the hangout for most of the unattached Homestake employees. Time wore down the endurance of most of the proprietors, and eventually the hotels began to close. The swanky "Smead" was built for the "moderns" and the tourist trade. Lead was proud of the Smead and its owner.

The Smead Hotel, however, had to go when the mine caved in, and most of that part of town had to be re-settled westward toward the head of Main Street. God built the mountains, but the mining moles worked underground and undermined the superstructure of the earth until it crumbled and fell. Subsidence swallowed the Smead Hotel and Long's Boarding House, inadvertently making space for new hotels and boarding houses for another generation.

Many citizens left Lead beginning in the 1900s; however, business owners were more likely to stay. The Homestake Store changed little, even in the personnel of managers and clerks. Though as time went by, many of the old-timers transplanted to cities with warmer climates. James Beck, of the hardware department, went to that promised land of California with the beginning of the Lead exodus. Joe Chamison stayed on for many years but finally moved to Butte, Montana. Oscar Silver and his family went west, settling in Los Angeles. Papa and Mother also eventually left Lead and moved to Los Angeles.

Through my story, I have shown you the birth and childhood of the town of Lead and its great mine. I feel a new Lead must rise out of the old and continue to give up its golden treasure to a busy world. With the end of the war, the world is being promised an awakening of the gold-mining industry. Lead has sent more than her quota of good men into the civil and military forces of the world, and I hope to soon see her resume her place in the mining world. People have said there could be sufficient gold to keep paying dividends for the next fifty years, and it appears there could be no end to the vastness of the rich, rich ore if the mine resumes operation. I hope, in a short time, to hear the humming of the Homestake stamps and the old tap, tap of those earlier days. Between those yesterdays and today, Sam McMaster and T.J. Grier's hands have folded across their breasts. Now other hands, that I will never know, will take over the work again.

As I bring this chapter to a close, I would be remiss not to credit the people who have encouraged and aided me in my undertaking. First, I would thank my mother for her diary and scrapbook that preserved articles written for Lead and other Minnesota newspapers. I am also thankful for the stories shared by my relatives and those of my childhood friends who assisted and encouraged me throughout this project.

I give sincere thanks to the following: A.E. Fuller, who gave me my first map of the Sidney Trail and Charles C. Haas who later created the maps used in this book. I owe a deep debt of gratitude for their help in establishing and substantiating the facts of my trips in and out of the Hills. I thank the SOUTH DAKOTA HISTORICAL REVIEW and the BLACK HILLS ENGINEER that provided geological facts and pre-settlement history that substantiated my own geological study. My thanks also goes to Professor L.C. Wimberly of the University of Nebraska; A.E. Sheldon, R.J. Latrom, and Myrtle D. Berry of the Nebraska Historical Society; and Dr. and Mrs. Rufus A. Lyman.

To these people and to the inhabitants of Lead, I owe my thanks. The men and women of that early mining town had few advantages in life, yet out of the muck and mire, they arose tall and stately as the beautiful pine trees that surrounded them. Many of the rough and calloused pioneers of that territory became prominent men and women who benefited the world at large. From the help of my own mother's hands, several young people in Lead received their first encouragement and secured financial aid that led them to a broader and better life. Few in the town knew of the gracious help given by my mother. I too gain satisfaction in the pleasure of knowing that several of my own pupils made great achievements. One became a trusted nurse in Los Angeles, and another served our country as a high official in the secret service during World War I. Lead had many outstanding citizens, but I cannot name them all.

I am proud to recall the good people of my childhood town and the beauty of the Dakota Territory. I hope that after reading my story, you have been able to replace any ill-preconceived notions about the inhabitants of a gold-mining town. It is my hope that you have now caught a glimpse of the rugged yet noble people who endured hardships with strength and integrity. These early pioneers and the majestic terrain, in which they struggled to live, no longer remain hidden solely in my memory. It is my hope that the beauty of the Black Hills and the town people of Lead will continue to live on in your thoughts as the pinecones of those great trees have found resting places in my heart.

EPILOGUE

Sarah Elizabeth and Charles William Taylor were married for 44-1/2 years. They had six children: Seth Charles Henry (born on April 4, 1900, and died on March 12, 1956 - a month shy of his 56th birthday); Marie Provo (born on May 16, 1902, and died on May 18, 1913, at the age of 11 due to Salmonella poisoning from drinking unpasteurized milk - the dairy claimed that the milk was pasteurized but it was not); Hutch Nordell (born on March 15, 1904, and died on October 13, 1918, at the age of 14 after being forced to participate in a foot race at school when not feeling well. After the race he suddenly collapsed and died); John William (born on December 21, 1906, and died on November 22, 1990, a month shy of his 84th birthday); James Ratliff (born and died on February 28, 1908); Beth Elaine (born on January 23, 1915, and died on March 16, 1980, at the age of 65).

Charles William served as the Superintendent of Schools in Ohiowa, NE, from 1898-1901 and School Superintendent in Geneva, NE, from 1901-1907. He was Secretary-Treasurer and Manager of the S.R. Smith Furniture Company in Lead, SD, from 1907-1908. He served as the Superintendent of City Schools in McCook, NE, from 1908-1911. From 1911-1927, he served as Professor of School Administration; Director of Teacher Training and was the Principal of the Teachers College High School at the University of Nebraska. He finished his career as the State Superintendent of Public Instruction of Nebraska in the State Capitol Building in Lincoln, NE, from 1927 until his death in 1943 after serving four terms.

Sarah Elizabeth loved to write. In 1939, she published a book of original poetry called <u>Hearth Stones</u>. An essay of hers entitled "Say What You Will" appeared in the fall 1944 edition of the <u>Prairie Schooner</u>. Later, two poems entitled "Smilin' Through" and "There Is No Death" were published in <u>The Muse of 1945</u>. On October 17, 1945, she sent her manuscript <u>Pinecones</u> "Pioneer Life in the Black Hills" to Mr. Lynn Carrick, Director of New York Office of the J.B. Lippincott Company. Her manuscript was never published. She was an avid genealogist, member of the Daughters of the American Revolution, the American Legion Auxiliary, Order of the Eastern Star, and a communicant member and active in the Ladies Alter Guild at St. Matthews Episcopal Church in Lincoln, NE. In 1923, she and Charles bought an island on Lake Vermilion, Minnesota, where they spent the summer months until Charles' death. The island property remains in the family today and five generations have enjoyed the beautiful sunsets and scenery of the lake.

Sarah Elizabeth "Sadie" died on May 8, 1962, while traveling in the Northwest with her daughter, Beth. She was survived by her son, John and her daughter, Beth, two daughters-in-law Mary Kathryn (wife of John) and Ruth (wife of Seth), two grandchildren, John William, Jr. "Jack" and Mary Elisabeth "Sissy" (children of John and Mary Kathryn), and six great-grandchildren. Her husband, four of their children, Marie, Hutch, James and Seth, as well as two grandsons, Seth "Shorty" Hutton and Charles "Chuck" William II, preceded her in death.

PHOTOS

Left to right - Sadie's Mother (Elizabeth Smith), Sadie and Sadie's Aunt (Sarah Bragg)
1893

Charles William, Sarah Elizabeth and their Children Seth, Marie, and Hutch
(1905)

Seth C.H. Taylor, age 11, with his Great Uncle Jack Bragg and his Grandmother
Eliza Smith while visiting them in Los Angeles in 1911

The Charles W. Taylor Family
Sarah Elizabeth, John William, Seth Charles Henry,
Beth Elaine, Hutch Nordell and Charles William
(1917)

Sadie's Uncle Jack Bragg
(1918)

Four Generations (left to right)
Elizabeth McLean Smith, Sarah Elizabeth Taylor, Charles William Taylor,
Ruth Hutton Taylor holding Seth Hutton Taylor, and Seth Charles Henry Taylor
(1923 or 1924)

The Charles William Taylor Family (left to right back row) Sarah Elizabeth, Seth Charles Henry and wife Ruth (left to right front row) John William and wife Mary Kathryn, Beth Elaine, Seth Hutton, Charles William holding John William, Jr. and Charles William II (1931)

Sarah Elizabeth "Sadie" Taylor 65 years old (1939)

Sarah Elizabeth with her 13-year-old granddaughter, Mary Elisabeth "Sissy" Taylor
on Sarah Elizabeth's front steps of her home in Lincoln, NE (1947)

Sarah Elizabeth Taylor kissing her granddaughter, Mary Elisabeth on her wedding day.
Left to right: Shirley Dewey (Maid of Honor), Walter R. Kurth (Groom), Mary Elisabeth
Taylor Kurth (Bride), Sarah Elizabeth (Grandmother of the Bride), Walter and Irene Kurth
(Parents of the Groom), and Mary Kathryn Taylor (Mother of the Bride)
August 23, 1958

RESOURCES

Ancestry: www.ancestry.com.

Baldwin, George P., ed. The Black Hills Illustrated. "Deadwood: Dakota Graphics." Black Hills Mining Men's Association, 1904.

Black Hills Mining Museum: www.blackhillsminingmuseum.com.

Find a Grave: www.findagrave.com.

Knight, Dwayne F. Steeples Above Stopes: "The Churches in the Gold Camps 1876-1976." Deadwood: Deadwood-Lead '76 Centennial Inc., 1976.

Lee, Bob, ed.; Stan and Wynn Lindstrom, assistant editors; with a new introduction by Bob Lee. Gold, Gals, Guns, Guts: "A History of Deadwood, Lead, and Spearfish, 1876-1976." South Dakota State Historical Society Press, Pierre, S.D. 2004.

Mitchell, Steven T. Nuggets to Neutrinos: "The Homestake Story." Xlibris Corporation, 2009.

Newspapers: www.newspapers.com.

Sanford Lab Homestake: www.sanfordlabhomestake.com.

The Adams Museum: www.deadwood.com/business/attractions/adams-museum

Toms, Donald D. The Flavor of Lead: "An Ethnic History." Lead Historic Preservation Commission, Lead, S.D., 2006.

Toms, Donald D., Kristie L. Schillinger, William J. Stone, eds. The Gold Belt Cities: "The City of Mills." Lead: Black Hills Mining Museum, 1993.

Toms, Donald D., William J. Stone, and Gretchen Motchenbacher, eds. The Gold Belt Cities: "Lead & Homestake." Lead: G.O.L.D. Unlimited, 1988.